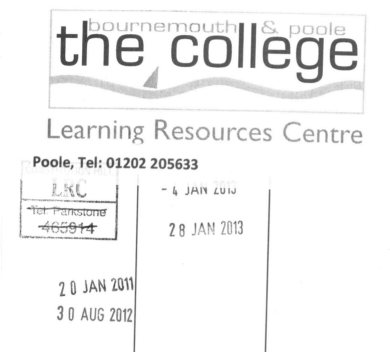

the college
bournemouth & poole

Learning Resources Centre

Poole, Tel: 01202 205633

This item must be returned to the LRC by the last date stamped, or fines will be charged. If not in demand it may be renewed by telephone or personal call. For telephone renewals, please be ready to quote your borrower number.

For Jodi—the greatest IRL and everywhere

VIRTUAL CULTURE

Identity and Communication
in Cybersociety

Edited by

STEVEN G. JONES

SAGE Publications
London • Thousand Oaks • New Delhi

First published 1997 Reprinted 1998, 2002

Permission to reproduce song lyrics from "Transmission", performed
and recorded by Joy Division, granted by Fractured Music/Factory
Comm. Ltd.

 SAGE Publications Ltd
6 Bonhill Street
London EC2A 4PU

SAGE Publications Inc.
2455 Teller Road
Thousand Oaks, California 91320

SAGE Publications India Pvt Ltd
32, M-Block Market
Greater Kailash – I
New Delhi 110 048

British Library Cataloguing in Publication data

A catalogue record for this book is available from the British Library

ISBN 0 7619 5525 9
ISBN 0 7619 5526 7 (pbk)

Library of Congress catalog record available

Typeset by Mayhew Typesetting, Rhayader, Powys,
Printed in Great Britain by The Cromwell Press Ltd, Trowbridge

Contents

Notes on contributors

Harris Breslow (harris@calumet.yorku.ca) received his doctorate from the Institute of Communications Research at the University of Illinois. He currently teaches philosophy and cultural history in the Mass Communications Programme at York University, Toronto, Canada. He is completing a manuscript on the relationship between architectural and economic spaces.

Dawn Dietrich (dietrich@cc.wwu.edu) is Assistant Professor of English at Western Washington University. She has published articles on postmodern performance and electronic culture and is currently at work on a book-length manuscript about theater practitioner Robert Wilson and the politics of the postmodern stage.

Nicole B. Ellison is a doctoral student at the Annenberg School for Communication at the University of Southern California, focusing on the social aspects of computer-mediated communication. Before attending graduate school, she worked at the Voyager Co. and other software development companies in Los Angeles, California.

Jan Fernback (fernback@rintintin.colorado.edu) is a doctoral candidate at the Center for Mass Media Research, School of Journalism and Mass Communication, University of Colorado. She is currently writing a dissertation on computer-mediated social relations which problematizes the concept of community as manifested in cyberspace. Her research interests include utopianism and new media technologies and the anthropology of cyberculture.

Steven G. Jones (steve-jones@utulsa.edu) is Professor and Chair of the Faculty of Communication at the University of Tulsa. A social historian of communication technology, his book *CyberSociety: Computer-Mediated Communication and Community* was published in 1995 and earned him critical acclaim. Jones has made presentations to scholarly and business groups about the Internet and social change and about the Internet's social and commercial uses. He also pursues research into popular music, youth culture, and communication. His first book, *Rock Formation: Technology, Music and Mass Communication*, was nominated for the BMI/Rolling Stone Gleason Award and the Association for Recorded Sound Collections Excellence in Historical Recorded Sound Research Award.

Richard C. MacKinnon (http://www.actlab.utexas.edu/~spartan/) after spending several years in Silicon Valley is a political scientist in the Government Department and the Advanced Communication Technologies Laboratory (ACTLAB) at the University of Texas at Austin. As a former police officer, he is able to draw on his law enforcement background to inform his theories for addressing computer-mediated crime and virtual offenders. His research interests are in the political anthropology, cultural study, and governance of virtual environments. He spends most of his online time dwelling in a community called Cybermind.

Margaret L. McLaughlin (mmclaugh@rcf.usc.edu) is Professor of Communication, Annenberg School for Communication, University of Southern California, and a member of the Faculty of the Integrated Media Systems Center. She is Co-Editor of the _Journal of Computer-Mediated Communication_ and serves on the Editorial Boards of _Text_, _Communication Research_, and _Progress in Communication Science_. She has written, edited, and co-edited several books, including _Conversation: How Talk is Organized_; _The Psychology of Tactical Communication_ and _Network and Net-Play: Virtual Groups on the Internet_ (1996). Her interests include discourse analysis, group communication, and computer-mediated communication.

Ananda Mitra (ananda@wfu.edu) is an assistant professor of communication at Wake Forest University in Winston-Salem, NC. He has published in the areas of critical studies, popular culture, and technology, particularly about the conditions in South East Asia and about South East Asian immigrants. His interest in the Internet stems from his personal use of the Net and in teaching courses in communication, technology, and culture.

Kerry K. Osborne (osborne@rcf.usc.edu) is a doctoral candidate in the Annenberg School of Communication, University of Southern California, Los Angeles. She has coauthored a number of articles on electronic communities and is currently researching Internet participation among the elderly. Additional interests include pragmatics of computer-mediated conversation and impression management on the World Wide Web.

Joseph Schmitz (schmitzja@centum.utulsa.edu) received his PhD from the Annenberg School of Communication at the University of Southern California in 1990 and presently teaches at the University of Tulsa. His research interests include the uses and social consequences of new communication technology and the study of these technologies within organizations.

David F. Shaw (shawd@ucsu.colorado.edu) is a doctoral candidate at the Center for Mass Media Research, in the School of Journalism and Mass Communication at the University of Colorado at Boulder, where he is writing his dissertation on the AIDS Memorial Quilt. He has received fellowships from the Swedish Institute, Stockholm, and the International Media Centre at the University of Salford, England, where he studied Swedish, European, and international media responses to AIDS.

Nessim Watson (Nessim1@aol.com) is an adjunct professor in the Communication Department of Westfield State College. His interests in modern communication, cultural studies, and the functioning of mass media systems are paired with a desire to infuse media literacy into secondary school systems and to provide students with an awareness of how culture influences our thoughts, beliefs, and actions. His current research involves how CMC technologies can be used to democratize both the cultural and political spheres of American society.

Susan Zickmund is Assistant Professor of Speech Communication at Augustana College. Her research on American fascism appears in _The Shepherd of the Discontented: Religion, Radicalism, and Rhetoric in the Discourse of Father Charles Coughlin_ and in contributions to _Religion and the Social Sciences_. She has ongoing collaborations with the Universität Bielefeld, Germany.

Preface

Since writing and editing *CyberSociety: Computer-Mediated Communication and Community* little time has passed according to the clock and calendar. On the Internet, though, ages have gone by. When *CyberSociety* was in press the World Wide Web was merely a cool application, an interesting way to use the network. Now it has become a full-blown medium of communication gaining widespread use, one on which we pin hopes, dreams, fortunes, and fantasies.

Still, *CyberSociety* is much more than a history of the Internet. I would like to believe its central themes and its examinations of social relationships online and their relationship, in turn, to ones offline remain relevant, and hopefully will continue to be so as long as we are interested in figuring out, as my colleague Joli Jensen might put it, what it means to live a valuable life.

Virtual Culture: Identity and Communication in Cybersociety is by no means an update or revision to *CyberSociety*, and though it shares some of the concerns and methods of the earlier book, its focus is quite a bit different, and I hope as relevant. Whereas *CyberSociety* concentrated on the nature of online communities and social formations, *Virtual Culture* converges on the nature of social and civic life online, and asks (fairly begs) the question: what is it about life offline that makes us so intent on living online?

In both the online and offline realms I am grateful to a number of people who have enriched not only this work but my thinking. In particular James Carey, Clifford Christians, Joli Jensen, and Ted Peterson are an inspiration. Sophy Craze and Kiren Shoman provided guidance, good care, and communication while I wrote and edited the book, and I am grateful to them, as I am to Margaret Seawell and others at Sage, for, without their help, you would not be reading it. Peggy Bowers at St Louis University, too, was very helpful as I sought to understand Charles Taylor's work.

I particularly wish to thank colleagues on the Faculty of Communication at the University of Tulsa, and must single out Jan Reynolds for her support and hard work on behalf of the entire faculty. I also owe a special thanks to Lewis Duncan, Tom Horne, and Lars Engle. Joe Schmitz is all one could hope for in a friend and colleague, and I am fortunate to share an appointment in the same department as he. Frank Christel, Barbara Geffen, Reed Davis, the staff in Computing and Information Resources, students at the university, and other faculty and staff there too numerous to mention, have made it a valuable and interesting learning environment, and have also provided serious fun. Al Soltow continues to provide wisdom and guidance—the next Leinie's is on me. Tom, Karla, Casey, Chris, and Abby White provided unserious fun, as did Rick Holzgrafe, Arthur Vandelay, the Utz family, Alan Smithee, and Milly and Lilly. A special hello and thanks goes to Laza, Sofia and Boris Sekulic, Elizabeth White, Mel Eberle, and Gary Szabo.

My parents, Sofia Jones and George Jones, have provided advice, comfort, and support in ever-greater quantity and quality, to the point where mere thanks are greatly inadequate.

Just as inadequate is any thanks I could give to Jodi White, who continues to bear with me and lift me up. I'll log off soon. Really. I promise.

Steven G. Jones
Tulsa, Oklahoma, USA
September 1996

Introduction

Steven G. Jones

Although the story of computer-mediated communication (CMC) and the Internet is still being written, we already know that there are (at least) two sides to it. The side we most commonly hear about is of their development and implementation, and this has been historically what we have heard most. We also hear much about Internet engineering, its business and commercial applications, its potential for entertainment. The side we hear less about (sometimes we hear nothing at all) is of the consequences of that development and implementation, of the uses to which we mean to put the technology, and the social outcomes we desire, and hence this book, *Virtual Culture: Identity and Communication in Cybersociety.*

But daily we become more savvy about technology. For instance, it seems quite commonplace to us that every technology has two sides to its consequences; on the one hand for every technology we develop in an attempt to improve life, we believe we also will, on the other hand, find life impoverished in some way. Such has been our experience with a variety of technologies, from nuclear power, with its capacity for generating electricity and for destruction, to the written word, with its capacity for preservation and dissemination of information and for its origination of silent readers. Once we are accustomed to a new technology we accept both sides, preferring, one suspects, to assume that as the technology is refined its negative consequences will also be better engineered. But our impatience shows through while we wait for those refinements, as this excerpt from a 1929 magazine article demonstrates:

> The average human being of to-day is not impressed by miracles. . . . He reads in a newspaper that plans are being made to connect New York with Tokio [*sic*] by telephone. "I doubt that it's practical," he may remark. But the next day he discovers that the thing has actually been accomplished. The day after that he himself calls up Tokio and, if there happens to be a few minutes' delay in putting the call through, he complains bitterly about the service. (Sherwood, 1929, p. 1)

It is likely that most people have had similar experiences. Once we see that something functions as it should, we believe it should function *even better.* And woe be if it does not function properly, as when a videocassette recorder mysteriously does not record a program for which we have set its timer, when we lose a connection while talking on our cellular telephone, it engenders is of greatest importance. His most telling comment is that the contemporary division of space brought about by highways is "seen as temporary, and communication . . . essential; the dwelling favors the open plan" (p. 125). I might add that the computer, its software and hardware, are seen in the same way, and perhaps we consider modern life less in terms of social mobility and more in terms of the "upgrade."

The grid systems we create, then, are structuring but not permanent, rigid but permeable; they flex. So it is with our attempts to map a grid of the Internet, the virtual, onto our existing grid of the non-virtual. We try to bend and twist both grids until they fit one on top of the other, but they always snap back into place and defy an easy interlock, perhaps like "smart" metals and plastics that regain their original shape on heating. Several essays in this book address the issue of the boundaries between the real and the virtual, assessing the shape and porousness of these grids, and we find that with the application of some intellectual heat they do not always spring back into old shapes but assume entirely new ones.

In regard to communication, we are, not surprisingly, also able to move more information more quickly than before, in different media (the link between communication and transportation is yet to be completely broken). Jackson (1985) is illuminating on this point too, as he notes that:

> Communication can be defined in several ways: it means passage from one place to another, and it means the transmitting of a message. In terms of the highway, it means an unending flow of traffic—perhaps much of it essentially aimless, a kind of search for some place or person to help reinforce our identity; it also means the signs and billboards and lights and signals—a chorus of communication such as no generation has ever before seen. (p. 46)

His description of the highway is as good a one of the Internet as I have found. The contributors to this volume examine the flow of traffic, but not for its own sake. Rather they seek to discover and critique that "search for some place or person" about which Jackson writes. The use of CMC and the Internet is part of what Jackson, extrapolating from a study done in Holland, sees as "the need for sociability, the need to use one's own personal possessions . . . the need to collect experiences, and the need to run dangers" (pp. 47–48).

There is another need, and it is the third area of our collective focus on communication technologies: storage. As we collect experience we must find someplace to put it. It seems nigh on impossible to continually add objects, symbols, and processes to our lives without letting others go, so what we try to do instead of subtract is store them. Whether the space is real or virtual, our capacity to keep filling it is undiminished (such is the nature of imagination), but our capacity to encompass it, in the sense of embracing it, putting our arms around it figuratively, to understand it, does not grow at the same pace. Having information and knowing what it means are entirely separate domains. As Ebben & Kramarae (1993) noted in a slightly different context, we must set aside our "assumption about education [as] rooted in the notion that knowledge is an accumulation of matter" (p. 21). What we sense is that we are *constituted* by information almost as much as we are constituted by blood, skin, and bone, and that, no matter the recording method we may use to externalize the memories and experiences we store, without us they would not make sense.

Conversely, without those memories and experiences our lives would not make sense either. Having "connections" does not simply mean hooking up a wire (or radio wave) from one place to another. In the old Eastern European sense of the term, "having connections" means having a thread that links us to others' thoughts, duties, rights, responsibilities, and obligations. It is, in truth, neither "who one knows" nor "what one knows" but the two combined. In its own way each essay in this book is concerned with connecting in that latter sense, and our collective concern should, by all means, focus there.

The present development of a global information infrastructure by way of the Internet brings these three strands (transportation, communication, storage) together in interesting ways. But what are the consequences for us as we invest them with those capacities? To invest in one area must mean that we disinvest in another. Richard Hoggart (1970) wrote that apart from the "expedient answers" technology may provide we are "in the area of value-judgments," for "every choice made opens *that* possibility to human beings or closes *that* one, makes *that* more likely or *that other* less likely" (p. 112). What do we choose to leave behind as we adopt and adapt to new media technology? What might we gain from our new investments? These are the questions raised in this book. They come from a variety of perspectives, engaging and joining theoretical work in sociology, political science, economics, communication, feminism, and history with observation and participation of the content and context of CMC and the Internet. The authors have kept a watchful eye on the landscape that we are forming with these technologies; sometimes that landscape is visible on our computer screens, and sometimes it is not. No matter where it may be visible it behooves us all to keep it in view, for it affects us all—and it promises to keep changing.

Note

1. Microsoft has in this advertising campaign asked a question that sounds like ones asked by myriad American college students and members of "Generation X" who can engage in a seemingly never-ending call-and-response round-robin based on two questions: "What do you want to do today?" followed by "I don't know, what do you want to do?" The dissipated *ennui* of these questions is similar to that of the Web surfer who, faced with an almost limitless array of sites to visit, is overwhelmed to boredom.

References

Carey, J.W. (1989). *Communication as culture*. Boston: Unwin & Hyman.
Curtis, I. (1980). Transmission. Fractured Music.

Ebben, M., & Kramarae, C. (1993). Women and information technologies: Creating a cyberspace of our own. In H.J. Taylor, C. Kramarae & M. Ebben (Eds), *Women, information technology, and scholarship* (pp. 15–27). Urbana: University of Illinois Center for Advanced Study.

Hoggart, R. (1970). Two ways of looking. In R. Hoggart, *Speaking to each other* (pp. 106–113). New York: Oxford University Press.

Jackson, J.B. (1980). *The necessity for ruins*. Amherst, MA: University of Massachusetts Press.

Jackson, J.B. (1985). The social landscape. In S. Yates (Ed.), *The essential landscape* (pp. 45–48). Albuquerque: University of New Mexico Press.

Sherwood, R.E. (1929, July). Beyond the talkies—television. *Scribner's, 24*, 1–8.

1

The Internet and its Social Landscape

Steven G. Jones

Whether it be film, television, radio, the Internet, virtually any medium of communication that relies on technology will at one time or another find itself deemed to be causing a "revolution." And just as quickly one will find some segments of society in opposition to that revolution.

Such is now the case with the evolution of technologies for computer-mediated communication (CMC), particularly the development of the Internet. Backlash toward these technologies has begun already and some decry the loss of personality that often accompanies the mediation of communication via computer; others lament the amount of time taken away from face-to-face interaction by technologies that require expertise, undivided attention, or even appear addictive. Clifford Stoll (1995) summarized the backlash best when he wrote, "bit by bit, my days dribble away, trickling out my modem" (p. 2).

Stoll's sense of life "dribbling away" is not surprising, for, to use James Carey's (1989) distinction between the "transmission" and "ritual" views of communication, transmission and transportation form the frame of reference for our thinking about communication. Most often we simply desire to know how much we can communicate, or "get across," most efficiently, economically, and rapidly. From that perspective Stoll's problem is that his life is but *dribbling* away and not speeding along his modem's connection. But from the point of view of "ritual," a perspective that claims communication "is the sacred ceremony that draws persons together in fellowship and commonality" (p. 18), Stoll's problem is that his days go by virtually without him, time passes through his modem without him noticing it.

In many, many ways, the transmission view dominates not only how the Western world thinks about communication but how it thinks about other aspects of life, and this may be most evident in the modern embrace of "progress," or what Carey characterized as "the mythos of the electronic revolution," the hope and belief that social ills will be overcome by advances in science and technology.

In *CyberSociety* (Jones, 1995) I sought to bring Carey's words to bear on our understanding of the historical roots and motivations for what had come to be known as the "information superhighway," the ongoing project of constructing the transportation infrastructure to maintain "progress" in industry. In this regard it is important that we do understand the transmission view of communication. It not only permeates history, in terms of the development of Western society, it continues to exert influence on the socio-economic structure of our communication media. As John Brinckerhoff Jackson wrote (1972) about the development of the Illinois Central Railroad in America:

> railroad-designed towns . . . represented an important development in our whole landscape. They and the new farms surrounding them were not, even in theory, part of a pattern of independent social spaces: they were integrated from the beginning into a well-designed economic process, into a linear system vividly symbolized by the lines of track and their accompanying telegraph wires. (p. 68)

The spread of railroads had sweeping consequences for social life even in areas that were not bisected by tracks. And now the Internet's development is similarly linear, though not symbolized by tracks and telegraph lines but by the personal computer, keyboard, and mouse. The Internet does not create independent social spaces *per se*, as it relies on an existing communication infrastructure and is integrated into current economic processes in the telecommunications industries. Is it any surprise that most people use the telephone system to access the Internet via modem, or that the promise of high-speed Internet connections comes via existing cable television installations? Like the telegraph wires that accompanied the railroad tracks, and the roads that followed the railroad tracks, *ad infinitum*, the Internet is a "piggy-backed" medium, one that follows paths we already know.

For the present analysis, it is most important to note that there was not only an industrial (and military) motivation for the creation of a communication infrastructure that has, in turn, led to the Internet's creation and growth, but a social one as well. Many of the technologies that are developed for business purposes are useful for social purposes (and vice versa), much to the chagrin of employers who find that the technology that was to have increased their workers' productivity has had the opposite effect and lowered it, while concomitantly increasing their socializing at work (Rice & Love, 1987; Schmitz & Fulk, 1991).

That the adoption of technology can have an effect opposite to the one intended should not be surprising, for we have become accustomed (perhaps from the very first time we must deal with the consequences of a thunderstorm that has cut power to our area and left us without refrigeration, lights, air conditioning, television, etc.) to the "trade-offs" that occur as we develop and implement technology. We may not realize the magnitude of those trade-offs until we lose access to the technologies to which we have become habituated. I raise these points not to argue that those trade-offs should necessarily prevent us from adopting technology, but rather to point out that, so long as technology works, we take the trade-offs for granted.

But when we are unable to avail ourselves of communication technology we are struck by the sudden intensity of the local, the immediate apprehension that we are in the here, and now, and unable to attend to matters beyond our physical reach. Space is at that moment something we inhabit rather than something through which we move. To put it colloquially, we feel it "close in" around us. And what startles is that very physical presence of space, that feeling of something, or some absence, pressing against you when the lights go out.

Ordinarily, however, we "feel" space as a fish likely "feels" water. It is our own physical medium, a part of us to such an extent we do not even notice it, though we move through it and exist within its presence. It is part and parcel of our capacity for movement, so much so that the conjoining of space and motion, the very dependence of our sense of space on motion, has caused Richard Sennett (1978) to note that mobility is a *sine qua non* of modern life:

> Today, we experience an ease of motion unknown to any prior urban civiliza-
> tion, and yet motion has become the most anxiety-laden of daily activities. The
> anxiety comes from the fact that we take unrestricted motion of the individual to
> be an absolute right. (p. 14)

One might well imagine, of course, that the term "auto-mobile" is derived from that sense that we believe we are granted the right of auto-mobility, irrespective of whether the medium is a highway or information super-highway . . . or social environment. For Carey's connection of the mythos of the electronic revolution to the Industrial Revolution connects not only the material aspects of those (essentially modern) stories, it connects their social and moral dimensions as well.

The Internet and Community

My own initial concerns about CMC, as I explained them in *CyberSociety* (Jones, 1995), were focused on issues of community. The concerns I had were centered on the question "Who are we when we are online?" and were oriented toward the communal, the social relationships we were seeking to foster via the Internet and CMC. In particular I wanted to examine emerging social formations online and determine whether they provide some of the things we desire offline, things like friendship, community, interaction, and public life, to determine whether the moral ideals we seek among one another, in community, are realized online.

Part of what motivated my interest and concern was that much was being made about the dual potentialities of the Internet. First, it could re-create community *as we had once known it*, rebuild for us the "great good place" (Oldenberg, 1991; Rheingold, 1993) we once knew but abandoned for "bowling alone" (Putnam, 1995). Second, it would not merely "get us all together," it would do so without our having to do expend much effort, since it would overcome space and time for us, and it would also enable us to communicate with one another. As J. MacGregor Wise points out in a forthcoming work, we have developed the belief that political, moral, and social problems are the result of a lack of communication, and that if we improve communication we will also solve the various problems that plague modern life. The Internet would thus make community *better*. It was to result in a community free of the constraints of space and time, and so free us to engage with fellow humans irrespective of geographic proximity and the clock, and it would construct that community from *communication*, rather than inhabitance and being, which do not guarantee communication. As Douglas Schuler (1996) put it:

> The old concept of community is obsolete in many ways and needs to be updated to meet today's challenges. The old or "traditional" community was often exclusive, inflexible, isolated, unchanging, monolithic, and homogeneous. A *new community*—one that is fundamentally devoted to democratic problem-solving—needs to be fashioned from the remnants of the old. (p. 9)

Schuler goes on to describe these new communities as having "a high degree of awareness . . . and principles and purpose" (p. 9), and focused around action, around "doing." In this conception, one growing in popularity, communities are not places to be, to engage in conversation (from the mundane to the momentous), they are groups of people seeking to achieve particular goals. This description is part of an older thread in conversations about computing. As Licklider and Taylor wrote in a 1968 essay that presaged much of computing's future:

> life will be happier for the on-line individual because the people with whom one interacts most strongly will be selected more by commonality of interests and goals than by accidents of proximity . . . communication will be more effective and productive, and therefore more enjoyable. (p. 31)

Licklider and Taylor, and for that matter Schuler also, do not address whether communication that is not goal-oriented can be enjoyable too. And what happens to those "selected" groups once their goals are achieved is open to question. In general, Schuler's call for new communities seems more like a call to form committees, or at best teams, and democracy itself is defined as problem-solving and not as a way of life. It is conceived of as a means to a material end rather than a set of moral values.

A similar call is made by Howard Rheingold (1991, p. 377), who envisions virtual reality providing the "learning by doing" that, he claims, John Dewey espoused. But that characterization is a perversion of Dewey's expectations for education, expectations grounded in hopes for social being and not simply the learning of trade and skill. As Jensen (1990) summarized, "For Dewey, education should reflect the life of the larger society, cultivating students as full social citizens, lively and responsive" (p. 146). Furthering his twist on Dewey, Rheingold organized Electric Minds, Inc., a media company formed to create the Social Web. Its goal, according to Rheingold, "is to be *the* global brand for community" (cited in McCoy, 1996).

Such rhetoric puts a different spin on the modern nostalgia for community. Instead of merely criticizing the deterioration of communities in modern life, it evokes a sense of lost opportunities that need to be again made available, if only we would work harder (or have more money with which to buy Rheingold's "brand" of community). It is therefore particularly responsive to the fragmentation of modern life along the lines of space and time, as it seeks to rally and reunite us in action and activity. But we should not overlook that it is we who, in our rush to overcome space and time, instead fragment them, and thus cause the ruptures we want healed. As Carey (1993) trenchantly points out in the title of an essay, "everything that rises must diverge." Both space and time are fragmented and divergent in the face of new technologies, made discontinuous by the very elements of control that we seek to utilize to make them less so, to make them, in fact, convergent. What Carey had observed was that:

> Divergence is not some random and unfortunate occurrence, a snake in our idyll of convergence, but a necessary consequence of the technological change we so eagerly support. We are living, engineering and hardware notwithstanding, in a period of enormous disarray in all our institutions and in much of our personal life as well. We exist in a "verge" in the sense Daniel Boorstin gave that word: a moment between two different forms of social life in which technology has dislodged all human relations and nothing stable has as yet replaced them. Media may be converging. . . . Social convergence does not follow the technical convergence, however. (p. 173)

And so it is that our hopes for convergence are dominating our common sense. The creation of the convergence, and hence stability, we seek requires that we cease to attempt to "save" or "overcome" space and time through use of technology. They are not to be "overcome," we are, rather, to live in them.

It also requires that we move beyond simply observing whether things look as if they are converging to understanding the outcomes of our observations, or, to put it another way, understanding whether the perception of difference and similarity makes a difference. For example, though it may *seem* as if convergence is occurring and societies around the world share symbols, ideas, language, etc., a pervasive sense of divergence remains. Zelinsky (1992) noted that a research study conducted in 1967 "failed to disclose any convergence, and indeed suggested the opposite trend":

> cultural distances seem to be shrinking; but modern man, torn loose from conventional bounds of place or social and biological descent, may well be feeling his way into a number of newly discovered dimensions. The opportunities for personal choice, more complete individuation, and the formation of new social and cultural entities may have been greatly enhanced. Thus although most places may have begun to look alike, in important ways not usually susceptible to casual visual observation they may have started down fundamentally different routes. In sharp contrast the communities of the premodern past may have displayed the greatest imaginable superficial differences, but the most striking isomorphisms are revealed to the persistent analyst. (pp. 87–88)

I would liken this to the present situation with the Internet, which, I believe, we have a tendency to understand mainly in spatial terms, observing it as if visually, through the use of visual metaphors, as if it were indeed a highway being constructed through our backyard. (It thankfully lacks the mess, trouble, and some of the disruption of roadwork, but it still employs eminent domain as our property is colonized.) We marvel at the sights and sounds brought into our homes and places of work and sometimes are dismayed at their intrusion into our lives, but we think less about the Internet's non-spatial features. We think more about its ability to "take us places" and less about its insertion into the mundane practices of our everyday life.

For us to change our thinking about the Internet, to gain a more critical awareness of it, we might turn toward Harold Innis's work concerning the social consequences of the fragmentation of modern society from what he termed the "bias" of communication, the structuring of space and time by communication. Now, of particular interest *vis-à-vis* the Internet is its bias toward time, and *not* space, though the Internet's principal and popular definition is as a "cyberspace." I believe the Internet does, in its way, have a bias toward space, as do other communication technologies. Yet it is a kind of "laissez-faire" bias, not one that structures space so much as one that entirely obliterates it as a sense-able construct and so renders it absurd. As Perkowitz (1996) noted in a review of E.M. Forster's *Howards End* and "The Machine Stops":

> Forster . . . realizes that the quality of personal connection depends on the quantity—often inversely. "The more people one knows the easier it becomes to replace them," Margaret sighs. "It's one of the curses of London." Too many connections, in other words, devalues each one in a kind of emotional inflation. (p. 87)

It is not that distance is made meaningless, but once we are all connected in cyberspace we are then infinitely distant from one another when we are not communicating.

The Internet's bias toward time, on the other hand, marks it as the latest in a series of mechanical developments arising from "the demands of industry on time" (Innis, 1951, p. 74). It is part of a process that has intruded into everyday life, into the social (see Lewis Mumford's writing for poignant examples), that demands efficiency and results in fragmentation and what Innis termed an "obsession with present-mindedness" (p. 87) and what Jeremy Rifkin (1987) calls "the new nanosecond culture." Perhaps its best description, and one that links the Internet's bias toward time to computing generally, is that of a software engineer who stated, "real time [is] no longer compelling" (Ullman, 1995, p. 133).

Of great value toward making a connection between the Internet's time bias and its social consequences is Benedict Anderson's (1983) analysis of the evolution of "simultaneity":

Our own conception of simultaneity has been a long time in the making, and its emergence is certainly connected . . . with the development of the secular sciences. . . . What has come to take the place of the mediaeval conception of simultaneity-along-time is, to borrow again from Benjamin, an idea of "homogeneous, empty time," in which simultaneity is, as it were, transverse, cross-time, marked not by prefiguring and fulfillment, but by temporal coincidence, and measured by clock and calendar. (p. 24)

Time is empty, according to Anderson, because we have less of a sense of its flow and a greater sense of its discontinuity—time is not a whole, it is a series of fragments that pass by, one to the other, in a serial lock-step. It is ours to fill and try to save rather than to experience and understand.

The Internet and Modern Life

Our sense of history and our imagination are necessarily related to the modern conception of time, for we see ourselves as moving through time, and to some extent outside of it, rather than living within it. It is well illustrated by the hold on our imagination of editing technologies, ones that allow us to manipulate images and sounds, space and time. As I stated in an earlier essay (Jones, 1994) on cyberpunk, hypertext, and symbolic process, "The point is not that art imitates life, life imitates art, and so on, but that *life itself can be edited*" (p. 86). Time is asynchronous, and nearly, perhaps only twenty minutes into the future, to borrow from Max Headroom, within our control.

Consequently, the Internet's insertion into modern life represents a further displacement, or divergence, between our sense of "lived" time (the time that passes according to our senses, the time of "being") and our sense of "social" or "functional" time (the time that we sense as a form of obligation, or as time for "doing," for "capturing," or what Stoll feels is being "dribbled away" against his wishes). Rifkin (1987) notes that:

The computer is a form of communication like script, print, and the telephone, but it is also a time tool, like the clock on the wall. . . . As a timepiece, the computer . . . establishes a new set of accelerated temporal demands on human behavior. . . . The ability to intuit the proper sequences of behavior, knowing how long things should take . . . becomes difficult and strained (pp. 27–28)

Computer makers continually speed up their machines, but few people I know find that accelerated central processing units save them much time, or, better, minimize their time for "doing" toward time for "being."

The Internet itself can, of course, provide some semblance of a place for "being," and lurking on mailing lists, Usenet newsgroups, Internet Relay Chat, etc., is evidence of at least that much. But these activities are biased toward an isolated form of being, for if one is lurking and not interacting, one is no more a part of the social than is a wallflower. "Being," in this sense, connotes a near-stasis in social terms. There is a remarkable parallel between lurking and reading (and, in fact, the primary activity of Internet use is reading, whether lurking or not). Reading, and print culture as Internet communities are similar to the type of assemblage Anderson believes was brought about with the advent of the newspaper in America:

> What were the characteristics of the first American newspapers, North or South? They began essentially as appendages of the market. Early gazettes contained— aside from news about the metropole—commercial news . . . as well as colonial political appointments, marriages of the wealthy, and so forth. In other words, what brought together, on the same page, *this* marriage with *that* ship, *this* price with *that* bishop, was the very structure of the colonial administration and market-system itself. In this way the newspaper . . . quite naturally, and even apolitically, created an imagined community among a specific assemblage of fellow-readers, to whom *these* ships, brides, bishops and prices belonged. (p. 62)

Similarly those who frequent Usenet newsgroups provide evidence that they feel the group and its messages "belong" to them (McLaughlin, Osborne, & Smith, 1995, p. 102), creating an inversion of traditional community power and possession. No longer do *we*, as members of the group, belong to the community, rather the community belongs to *us*. Our sense of identity is not only derived from our identification with the group, it is derived from our understanding of the group identity. In this sense the Internet continues a trend toward marketing initiated by the development of the printing press and sped forward by additional communication technologies, creating what Beniger (1987) has called "pseudo-communities," the integration of diverse groups by means of mass communication and mass production. In conjunction with the development of the conception of "homogeneous, empty time," the fractured narratives produced by the newspaper, and now the Internet, prove a powerful force for bringing people together:

> This new synchronic novelty could arise historically only when substantial groups of people were in a position to think of themselves as living lives *parallel* to those of other substantial groups of people—if never meeting, yet certainly proceeding along the same trajectory. . . . One could be fully aware of sharing a language and a religious faith . . . customs and traditions, without any great expectation of ever meeting one's partners. (Anderson, 1983, p. 188)

Though to some extent these narratives may feel like community, they are its opposite, at least as far as we have thus far known it in our history, for community relies on what I previously referred to as "inhabitance," as being not just in the same place at the same time in interaction with others but as being *a part of* that place, as if one is a part of the landscape. But instead of inhabitance there is recognition, the understanding that, first, there are others like us, and, second, that others know we exist. Consequently, if we are to create a sense of community beyond mere recognition, we require far more than its construction, physical or virtual—we also require human occupancy, commitment, interaction, and living among and with others. We require a counterbalance to the spectacle that is created when one thing is juxtaposed among different others as in a newspaper or department store (Sennett, 1978, p. 144). Garrison Keillor (1996) acknowledges, for instance, that "it isn't opinions that make people, it's geography," and even if that is not so, it is important to note the desire for community and stability it makes clear.

But the sense of community that is created on the Internet is in large part incidental to activity that takes place therein, or, to put a different spin on a popular phrase, on the Internet community is what happens when one is making other plans. We are struck, as we use the Internet, by the sense that there are others out there *like us*. That sense is amplified by the coincidental increase, brought about by our consumption of other media, of the feeling that the world "out there" is growing ever stranger and is less likely to resemble us as time goes on. The Internet seren-dipitously brings to us, in our living-rooms and offices, a sense of connec-tedness, but it is an aimless connectedness, a kind which reassures that between "us" and "them" there may be some common ground after all. And, once reassured, anything more brings us too close to having to go "out there."

That aimless connectedness may make Internet communities no better or worse than offline ones, but it does make them different. As Anderson (1983) noted in *Imagined Communities*, "Communities are to be distin-guished, not by their falsity/genuineness, but by the style in which they are imagined" (p. 6). The Internet's communities are imagined in two ways inimical to human communities. First, they thrive on the "meanwhile," they are forged from the sense that they exist, but we rarely directly apprehend them, and we see them only out of the corner of our eye. As my colleague Joe Schmitz has pointed out, in many instances they can be of great significance to people. Of course the popular press is fond of pub-lishing reports of people whose personal lives crumble as a consequence of their life online. Naturally we understand online life only in relation to its offline counterpart, and so our comparisons are somewhat limiting, as is, therefore, our ability to measure "significance" in these terms. We think, and sometimes feel, we belong to Internet communities, but we are not sure quite how or in what ways, or whether belonging *matters* (beyond its capacity to have a negative effect on life offline).

Second, they are imagined as parallel, rather than serial, groupings of people, which is to say that they are not composed of people who are necessarily connected, even by interest, but are rather groupings of people headed in the same direction, for a time. They may read the same things, occupy the same chat rooms for a time, view the same World Wide Web pages, in fact have the same interests and imagine that they are part of larger groups, "Internet users" in the main and subgroups from that, but they are the "old men who fill the reading-rooms of the branch public libraries" in Hoggart's description. As one Internet user put it, being online "is a time to be alone and yet be with others" (Bennahum, 1994, p. 23).

Now, clearly, like Hoggart's characters, there are those who are finding at least some, if not all, of the community interaction and belonging that they are looking for in the interactions they experience online. If there is any doubt of that one need only examine some of the chapters in mobility. We should pay significantly more attention to it in regard to the question "Can . . . civic life flourish in a mobile, multicultural society?" Scholars from differing traditions have been assessing the phenomenon of mobility from many perspectives. Perhaps its most eloquent recent naming is as "liquescence," the dissolution of the "once unquestioned markers of stability" (Critical Art Ensemble, 1994, p. 11), but it has also been characterized as a shift in meaning, or as the prevalence and primacy of "flow," or "obscenity," an era in which "there is no longer any metaphor, rather metamorphosis" (Baudrillard, 1987, p. 75), or, in Marshall Berman's (1988) poignant reflections on Marx's phrase, a time when "all that is solid melts into air." Irrespective of its name, the very act of naming it points to its antecedent, and leads to assertions such as David Reisman's (1961) that in less industrialized societies "a person rises as a cork does in water: it is simply a matter of time, and little *in him* needs to change" (p. 39).

Reisman's assertion stands in stark contrast to an increase in social mobility after the Industrial Revolution, as Sennett explains in his superb analysis of the social psychology of capitalism, when the opportunity to continually reinvent oneself flourished. Such reinvention is part and parcel of mobility, of the easing of the "burden of respectability," and part of the evolution of the concept of time as "homogeneous, empty time." Once time is "empty" in this sense, it is as if society, as Carey (1989) notes, becomes "exempt from history" (p. 119). Though I may be stretching his point, I believe Carey is correct at the individual as well as social level. Just as important, when space is "full," in the sense that there are no lands left to be discovered, "when," as Reisman (1961) puts it, "the basic physical plant of a society is felt to be built" (p. 46), the work that leads toward progress turns precisely toward personality. To again borrow from Reisman, "the product now in demand is neither a staple nor a machine; it is a personality" (p. 46). Hence the great importance of the Internet in contemporary Western society: the Internet constitutes a new frontier, and since it is a cyberspatial frontier it can be conceived as limitless. But it also provides greater opportunity for social mobility, for it is a particularly "human constructed" frontier, one that "was created by its pioneers" (Miller, 1995, p. 51). To put it another way, cyberspace is promoted as social space because it is made by people, and thus as the "new public space" it conjoins traditional mythic narratives of progress with the strong modern impulses toward self-fulfillment and personal development.

There is an illusory unification of the atomism–holism debate I have already mentioned, but it is not a resolution and it is illusory because in either instance (as the communal colonizing of a new frontier or self-development) it is self-centered and provides for no strong bonds to others. De Tocqueville (1835/1956), I believe, sensed something of this sort very early on in American history when he sought to illustrate the consequences of social mobility and introduced a fundamental dichotomy between the social and the individual:

> Amongst aristocratic nations, the different classes are like vast enclosures, out of which it is impossible to get, into which it is impossible to enter. These classes have no communication with each other, but within them men necessarily live in daily contact.
>
> But when neither law nor custom professes to establish frequent and habitual relations between certain men, their intercourse originates in the accidental similarity of opinions and tastes; hence private society is infinitely varied. In democracies, where the members of the community never differ much from each other, and naturally stand so near that they may all at any time be confounded in one general mass, numerous artificial and arbitrary distinctions spring up, by means of which every man hopes to keep himself aloof, lest he should be carried away against his will in the crowd. (p. 248)

De Tocqueville's description of social relations originating "in the accidental similarity of opinions and tastes" is a particularly appropriate description of much activity online, identifying the feeling one gets upon serendipitously stumbling across a community of interest that matches one's own tastes and opinions. That feeling is important, because it helps allay our concerns about individualism, what Charles Taylor (1992) has called one of "three malaises" that, along with instrumental reason, and the consequences of it and individualism for political life, occupy much of the thinking about modern society. Placed against that concern is one that de Tocqueville identifies, losing oneself in the crowd, becoming an indistinguishable part of a mass audience, and thus the dichotomy: how do we maintain a balance between being ourselves, individuals, and satiate our need to be social, like others, simultaneously? De Tocqueville (1835/ 1956) provides a clue:

> In aristocracies, men are separated from each other by lofty stationary barriers; in democracies, they are divided by many small and almost invisible threads, which are constantly broken or moved from place to place. (p. 248)

Those "small and almost invisible threads" are not unlike the links we create online, connections that allow us to interact, but are not sufficiently strong to keep us in place, whether that place be a physical location or a social class. Nor would it seem that we wish to be kept in place, given the modern desire for mobility. But these threads are all that is left to link us to what Taylor (1992) called our "place in the chain of being" (p. 3).[2] For an example of what occurs without those links, and in a remarkable echo of Hoggart's "old men" in the reading-room, Taylor cites "Nietzsche's 'last men' . . . [who] have no aspiration left in life but to a 'pitiable comfort'" (p. 4). These characters suffer from, among other things, a lack of recognition, and thus, as Taylor points out, a lack of dignity.

The Internet and Civil Society

Taylor's insight highlights the second issue that I wish to emphasize from Jensen's comments, one related to moral values. However weak or strong the "small and almost invisible threads" may be, it is clear that modern society is firmly of the belief that communication itself has the power to affect moral life. Carey properly situates the modern espousal of progress as having "much in common with the outlook of the Industrial Revolution . . . moral as well as material" (p. 114), well illustrated in the work of Emerson and Whitman and in

> A typical passage of the era . . . from an address by Charles Fraser to the Mercantile Library Association of Charleston, South Carolina, [investing] machinery with metaphysical properties: "An agent was at hand to bring everything into harmonious cooperation . . . triumphing over space and time . . . to subdue prejudice and to unite every part of our land in rapid and friendly communication; and that great motive agent was steam." (p. 120)

Both an ideal of a civil society and an idealized version of it are contained in that passage, and it evinces a profoundly political moral belief, for it expresses the notion "that, like Michelangelo chipping away at the block of marble, new technologies will make the world more nearly what it was meant to be all along" (Marvin, 1988, p. 235). It is a belief that Internet users share, and the pages of *Wired, Mondo 2000*, online discussions, Internet-related periodicals, are replete with its expression. But how will this belief be realized, and why via communication?

I find that we imagine it will happen because of our belief that communication reconciles the inner voice, to which we are told to be true (in search of our "authentic" self, as Taylor has it), and the outer voices that both enable us to live in the world and provide a mechanism by which we understand our social relations—and thus understand the social dimension of the authentic self. This, too, is the case with our belief in democracy. Elgin (1991) claimed that "the most powerful and direct way to revitalize our democracy is by improving our ability to know our own minds as a community of citizens" (p. 28). We search as much for our "authentic" collective self as for the individual one (and perhaps therefore pay such close attention to "public opinion").

Viewed from another angle, it is as if communication has taken the place of what Taylor (1992) has called "honour":

> In . . . earlier societies, what we would now call a person's identity was largely fixed by his or her social position. That is, the background that made sense of what the person recognized as important was to a great extent determined by his or her place in society and whatever role or activities attached to this. The coming of a democratic society doesn't by itself do away with this, because people can still define themselves by their social roles. But what does decisively undermine this socially derived identification is the ideal of authenticity itself. By definition this cannot be socially derived but must be inwardly generated. (p. 47)

This creates, of course, a paradox. Communication at once fixes our identities but also provides us with mutability and mobility. It can do so because it provides the means of self-expression, means which not only express but also articulate and circulate and, ultimately, transcend that self. In CMC (real-time or not) our words become our "seconds," alter-egos whose lives we follow as they move from one message thread to another, continually quoted (and thus alive) or archived (at rest) or for-gotten (and thus dead). Our *selves*, on the other hand, log on to see what our words have wrought, what other words/lives (from other selves) they may have generated.

To the extent that cyberspace provides us with some new form of public space, it is likely that it affords us a place for expression. What we tend to forget is that our actions and activities *vis-à-vis* self-expression have multiple trajectories, effects in more than one sphere of life, and sometimes contradictory ones, or, as the philosopher Alfred Schütz (1967) put it, we live in "multiple realities" that we conceive "more or less disconnectedly, and when dealing with one of them [we] forget for the time being its relations to the rest" (p. 207).

The Internet provides a fertile medium for the growth of multiple realities and multiple identities (see Turkle, 1984, 1995, for masterful accounts of identity online and in interaction with computers). Of course, the multiplicity of which I speak is not solely of our own making, as Schütz himself asserts, and it is not solely of our own apprehension. It is a multiplicity that in part derives from our own experience and from the experience of others, mediated via language and communication. Its most visible manifestation is in the "this-and-that"-ness of mediation described by Benedict Anderson, and it is now very visible on the Internet, within which the juxtaposition of Web pages, newsgroups, mailing lists, is infinite and immediate, since there is no space in which to put things side by side.

The Internet can thus be understood as another step in the evolution of the media of mass communication which, with the advent of the printing press and newspaper, first mixed together multiple realities in immediate fashion, giving the impression that multiple realities are of a single time and space, sometimes in pleasing juxtaposition and sometimes with terrifying randomness. And so in its multiplicity the Internet makes Anderson's "homogeneous, empty time" still more discontinuous by filling it with a never-ending "vivid present," as Schütz calls it. The Internet is another in a line of modern technologies that undermine the traditional notions of civil society that require unity and shun multiplicity while giving the impression that they in fact re-create such a society. The Internet brings us together, but the best we can do, overwhelmed by the vastness of all that it seems to encompass, is to ask, as does Schuler by focusing on purposive action, how to organize its content lest it "disturb the funda-mental idea of a single best cultural order" (Marvin, 1988, p. 192). Perhaps the single biggest difficulty facing the World Wide Web, and the Internet generally, at present is precisely the inability to organize and catalogue its contents, despite the proliferation of "search engines" for indexing Web sites and Usenet newsgroups. What is important, though, is not so much the failure or success of any such project, but that it is undertaken in the first place, for it provides evidence of the drive to organize cultural experience (Fuller & Jenkins, 1995) into the single order Marvin notes.

changes in public life of which it is both a part and a cause. There is a loss of a sense of participation in civil life and a loss of a sense of life within a unified world. The Internet, via communication, promises a single system by which we will all connect and participate, hence the propensity to claim it as the ultimate flowering of participatory democracy. But if there is additional participation it is in the guise of organization, in the sense that Lewis Mumford (1962) meant when he wrote:

> By isolating simple systems and simple causal sequences the sciences created confidence in the possibility of finding a similar type of order in every experience: it was, indeed, by the success of science in the realm of the inorganic that we have acquired whatever belief we may legitimately entertain in the possibility of achieving similar understanding and control in the vastly more complex domain of life. (p. 327)

Think, for instance, of the word "join." It has two important definitions for the present argument. One is to "put together," to combine, to, basically, organize. Another is to "come together" in the sense of associating. The first leads to stasis, *regardless of the number of connections made between disparate elements now organized.* The second is dynamic, and to an extent relies on the notion that, in fact, relationships are *out of control*, that associations are made, broken, remade, and sometimes, though infrequently, permanent. The Internet furthers the human will to organize towards stasis. Its best example, the World Wide Web, exists as a set of connections from one text to another, providing for choice in navigation from text to text. The Web is problematic, for it at once provides connection, but it does not provide archiving. Scholars (such as ones contributing to this very book) are, for instance, grappling with the difficulties of a medium that does not readily provide them with a means of citation. How do we maintain the associations that a citation system provides? One scholar has said:

> Before now, we were relying on 600 years of the print record and its elaborate infrastructure to guide the citation of a printed work. A reader who wishes to locate a book can take a few pieces of information—the author's name and title—to a library or bookstore anywhere in the world and find out if it's available. You don't have that infrastructure in the electronic world. (Guernsey, 1996, p. A18)

The same person went on to say that "The problem is made more critical . . . when one considers that challenges posed by online resources that may move or disappear in a short time" (A18). A Web author may provide links to documents that may themselves change location, and thus the ever-shifting dynamics of the medium make it more clearly one that is, in fact, out of control.

Still, its users are given choices, ones that are mostly static because they are pre-set and structured, determined for the user by the text's author. They are choices, based on forethought by authors' choices, given in anticipation of their results, and choices that are essentially binary: either I will connect to this page or to another, depending on which one makes "sense."

Such is also the work of classification and organization (Darnton, 1985), the choosing of one form of order over another (or simply over chaos and randomness). Thanks to the Internet, Steinberg (1996) claims, "the long-moribund fields of knowledge organization and information retrieval are, once again, showing signs of life" (p. 109). In social terms, such organization is often successful at putting people together, enabling cooperation, but it does little to foster *association* in the sense of intimacy and fellowship. The former is an intellectual process and one of action, the latter is an act of humanity and reflection—and community.

This distinction is, I believe, of critical importance, for it gets to the heart of social relations as process, as ritual (to borrow again from Carey) as opposed to an understanding of them as solely grounded in action. What is lacking in regard to citizenship and public life not only on the Internet but in modern society generally is an ability to transcend action, not only to provide a response but to have responsibility. Taylor (1995) pointed out the closing off of these opportunities in the eighteenth century when the public sphere, as he calls it, emerged as a political organization:

> [In] the eighteenth-century public sphere . . . the members of society come together and pursue a common end; they form and understand themselves to form an association, which is nevertheless not constituted by a political structure.
>
> By contrast, in projecting a public sphere, our eighteenth century forbears [*sic*] were placing themselves in an association, this common space of discussion, which owed nothing to political structures, but was seen as forming a society outside the state. (p. 266)

I cannot be certain whether or not Taylor intentionally used the term "projecting," but it is critical to understand that the distinction Taylor makes encompasses not only the notion of a post-eighteenth-century formation of an extra-political polity but one that is, in fact, *projected*, by way of public opinion and other mediated constructs as I have discussed earlier. The Internet, too, projects itself as a public sphere, and as one outside political structures, but only *vis-à-vis* its users' (and structure's) blockage of regulation and not in regard to its communities. Were it otherwise and the Internet were not a public space it could not be hyped as a tool for democracy. And it *is* a political enterprise, for as Sclove (1995) put it, "technologies . . . qualify as social structures by virtue of being social creations . . . [and] shape and help constitute a society's fundamental political relationships and processes" (p. 89).

But whether political or not, the mere fact of the Internet's claim to "freedom," or independence, does not guarantee it an existence beyond its users' activities. That it is a projection, and one outside the state, only lends to the sense that participation, that sense of one's voice being heard, is diminished, that Dewey's (1927) call for each to have "a responsible share" goes unheeded. As Carey (1991) claimed, "only when citizens can speak and act with some promise that their fellows will see and hear and

of hard disk storage media need occasional reformatting, a near-ritual erasing of information.

Restoration is what I believe we really seek from new technologies of communication. One telling instance of this occurred when Josh Grotstein, Prodigy's senior vice president for content, told of the stereotypically American "down-home" the Andy Griffith-like feeling Prodigy's online game players sought: "We're learning that something as simple as checkers is more than checkers. . . . What it turns out to be is like sitting on the porch talking to someone" (cited in Hafner, 1996). Yet this is an unsatisfying restoration because it is entirely made by us. There may be a game of checkers, there may be talking, but there is no porch, and thus there is no horizon, no landscape, no setting, no perspective. In *The Essential Landscape*, a book of photographs and essays focusing on New Mexico, Jackson (1985) pointed out that we used to search for our identity within our environment, that "We used to believe that a truly harmonious relationship would result when man took his identity from his setting. . . . Now we have begun to search for identity in other ways; and more and more we are inclined to manipulate the environment, use it as a tool for creating our identity" (p. 45). Of course, the Internet is the ultimate such tool. It does not even require the pre-existence of a natural environment, we provide it with one from our imagination—hence cyberspace.

If it is the case that we are inventing landscapes from whole cloth, and I believe it to be, then we are doing both our history and ourselves a disservice. We are not "redeeming what has been neglected," as Jackson (1980, p. 102) claims is best. Redemption, in this sense, comes not from merely incorporating history and its structures into the present, but from having a love for "what happened in this particular place and might happen yet again" (Carey, 1991, p. 109). We are instead continuing our neglect of Tillich's "beside-each-otherness" that matters to us as human beings, and that neglect leads to an "against-each-otherness" that Tillich called injustice, for it separates us from our sense of time and, thus, our sense of the way we affect each other.

As Sherry Turkle (1995) noted, "what matters now is the ability to adapt and change—to new jobs, new career directions, new gender roles, new technologies" (p. 255). This will likely continue to matter, but we should know by now that the Internet has not by itself brought about the contemporary situation Turkle describes. Instead, it is a technological response to the existence of Schütz's "multiple realities," a technological version of what Turkle calls the "protean" self. This is where our greatest difficulty reconciling the Internet and the social may be. Schütz (1967) boldly states, "I find myself in my everyday life within a world not of my own making" (p. 329), and so it really is not the "making" that need be our primary concern. Within the multiple realities of everyday life some are made by us, and others are not, some seem more real or natural and some seem as dreams. Reality is in essence out of control, not in the sense that it is purely chaotic but in the sense that it is uncontrollable. Such is life, and such is our use of communication technology in the apprehension of those realities and in the practice of life. Life itself is never either just simple or complex, though we may wish it were *simpler*. It is a combination of those, perhaps we may call it a complex of simplicities, and any technologies, not just the Internet, which promise to reduce that complex to a singularity, or at least a unity, will only deepen our sense of loss and estrangement from life and from others.

Notes

1. It would be interesting to reframe this debate in terms of bits, as opposed to atoms, along the lines of Nicholas Negroponte's (1995) discussion of life in the age of digital technologies, though such reframing would, I believe, not alter Taylor's persuasive use of the debate as an illustration of the dichotomy between the individual and society.

2. I am indebted to my colleague Joe Schmitz (1996) for pointing out the importance of work-related "chains of being" that exist in modern life, and that "our organizations—and increasingly both for men and women—provide lasting structures, goals and 'persons' to 'play with.' Perhaps this leads to a chronic and dysfunctional dependence on the workplace." This is a particularly important observation given the incorporation of a traditionally work-oriented technology, the computer, into the home.

References

American Library Association et al. v. United States Department of Justice. Civil Action No. 96-963 (1996). United States District Court for the Eastern District of Pennsylvania.

Anderson, B. (1983). *Imagined communities: Reflections on the origin and spread of nationalism.* London: Verso.

Barlow, J.P. (1996, September 14). Conversation with the author, Vienna, Austria.

Baudrillard, J. (1987). *Forget Foucault* (N. Dufresne, Trans.). New York: Semiotext(e).

Beniger, J. (1987). Personalization of mass media and the growth of pseudo-community. *Communication Research, 14*(3), 352–371.

Bennahum, D. (1994, June). Fly me to the MOO. *Lingua Franca, 1,* 22–36.

Berman, M. (1988). *All that is solid melts into air: The experience of modernity.* New York: Penguin.

Breslow, H. (1996, August 31). Telephone conversation with the author.

Carey, J.W. (1989). *Communication as culture.* Boston: Unwin & Hyman.

Carey, J.W. (1991). "A Republic if you can keep it": Liberty and public life in the age of Glasnost. In R. Arsenault (Ed.), *Crucible of liberty: 200 years of the Bill of Rights* (pp. 108–128). New York: Free Press.

Carey, J.W. (1993). Everything that rises must diverge: Notes on communications, technology and the symbolic construction of the social. In P. Gaunt (Ed.), *Beyond agendas* (pp. 171–184). Westport, CT: Greenwood Press.

Critical Art Ensemble (1994). *The electronic disturbance.* Brooklyn, NY: Autonomedia.

Darnton, R. (1985). *The great cat massacre and other episodes in French cultural history.* New York: Random House.

Detweiler, R.A. (1996, June 28). Democracy and decency on the Internet. *The Chronicle of Higher Education,* p. A-40.

Dewey, J. (1927). *The public and its problems.* New York: Henry Holt and Company.

Dordick, H.S., & Wang, G. (1993). *The information society.* Newbury Park, CA: Sage.

Eisenstein, E. (1983). *The printing revolution in early modern Europe.* Cambridge: Cambridge University Press.

Elgin, D. (1991, Summer). Conscious democracy through electronic town meetings. *Whole Earth Review,* pp. 28–29.

Fuller, M., & Jenkins, H. (1995). Nintendo® and new world travel writing: A dialogue. In S.G. Jones (Ed.), *CyberSociety: Computer-mediated communication and community* (pp. 57–72). Thousand Oaks, CA: Sage.

Goody, J. (1975). *Literacy in traditional societies.* Cambridge: Cambridge University Press.

Guernsey, L. (1996, January 12). Cyberspace citations. *The Chronicle of Higher Education,* pp. A-18–A-21.

Hafner, K. (1996, August 12). Log on and shoot. *Newsweek,* pp. 58–59.

Hoggart, R. (1957). *The uses of literacy.* Boston: Beacon Press.

Innis, H.A. (1951). *The bias of communication.* Toronto: University of Toronto Press.

Jackson, J.B. (1972). *American space.* New York: W.W. Norton & Company, Inc.

Jackson, J.B. (1980). *The necessity for ruins.* Amherst, MA: University of Massachusetts Press.

Jackson, J.B. (1985). The social landscape. In S. Yates (Ed.), *The essential landscape* (pp. 45–48). Albuquerque: University of New Mexico Press.

Jensen, J. (1990). *Redeeming modernity.* Newbury Park, CA: Sage.

Jones, S.G. (1994). Hyper-punk: Cyberpunk and information technology. *Journal of Popular Culture, 28*(2), 81–92.

Jones, S.G. (Ed.) (1995). *CyberSociety: Computer-mediated communication and community.* Thousand Oaks, CA: Sage.

Keillor, G. (1996, August 5). *Urban Landscapes: Minneapolis.* Disney Network Cable Television.

Leonard, A. (1996, April). Bots are hot! *Wired,* pp. 114–117, 166–172.

Licklider, J.C.R., & Taylor, R.W. (1968, April). The computer as a communication device. *Science & Technology,* 21–31.

Marvin, C. (1988). *When old technologies were new.* Oxford: Oxford University Press.

McCoy, J. (1996, August 5). Howard Rheingold launches Electric Minds, Inc. PR Newswire press release.

McLaughlin, M.L., Osborne, K.K., & Smith, C.B. (1995). Standards of conduct on Usenet. In S.G. Jones (Ed.), *CyberSociety: Computer-mediated communication and community* (pp. 90–111). Thousand Oaks, CA: Sage.

Miller, L. (1995). Women and children first: Gender and the settling of the electronic frontier. In J. Brook & I.A. Boal (Eds.), *Resisting the virtual life* (pp. 49–58). San Francisco: City Lights Books.

Mills, C.W. (1956). *The power elite.* New York: Oxford University Press.

Mumford, L. (1962). *Technics and civilization.* New York: Harcourt, Brace & World, Inc.

Negroponte, N. (1995). *Being digital.* New York: Knopf.

Oldenberg, R. (1991). *The great good place: Cafes, coffee shops, community centers, beauty parlors, general stores, bars, hangouts, and how they get you through the day.* New York: Paragon House.

Ong, W.J. (1982). *Orality and literacy.* London: Methuen & Co.

Pauly, J.J. (1986). The uses of tone: On rereading Richard Hoggart. *Critical Studies in Mass Communication, 3*(1), 102–106.

Perkowitz, S. (1996, May–June). Connecting with E.M. Forster. *The American Prospect, 26,* 86–89.

Plant, S. (1996). On the matrix: Cyberfeminist simulations. In R. Shields (Ed.), *Cultures of Internet* (pp. 170–183). London: Sage.

Putnam, R.D. (1995). Bowling alone: America's declining social capital. *Journal of Democracy, 6*(1), 65–78.

Reisman, D. (1961). *The lonely crowd.* New Haven, CT: Yale University Press.

Rheingold, H. (1991). *Virtual reality.* New York: Touchstone Books.

Rheingold, H. (1993). *The virtual community: Homesteading on the electronic frontier.* Reading, MA: Addison-Wesley.

Rice, R.E., & Love, G. (1987). Electronic emotion: Socioemotional content in a computer-mediated network. *Communication Research, 14,* 85–108.

Rifkin, J. (1987). *Time wars.* New York: Touchstone Books.

Rushkoff, D. (1994). *Cyberia.* San Francisco: HarperSanFrancisco.

Schmitz, J. (1996, August 2). Conversation with the author.

Schmitz, J., & Fulk, J. (1991). Organizational colleagues, media richness, and electronic mail. *Communication Research, 18,* 487–523.

Schuler, D. (1996). *New community networks.* New York: ACM Press.

Schütz, A. (1967). *Collected papers, vol. I.* M. Nortenson, Ed. The Hague: Martinus Nijhoff.

Sclove, R.E. (1995). Making technology democratic. In J. Brook & I.A. Boal (Eds.), *Resisting the virtual life* (pp. 85–101). San Francisco: City Lights Books.

Sennett, R. (1978). *The fall of public man.* New York: Vintage Books.

Shields, R. (1996). Virtual spaces, real histories and living bodies. In R. Shields (Ed.), *Cultures of Internet* (pp. 1–10). London: Sage.

Steinberg, S. (1996, May). Seek and ye shall find. *Wired,* pp. 108–114, 172–182.

Stoll, C. (1995). *Silicon snake oil.* New York: Doubleday.

Taylor, C. (1992). *The ethics of authenticity.* Cambridge, MA: Harvard University Press.

Taylor, C. (1995). *Philosophical arguments.* Cambridge, MA: Harvard University Press.

de Tocqueville, A. (1835/1956). *Democracy in America.* New York: Mentor Books. (Original work published 1835.)

Tillich, P. (1959) *Theology of culture.* New York: Oxford University Press.

Turkle, S. (1984). *The second self.* New York: Touchstone Books.

Turkle, S. (1995). *Life on the screen.* New York: Simon & Schuster.

Ullman, E. (1995). Out of time: Reflections on the programming life. In J. Brook & I.A. Boal (Eds.), *Resisting the virtual life* (pp. 131–144). San Francisco: City Lights Books.

Williams, R. (1989). *Resources of hope.* London: Verso.

Wise, J.M. (forthcoming). *Technology and social space.*

Zelinsky, W. (1992). *The cultural geography of the United States.* Englewood Cliffs, NJ: Prentice Hall.

creates a safety net. In cyberspace, we tend to be bolder, riskier, sometimes more rude, sometimes more kind, but the silence is broken nevertheless. We might be alone at our computers as we type, but we are participating in some form of public life; the form of public life that comes about after the mistrust of our neighbors and our intense desires for privacy force us to re-examine our atomized lives. The exciting sense of possibility permeates cyberspace.

Walzer (1986) has argued that public space can be "open-minded," when it is designed for multiple, even unforeseen purposes, and when its users are prepared to tolerate the broad utility of the space. Open minded space is a "breeding ground for mutual respect, political solidarity, civil discourse" (p. 472). Cyberspace has this "open-minded" quality; users of all stripes flock there, with only the rules of social propriety and "netiquette" to guide them, and engage with one another. Flaming and virtual harassment in cyberspace, like the Spanish Inquisition's *auto-da-fé* ceremony of public torture, illustrate the dark character of CMC's public arena, but this darkness is often the price exacted for the tolerance required to realize and maintain truly open-minded space.

When Habermas (1962/1989) conceived of the public sphere as a realm in which rational public debate helps to shape participatory democracy, he noted that the nature and limits of public space were partially determined by the concomitant social configurations of the day. Thus, cyberspace may serve as a public sphere of sorts, comparable to the seventeenth-century coffee houses of Britain and salons of Paris or to the eighteenth-century press of England and the United States. IRC chat rooms, Usenet groups, listserves, and other subscriber-supported bulletin boards serve as institutionalized forums for public exchange and debate on an assortment of issues. Despite Habermas's idealized exposition of the public sphere and its overemphasis on the value of Enlightenment rationality, his notion of the public sphere remains a useful construct for examining the spatial nature of CMC technology.

Habermas argues that the rational formation of public opinion and public policy is based on a debate within a public sphere of competing ideas. However, Habermas critic Fraser (1990) contends that his concept of the public sphere functioned not as a true realm for public debate, but as a refuge for propertied, bourgeois men to practice their own skills of governance. Women and non-propertied classes were banned from this elitist public space, thereby diminishing the potential for the debaters of the eighteenth- or nineteenth-century collectivity to engage in confrontational discourse. In contemporary America, Fraser asserts that coexisting public spheres of counterpublics—such as gays, feminists, labor organizers, anarchists, and a variety of other factions—tend to form in response to their exclusion from the dominant sphere of public debate. Thus, a multiplicity of public spheres based on collective identities and interests has emerged within the United States, where an authentic public realm that considers the interests of all citizens in a democracy has, for all intents and purposes, never existed. This multiplicity of public spheres is represented in cyberspace, where dissonance is welcome, a plurality of constituent voices enriches public space, and tolerance of flaming and hostile behaviors is exhibited.

From the Virtual Town Meeting to the Online Handshake

Whatever occurs in the space itself, CMC users can assert victory in humanity's ancient struggle with nature by overcoming the constraints of geographical boundaries and form reimagined social configurations. Cyberspace is *public* space; at the same time, cyberspace is *private* space where, via e-mail, two users can argue politics or fall in love, or several users on a private listserver can strategize a meeting or discuss the finer points of a classroom lecture. As Jones (1995) argues:

> Computer-mediated communication will, it is said, lead us toward a new community: global, local, and everything in between. But the presence of chaos inexorably draws us away from that ideal as the need for control becomes greater and greater. (p. 13)

Nevertheless, new and reproduced patterns of social relations are evident in cyberspace as the desire to control virtual space results in the formation of so-called "cybercommunities." The character, boundaries, practical manifestations, power relations, artifacts, and even the very existence of virtual communities have been explored in great detail (see particularly Jones, 1995). However, community is a term which seems readily definable to the general public but is infinitely complex and amorphous in academic discourse. It has descriptive, normative, and ideological connotations. A community is a bounded territory of sorts (whether physical or ideological), but it can also refer to a sense of common character, identity, or interests as with the "gay community" or "virtual community." Thus, the term "community" encompasses both material and symbolic dimensions; for example, the European Community was created to foster the economic interests of its constituent nations, while the New Age community of Santa Fe, New Mexico, exists around a core of symbolic, quasi-religious interests. Many scholars have debated the constitution of community and its importance within our public culture.

As well, social commentators from Howard Rheingold and John Perry Barlow to Richard Sennett have vilified the perceived decline of "community" in post-industrial America. The popularization of CMC has led to its being heralded as a means toward realizing the dreams of the communitarian movement in the United States. We tend to think of communities in the somewhat romanticized terms laid out by Ferdinand Tönnies and Georg Simmel during the late nineteenth century—as places where social interaction, shared value systems, and shared symbol systems governed the sense of community characterized by an organic notion of fellowship, custom, understanding, and consensus. More contemporary theorists argue that community encompasses the social, economic, political, and cultural—solidarity and social interaction, the production and consumption of goods, the collective formation of goals and implementation of policy, and the shared experiences and symbolic constructions that bind us culturally. These conceptions indicate that the notion of community is dynamic and evolves as society evolves, and that it is particularly pertinent in light of the emergence of CMC technology.

Perhaps the pre-eminent popular theorist about community in cyberspace, Howard Rheingold (1993), has advanced his notion of "virtual community" as "social aggregations that emerge from the [Internet] when enough people carry on those public discussions long enough, with sufficient human feeling, to form webs of personal relationships in cyberspace" (p. 5). Rheingold has argued, in the face of criticism of this notion of "placeless" community, that virtual community is real, that it speaks to vast numbers of disenfranchised people who yearn for a more organic type of community amid the confusion and chaos of post-industrial society. People need contact with one another, he says, whether it be in cyberspace or in a coffee shop. Rheingold sees virtual communities as places where people gather for conviviality—these are the places where community is built and sustained. For Rheingold, then, virtual communities harken back in nature to the fellowship, folk traditions, and cultural homogeneity of Tönnies' (1887/1957) traditional *Gemeinschaft* or even to Dewey's (1927) vision of the Great Community as a realm in which individual action fuels the collective good. Virtual communities, according to Rheingold, perform the functions of traditional, *Gemeinschaft*-like community. His virtual community is a folksy place where anyone can drop in, have a friendly chat, receive some advice about a problem, argue politics, and interact with other people who might otherwise remain strangers.

But what is the real interest driving a virtual community? Does a group of like-minded individuals constitute a true collectivity? If so, what is that collectivity's foundation? What is its charter? Rheingold wants us to believe that our need for human association and a sense of belonging is so strong that we will seek to build communities of interest in cyberspace because we might not be able to build them elsewhere. It may be that the symbolic value of virtual community is enough to sustain us in an era when physical community building is hampered by distrust or fear of (or, worse, insouciance for) our neighbors. Or, these virtual communities may serve as models for future efforts at physical community building. Ideologically, community within cyberspace appears to emphasize a shared belief in the principles of free speech, individualism, equality, and open access—the same symbolic interests that define the character of American democracy. Experientially, community within cyberspace emphasizes a community of interests that may lead to a communal spirit and apparent social bonding. These communities can be purely instrumental in nature—that is, they may never extend beyond talking to one another; or, they may promote action—that is, virtual communities may manifest themselves in real political action, such as educational or political caucuses.

However, communities of interest are closed places—they can become self-seeking, atomized, even solipsistic communities that lack a social role in the larger collectivity. Members don't necessarily have a sense of belonging to anything larger than the community itself, which adheres to an agenda shaped by the content of a discussion group. Roots in a virtual community are shallow at best; with a small investment of time and frequency of "virtual" interaction, members can establish themselves forcefully within the community. Just as easily, though, they can disassociate themselves with the community by refusing to log on, thereby leaving the community with much less trauma than what might accompany leaving a physical community. Moreover, the word "community" is seldom used in a pejorative sense; rather, community is a feeling of belonging and solidarity that we all purportedly seek, whether online or in a physical sense. Both Marshall Berman (1988) and Richard Sennett (1977) talk, however, of the disfunctionality of community—its oppressive and stifling nature. In *All That is Solid Melts Into Air*, Berman uses a section from Goethe's *Faust* to illustrate the oppressiveness of community. Faust's lover, Gretchen, is scorned by the quaint, small-town virtuous community in which she lives when it becomes public knowledge that she is no longer pure. As a series of tragedies befall her (leading ultimately to her death) she becomes the embodiment of the human foundation that must waver and finally give way to the confining, overbearing *Gemeinschaft*. Berman (1988) argues that the onset of modernity frees us all from the confinement of this now archaic form of social existence, claiming:

> Our century has been prolific in constructing idealized fantasies of life in tradition-bound small towns. The most popular and influential of these fantasies is elaborated in Ferdinand Tönnies' *Gemeinschaft und Gesellschaft*. . . . Goethe's Gretchen tragedy gives us what must be the most devastating portrait in all literature of a *Gemeinschaft*. His portrait should etch in our minds forever the cruelty and brutality of so many of the forms of life that modernization has wiped out. So long as we remember Gretchen's fate, we will be immune to nostalgic yearning for the worlds we have lost. (p. 60)

Similarly, Sennett (1977) argues in *The Fall of Public Man* that community has become enmeshed in the cult of personality—that we seek to understand social intercourse in terms of personal feelings rather than in rational or objective terms. As public culture declined with the rise of industrialization, urbanization, and mass society, Sennett claims that people began exhibiting a nostalgic desire for a romanticized notion of community as "like-minded individuals." He calls this form of community "destructive gemeinschaft," where emotional relations between people take precedence over collective action. Thus, he argues, "community in society became akin to an engine which runs only in neutral gear" (p. 239). This "destructive gemeinschaft" has a moralistic tone about it; when controversy arises within the community, emotions are stirred, moralistic rhetoric is employed, the collective personality is asserted, and the controversy revolves no longer around an issue *per se*, but around the integrity and character of the collectivity itself. Members of a community must believe in themselves, their collective personality, by downgrading their enemies and asserting who "they" are. Sennett's thoughts apply in contemporary America by illustrating the regressive nature of identity politics; the rhetoric is universal, but the community interests are specialized. Ultimately, then, Sennett echoes Berman's sentiments:

> Far from destroying fraternal community, 19th Century cosmopolitan culture made community seem too valuable. Cities appear in present-day clichés as the ultimate in empty personality. In fact, the lack of a strong, impersonal culture in the modern city instead has aroused a passion for fantasized intimate disclosure between people. Myths of an absence of community, like those of the soulless or vicious crowd, serve the function of goading men to seek out community in terms of a created common self. The more the myth of empty impersonality, in popular forms, becomes the common sense of a society, the more will that populace feel morally justified in destroying the essence of urbanity, which is that men can act together, without the compulsion to be the same. (p. 255)

What's missing in virtual communities, then, is the sense of individuality that can operate within the collectivity. According to Dewey, the individual's full potential cannot be realized without the context of the community to guide it. That community is constituted by true democracy; a democracy which may or may not exist within virtual communities. Simmel (1950) argued that individual identity is based in part on social existence, therefore the individual cannot be "actualized" without a sense of contributing to the greater collectivity. To what extent do most virtual communities provide individuals with opportunities to contribute to the greater collectivity? Etzioni (1991) and Bellah, Madsen, Sullivan, Swidler, & Tipton (1985) echo these ideas, claiming that individuals can subvert hyper-individualistic, selfish tendencies in favor of realizing the benefits of acting responsibly within a moralistic, transcendent social order. Do these benefits exist in virtual communities of interest? As Jones (1995) has stated with regard to these notions:

> The manner in which we seek to find community, empowerment, and political action all embedded in our ability to use CMC is thereby troubling. No one medium, no one technology, has been able to provide those elements in combination, and often we have been unable to find them in any media. (p. 33)

It may be, then, that Dewey's true democracy and Simmel's actualized individual identity are found in cyberspace not so much within the content of virtual communities, but within the actual structure of social relations that constitute the use of CMC. Whether we look for active community in cyberspace or whether we seek refuge rather than rational or confrontational discourse, the structure of social relations in the virtual realm and the nature of virtual space itself have notable implications for the collectivity of CMC users.

The CMC Collectivity

With the rise of industrial society, the nature of social relations was transfigured from a homogeneous social order of mechanical solidarity (based on the similarity of individuals, prevalent in pre-industrial societies) toward an organic solidarity (based on heterogeneity of individuals that arises with a well-articulated division of labor in industrial nations). And, as postmodern theorists argue, a similar cultural shift has transpired with the rise of post-industrial society; the cultural salience of local knowledge and meaning has supplanted that of the authoritarian metanarrative. Certain religious and cultural interests have retreated to tribalism in the wake of multiculturalism, diversity, and identity politics. An almost xenophobic manifestation of these ideals is evident in walled neighborhoods that offer "security and protection" from outsiders, while renewed interest is proliferating in self-sustaining communities such as the Amish, who offer models of communitarian social existence. Clearly, the "idealized" notion of community is occupying the American public psyche at present.

The ideas of community espoused by the new communitarian movement proponents, such as Etzioni and Bellah, illustrate this preoccupation as they focus on a shift away from truly collectivist notions of community. The communitarian form of community would be characterized by self-reliance in concert with a social yearning for the meaning found in a community. But nostalgic community rhetoric is not limited to social experience. Indeed, business and economic institutions in the United States are incorporating expanded notions of community into their commercial and business practices. Community is marketed in the service sector through the commodification of the symbolic aspects of religious community, for example. Purchasing crystals, books on Eastern spirituality, and homeopathic remedies allows one to possess the products that designate symbolic membership in the New Age community. Similarly, one can claim membership in the gay community by purchasing rainbow flag paraphernalia. The service sector also markets community in advertising campaigns with evocations of the romantic legacy left by close-knit communities of a bygone era. TeleCommunications, Inc. is now positioning itself as an arbiter of this form of community in its advertising campaign that highlights the cable industry's unique ability to bring online community into households. In the realm of economics, multinational trade partnerships (such as NAFTA) may transcend national boundaries, yet they are moved through legislatures with the help of community-oriented rhetoric that emphasizes mutual gain and fellowship.

Nevertheless, a tension between individuality and collectivity underlies all concepts of community. The mythos of American democratic ideology emphasizes the primacy of the individual in social relations, yet the American collectivity is defined as an inclusive sphere of diverse interests. In *The Social Contract*, Rousseau observed that tensions exist between humanity's natural state of independence and the inevitability of social existence. The problem, as Rousseau saw it and as it exists in contemporary America, is reconciling the good of the collectivity with the free will of the individual. The social contract we make is to relinquish some of our natural freedom to live in a collectivity where universal protection, civil liberty, and the collective good are emphasized. Rousseau noted that, when we forget the common good and majorities galvanize around special or private interests, we degenerate as a society into factions where we have fewer civil liberties.

Unfortunately, the complexity of industrial and post-industrial eras make the conditions for Rousseau's contract anachronistic. Regardless of the ideological significance Americans as a nation place on the notion of public life and unimpeded public discourse, the concept of a true integrated collectivity is anathema to the principles of freedom, equality, individuality. Establishing solidarity among a nation of autonomous social beings obfuscates the nature of citizenship and of collective identity.

Again, Dewey's (1927) social philosophy does not forsake the individual for the collective; he argues that true self-knowledge is gained only through the experience of community life and that democracy as a way of life requires individual participation in the creation of collective life. Thus, he tended to romanticize the notion that the Great Society could become the Great Community—that a "scattered, mobile and manifold" public could define itself as an authentic democracy. Dewey's vision of the Great Community is one in which individual activity fuels a sense of collective "good" that is shared and relished by all in the community, which in turn fuels the "liberation of potentialities" of community members; Dewey's Great Community is synonymous with his notion of democracy as a way of life.

Dewey argued that the ideas of fraternity, liberty, and equality were "hopeless abstractions" if they were separated from community existence. Equality without community becomes a mechanized form of identity that cannot be realized; fraternity without community becomes meaningless; and liberty without community becomes isolationism from social links that decays into anarchy. Dewey's great strength, then, is his insistence on individual growth and association within public life. His philosophy separates him from classical liberal theorists who argue that individuals are islands of reason, liberated from external constraints. Our humanity rests on our ability to function as individuals within a community, according to Dewey.

Similarly, Etzioni (1991) espouses the notion of a "responsive community" in which members can affirm their values in a non-coercive environment that "appeals to the 'nobler' part of the self" (p. 147). This entails a symbiotic relationship between individuals and the community that seeks to revive values, institutions, social bonds, and responsibilities in a manner that recognizes the individual but does not retreat into moralism or authoritarianism. Etzioni's communitarian agenda seems to address the concerns of Tönnies and Simmel; its charter is to regroup moral foundations in Western society. Etzioni laments the loss of these moral foundations that seemed clear, yet puritanical and authoritarian in the 1950s. Communitarians do not advocate a return to the morality of 1950s America, but rather a revitalizing of the values of citizenship that have remained so amorphous since "traditional" morality was undermined in 1960s America. The late stages of Enlightenment thinking that embraced radical individualism led to multiculturalism, special interests, and identity politics so that the notion of a shared public interest or community has withered away, according to Etzioni (1993), who argues:

> When the term community is used, the first notion that typically comes to mind is a place in which people know and care for one another—the kind of place in which people do not merely ask, "How are you?" as a formality but care about the answer. This we-ness (which cynics have belittled as a "warm, fuzzy" sense of community) is indeed part of its essence. Our focus here, though, is on another element of community, crucial for the issues at hand: communities speak to us in moral voices. They lay claims on their members. Indeed, they are the most important sustaining source of moral voices other than the inner self. (p. 31)

This "moral voice" of communities provides the social cement that holds together the moral order but does not supersede the values of society or even of humanity in general (such as "do unto others"). Etzioni (1993) argues that this morality is merely suasive, not coercive, and can be reinforced in social institutions such as schools, since religion, family, and neighborhoods have been failing to provide a moral infrastructure within communities.

Bellah et al. (1985) echo some of Etzioni's ideas, but they argue that hyper-individualism, rather than urbanization or a lack of morality, has obscured the idea of community in contemporary society. They posit that the rhetoric of individualism has become the primary language in the United States, whereas the language of traditional communities has become secondary to our culture, and is used only when the first seems inadequate. The language of individualism urges us to break from the past and reinvent ourselves, to "pull ourselves up by our own bootstraps"— Bellah et al. (1985) claim that this leads to life "somewhere between the empty and constituted self" (p. 154).

Like Etzioni and Dewey, Bellah et al. examine the conflict between individualism and the need for community, but they claim that community cannot be understood as an arrangement that merely serves to fulfill individual needs. So-called "communities of interest," they argue, are simply aggregations of self-interested, self-seeking individuals who join together to augment individual good. These communities of interest are places where "history and hope are forgotten and community means only the gathering of the similar, [and] community degenerates into lifestyle enclave" (Bellah et al., 1985, p. 154). Real community, however, is a "context within which personal identity is formed, a place where fluent self-awareness follows the currents of communal conversation and contributes to them" (p. 135). This argument resembles Simmel's notion that the individual is not wholly constituted by virtue of his or her role as an individual *per se* or as a social being *per se*. It is our communal context, our social existence, that shapes our individuality. Bellah et al. see the desire for self-reliance in concert with a social yearning for the meaning found in community to be a true paradox of contemporary Western culture.

Virtual Community as Collectivity

How then, can we conceive of virtual community as collectivity in the United States? How are the tensions between the ideals of individualism and the nature of collective life manifested in virtual communities? Although virtual communities of interest have been formed with a demonstrated sense of solidarity, have they nonetheless contributed to the fragmented cultural and political landscape of the United States that is replete with identity politics and the unfulfilled promise of a renewed public life? I argue instead that there is a *collectivity* of CMC users. This collectivity is driven by the principles of democracy and egalitarianism in its use of CMC, not necessarily in terms of the content of postings in cyberspace. The CMC collectivity is thus concerned with censorship and other types of restrictive regulations in cyberspace, and it is these concerns, these formal issues, which bind the collectivity. In Rousseau's terms, the CMC collectivity seems to be concerned with a "common good"; it tolerates the rhetoric of factionalism and tribalism in order to maintain what it sees as the universal desire for a cybercommunity that can be accessed by all who want to enter and that is free of overtly commercialized private interests.

There is a "virtual ideology" in cyberspace which is collectivist in orientation. There is a strong sense among users that, despite the tolerance needed for the space to be open-minded and despite the potential for oppressiveness, virtual interaction gives users back some of their humanity—a humanity which is authentically expressed among its constituents via a mass medium whose content is not wholly determined by corporate executives. It is an ideology that characterizes collectivist rhetoric as something positive, not something anti-American or anti-democratic. Mark Slouka (1995) has observed that the cultural fascination with cyberspace is partially the result of a deep need in humans to regain control in an alternative world since the "real" one has been "paved over, malled over" (p. 37) and has become devoid of community spirit. Further, the "community" of CMC users adhere to certain predetermined behavioral norms which advance the interests of the collectivity, such as netiquette and FAQ (Frequently Asked Question) files on Usenet and in MUDs (Multi-User Domains). MacKinnon (1995) has argued that these devices serve as Hobbes' *Leviathan*—that is, we need governmental inter-ference to protect humankind from our own evil natures, thus moderated groups in Usenet and netiquette serve as our "social contract" in cyberspace.

Kapor (1993) supports the concept of a virtual ideology that is collec-tivist in nature:

> Life in cyberspace is often conducted in primitive, frontier conditions, but it is a life which, at its best, is more egalitarian than elitist, and more decentralized than hierarchical. It serves individuals and communities, not mass audiences. . . . In fact, cyberspace seems to be shaping up exactly like Thomas Jefferson would have wanted: founded on the primacy of individual liberty and a commitment to pluralism, diversity, and community. (p. 53)

Although he acknowledges the optimism of this statement, Kapor claims that cyberspace *will* maintain some qualities of this Jeffersonian ideal if the government intervenes only by asserting its authority to redress the short-comings of private enterprise in cyberspace. Indeed, Kapor's thinking is consistent with Vice-President Gore's vision for the National Information Infrastructure, which includes CMC. Winner (1984), however, argues that this type of optimism needs to be checked:

> Where . . . is any motion toward increased democratization and social equality or the dawn of a cultural renaissance? Current developments in the information age suggest an increase in power by those who already have a great deal of power, an enhanced centralization of control by those already prepared for control and an augmentation of wealth by the already wealthy. Far from demonstrating a revolution in patterns of social and political influence, empirical studies of computers and social change . . . usually show powerful groups adapting computerized methods to retain control. (p. 92)

What Kapor sees, according to Winner, is naive since social equality, participatory democracy, and decentralized control will not be realized in a society hampered by its refusal to address CMC policy-making from an informed vantage. Questions of access to CMC technology by those other than the technological elite as well as questions of censorship, libel, copy-right infringement, and other legal quandaries still plague the development of cyberspace. Nonetheless, the ideals of openness, freedom, and tolerance pervade the collective consciousness of the community of CMC users.

Dissent within the Online Collectivity

Collectivist rhetoric has permeated the online community to a great degree since the passage of the Communications Decency Act (CDA) in February 1996 made it a crime to post "indecent, obscene, lewd, lascivious, filthy" material on the Internet in an attempt to protect minors from accessing it. While private online service providers, such as CompuServe, America Online, and Prodigy have enforced similarly established public-posting guidelines for years, the CDA represents the first attempt to overtly censor material over the decentralized Internet. All three of these commercial service providers have been embroiled in legal disputes regarding freedom of expression in public forums.

In 1990, Prodigy attempted to exercise control over the content of messages posted by subscribers on Prodigy's moderated public bulletin boards. After deciding to place limits on the number of messages subscribers could send each month, Prodigy was overwhelmed with messages from angry customers, some of which implored subscribers to boycott products and services advertised on Prodigy. Some of these messages were posted to the bulletin boards while others were quashed. When the protesting subscribers sent private e-mail messages to other members urging action against Prodigy, the service provider responded by revoking the senders' subscriptions. The incident led to cries of censorship from those asserting that the service is a common carrier, like the telephone wires, and that messages carried on those lines may not be interfered with. Others asserted, however, that Prodigy, as a commercial, private service provider, can act as a newspaper and publish whichever "letters to the editor" it deems fit or as a broadcast outlet that is regulated based on the notion that spectrum scarcity necessitates access and control of content.

The case raises free speech issues that have yet to be resolved in the halls of cyberspace. The Internet is still a public forum and thus has been regarded as a common carrier. But private service providers who act as publishers must take care to equitably decide which messages are posted and which are not. Stene (1995) suggests that the development of First Amendment law as applied in cyberspace is much more precarious than imagined. For example, Stene claims that the scope of the law changes when publishers, attorneys, and scholars no longer hold sole domain over First Amendment issues:

> As each person logs on to the Net, another publisher is born to this world, capable of libeling another individual to tens of thousands of people with a simple "send" command. . . . [T]he First Amendment must now be understood to be that which the majority of the people on the Net *believe* it to be, not as how it has historically been determined by the Court. (p. 3)

The legal morass created by this issue is illustrated in another Prodigy case. In 1991 the service provider allowed anti-Semitic messages which suggested that the Holocaust was a myth to be posted on its moderated bulletin boards. When the Anti-Defamation League of B'nai B'rith protested, Prodigy claimed that it had agreed to ban material that is "grossly repugnant to community standards" (Feder, 1991, p. 21). Nonetheless, it continued to allow postings questioning the truth of the Holocaust.

In a similar case, *Cubby* v. *CompuServe*, a New York federal district court ruled that CompuServe was not liable in a libel suit filed against the service provider regarding content it distributed via a newsletter. Thus, private service providers are not responsible for content disseminated in publications over their networks; rather they are merely distributors like libraries or bookstores. But for the Internet (now regarded as a common carrier), companies can be sued in other countries for distributing defamatory material via the World Wide Web. For example, a company that posts material critical of the government in Singapore can be held liable for defamation in Singapore (Edupage, 1996). These types of measures will become all too common if the CDA is deemed enforceable.

Presently, members of the CMC collectivity who want to uphold democratic ideals in cyberspace are claiming that the enforcement of the CDA will have a "chilling effect" on the future of electronic communication. Evidence of this chilling effect already abounds. CompuServe has eradicated 200 sexually oriented newsgroups from its service, citing "pressure" from German authorities, which claimed that the "indecent" content breached its laws. Because CompuServe could not drop the newsgroups only in Germany, all users lost access. The groups that were dropped included all of the alt.gay and alt.homosexual newsgroups, which amounted to 90 percent of homosexual Usenet content. Despite later assurances from German authorities that they disapprove of Internet regulation and that the "pressure" had been exerted by a lone bureaucrat, CompuServe has not reinstated the lost newsgroups (Telecom Post #22, 1996). Similarly, a bill has passed in the New York State legislature that grants liability to Internet Service Providers for content disseminated on their networks. The bill prohibits the knowing distribution of content that depicts "actual or simulated nudity, [or] sexual conduct" that is "deemed harmful to minors." The bill makes no distinction between public forums and private e-mail, making this form of communication illegal on discussion groups, e-mail, and Web pages (Telecom Post #22, 1996).

Government policy regarding privacy, free speech, and other civil liberties in cyberspace has lagged behind the developments of CMC technology, as these examples illustrate. Yet there exists within the CMC collectivity the profound adherence to the notion that freedom of expression is essential to individual liberty and free will. While these issues tend to stir the embers of the individualist/collectivist tensions, civic-minded Net citizens seem to constitute the CMC collectivity. Most members of the collective accept moderated newsgroups not as censorship or prior restraint, but as a concession they are willing to make to ensure the common good of the collectivity. This accepted virtual ideology, in concert with the lack of informed governmental policy regarding freedom of expression in cyberspace, has led to the creation of several groups, most notably the Electronic Frontier Foundation (EFF) and the Computer Professionals for Social Responsibility (CPSR), to pursue civil liberties in cyberspace. The Electronic Frontier Foundation, founded by Mitchell Kapor and John Perry Barlow, encourages policy-makers to adopt an open agenda for telecommunications; provides support for legal perspectives on the developing CMC frontier; and supports public interest litigation (such as anti-CDA measures) to preserve First Amendment guarantees in cyberspace (Cisler, 1990). The EFF and

CPSR recognize that lines separating public and private in cyberspace are all but clear. For example, although private e-mail is protected from unauthorized governmental interception by the 1986 Electronic Communications Privacy Act, private companies may choose to monitor their employees' e-mail exchanges. But insofar as cyberspace is considered public space, these agencies seem to have the support of the CMC collectivity to uphold the tenets of virtual ideology.

Kapor (1991) has argued that CMC discussion groups serve as one of the most potent uses of First Amendment freedoms of association and expression. He has also observed that CMC is a hybrid of sorts and thus does not follow one regulatory media model. CMC contains elements of publishing, telephone calls, and even broadcasting. Cyberspace is both public and private, the communication is one-to-one, one-to-many, and many-to-many. And, because cyberspace is open-minded space, its users will develop it in new ways regardless of what restrictions commercial service providers attempt to impose on it. Kapor (1991) supports regulatory policy commensurate with these contentions:

> We know that electronic freedom of speech, whether in public or private systems, cannot be absolute. In face-to-face conversation and printed matter today, it is commonly agreed that freedom of speech does not cover the communications inherent in criminal conspiracy, fraud, libel, indictment to lawless action and copyright infringement. (pp. 162, 164)

The collectivist virtual ideology does not expect that freedom in cyberspace will be absolute. Members of the CMC collectivity know that power is exercised quite differently in cyberspace than in traditional mediated environments limited by space or spectrum allocation. For example, free speech principles go only so far, according to Wiener (1994), when unmoderated newsgroup discussions degrade into flame wars, propaganda, or just utter nonsense. Garbage posts often result in censorship. And, with the expansion of the Internet in its current anarchic state (governed only by threats of the CDA, netiquette, and moderators), a few sociopaths can ruin the CMC environment for all. But the sense of common good that drives the collectivity of CMC users tolerates the boundaries drawn by the desire to maintain the *whole* in the face of its potentially drastic restructuring amid regulatory constraints. Wiener (1994) argues that moderation is not necessarily censorship because newsgroups operate like a letters-to-the-editor column where lucid postings are forwarded and clearly irrelevant or malicious posts are squelched.

Moreover, sanctions against errant posters to moderated newsgroups are part of the social contract, which states that absolute individual freedom must be given up in order to preserve civil liberty and to guarantee the rights to speak within the CMC environment. Free speech has a price according to established law; it also has a price in cyberspace. True dissenters in cyberspace are those who don't put faith in the collectivist rhetoric of the CMC community. Nonetheless, the groups that would appear to be the harshest dissenters—hackers, neo-Nazi propagandists, anarchists—are the ones who tend to benefit most from the First Amendment guarantees in cyberspace. Their speech is staunchly protected under the First Amendment until such time as the CDA should take effect. And, although criminal hackers have been targeted by federal law enforcement groups as potential threats to commercial security, racist propaganda, recipes for illegal synthetic drugs and bombs, and pornography freely circulate in both the public and private reaches of cyberspace.

Still, there exists a general fear and misunderstanding surrounding the limits of cyberspace. The public seems frightened by the possibility that terrorists or drug cartels could organize via computer and execute criminal acts over the phone lines. Popular movies such as *War Games* and *Hackers* fuel public perceptions that computer hackers can, with a few keystrokes, jeopardize national security or international commerce or that cyber-pedophiles will cause irreparable harm to our children. In part, this public fear inspired policy-makers to adopt the CDA. Although children have easily been able to acquire pornography for decades, the thought of them receiving it via the mysterious tangle of telephone wires and the black hole that is cyberspace seems more insidious to a public that has been bombarded with too many popular depictions of a dark, technocratic, inhumane future.

As dissenters within the collective, hackers have an unusual status. Some hackers, such as Kevin Mitnick, and groups of hackers, such as the Legion of Doom and the Lords of Chaos, have been convicted of computer crimes ranging from diverting money from corporate to personal accounts to stealing credit card numbers (Sterling, 1992). Indeed, hackers have been declared "enemies of the state" in part, as Ross (1991) claims, to legitimize the notion that hackers threaten free and open information exchange. Hackers have an ideology all their own, however. The hacker ethic is generally one that is against the privatization of the CMC collective and for the democratization of cyberspace. Hacking is a countercultural activity, one that rejects the Luddite character of past countercultural movements, so that, Ross (1991) contends, there has been

> a shift in the relation of countercultural activity to technology, a shift in which a software-based technoculture, organized around outlawed libertarian principles about free access to information and communication, has come to replace a dissenting culture organized around the demonizing of abject hardware structures. (p. 120)

Hacking is a counterculture in the broader sense, but not necessarily with regard to the collective CMC culture. With so many Usenet newsgroups and Web pages devoted to the art of hacking, such as alt.hackers, alt.2600, alt.2600.hackerz, alt.2600.moderated, alt.hackers.discuss, alt.hackers.malicious, and the hackers' Jargon File at Uniform Resource Locator (URL) http://fount.journalism.wisc.edu/jargon/jarg-intro.html, it is a small investment of time for the novice to become a professional steeped

in the requisite expert knowledge. The hacking cyber-subculture is dis-
affected from the larger cyberculture in part, but it is still associated with
legitimate high-tech industrial needs since the hacker expertise can be used
in business to safeguard against invasions by foreign hackers. So hackers
occupy a unique position within the CMC collective culture as a sub-
culture of rebels and as protectors of civil liberties and the democratic
right to openness and freedom (Ross, 1991). The targets of hacker efforts,
Ross observes, are usually "official" computer systems—defense and intelligence agencies, police, and the armed forces—attacked in defense of civil
liberties imperiled by centralized bureaucracy of the military–industrial
complex. There is nothing to prevent hackers from partially disabling the
CMC environment itself through the introduction of crippling viruses.
Instead, they seem to embrace the Jeffersonian ideals that Kapor (1993)
advocates. And, often times, hackers are not true criminals but joyriding
kids who want to taste the forbidden fruit of trespassing in cyberspace.

Thus, dissent within the CMC collectivity can be seen as a championing
of the ideals of egalitarianism, openness, and freedom of expression in
terms of content. Calls for public activism are rampant in cyberspace—
protests against government regulation of the Internet, against other
proposed governmental legislation, and even against corporate environmental policies can be monitored and debated via listservers and Usenet
groups such as alt.activism and misc.progressive. But in formal terms,
dissent within the CMC collectivity takes on this character as well; hackers
revolt against principles and practices that tend to violate the collectivist
virtual ideology rather than undermine it, and widespread civil dis-
obedience on the Internet, in the form of intentional violation of the
restrictions imposed by the CDA, is likely in the event that the CDA is
eventually upheld.

Virtual Agora, Underground Newspaper, or Cybercommunity?

If we regard CMC to be nothing more than a new mode of communication, an underground newspaper of sorts, the implications of the issues
raised in this chapter are not particularly far-reaching. The ideas of
community, collectivist virtual ideology, freedom of expression and dissent
within the pages of a virtual newspaper are important, but the readers of a
newspaper do not have the personal investment and commitment to a way
of life that participants in a community do. If we think of the CMC
environment as a virtual agora, a *place* where people reside in a bodiless
form, where social structure and meaning exist, and where action can
spring forth, these ideas become more significant. CMC will not likely
transcend the contemporary manifestation of democracy in the United
States if it is regarded as nothing more than a counterpart of current
communication technology. But, treated as a place where the virtual
collectivity is socially constructed, CMC has the potential to help us

translate some of the ideology of virtual existence into our collective American psyche.

There is no question that virtual existence can be observed through traditional ethnographic means—by examining events, artifacts, and social relations. But a more complete picture of cyberspace considers virtual ideology, the place of the individual within the collective, and the power struggle that unfolds as boundaries are renegotiated, broken, and formed anew. The online collectivity does indeed reproduce existing structures, but it also undermines them and raises new possibilities for resistance *from the collective* and against the culture writ large. The content of discourse within the CMC collective is so diverse that the nature of dissent in cyberspace seems to indicate an embrace of postmodern notions of multinarrative discourse within a decentralized, fragmented public sphere that knows no definitive national boundaries, but rather institutional and socially constructed ones. Dissonance within the online collective in part focuses on the formation of the collective itself. People yearning for some new type of communal bonding, a new form of experiencing human contact, or a new form of social existence within an essentially lawless frontier themselves constitute a dissenting voice on the landscape of cultural experience. For some, their experiential lives in cyberspace, their embrace of the collectivist virtual ideology, and their willingness to follow the norms and social expectations that comprise the virtual social contract constitute a rejection of the overly individualistic character of contemporary American social existence. For these members of the collective (including hackers, civil libertarians, and anarchists), cyberculture and virtual ideology are real constructs from which meaning is derived.

References

Bellah, R., Madsen, R., Sullivan, W.M., Swidler, A., & Tipton, S.M. (1985). *Habits of the heart: individualism and commitment in American life.* New York: Harper & Row.

Benedikt, M. (1991). Cyberspace: Some proposals. In M. Benedikt (Ed.), *Cyberspace: First Steps* (pp. 119–224). Cambridge, MA: MIT Press.

Berman, M. (1988). *All that is solid melts into air. The experience of modernity.* New York: Penguin.

Carey, J. (1995). The press, public opinion, and public discourse. In T. Glasser & C. Salmon (Eds.), *Public opinion and the communication of consent* (pp. 373–402). New York: Guilford.

Cisler, S. (1990). An essay on the openness of networks, electronic free speech, and the security of computers. *Online, 14*(6), 101–104.

Cubby v. *CompuServe*, 766 F. Supp. 135 (SDNY 1991).

Dewey, J. (1927). *The public and its problems.* New York: Henry Holt.

Edupage (1996, February 27). *Educom,* educom@elanor.oit.unc.edu.

Etzioni, A. (1991). *A responsive society: Collected essays on guiding deliberate social change.* San Francisco: Jossey-Bass.

Etzioni, A. (1993). *The spirit of community: Rights, responsibilities, and the communitarian agenda.* New York: Crown.

alt.music.indigo-girls. That's not a community; it's a fan club. Newsgroups, mailing lists, chat rooms—call them what you will—the Internet's virtual communities are not communities in almost any sense of the word. A community is people who have greater things in common than a fascination with a narrowly defined topic. (Snyder, 1996, p. 92)

It is such critiques that make the question of the Internet community so troublesome. While Anderson could have argued for the Internet to be a forum for the production of community, many others would be hard-pressed to agree, since by the very nature of the technology, the use of a computer monitor and a keyboard, participation through the Internet becomes an individualized activity where the "human touch" is often lacking. Indeed it can be argued that such humanization would detract from the notion of community because it is antithetical to the way we have been naturalized to think of communities. These arguments are central to technophobes who have argued that technology is dehumanizing and consequently the application of technology would transform the culture and everyday life of people (see, e.g., the arguments of Neil Postman, 1993). However, it is also true that every technological invention and adaptation, from fire to the Internet, has transformed the way in which humans relate to each other and form communities. Consequently, it is relatively difficult (and perhaps fruitless) to arrive at a definitive description of community because that itself is a provisional construct changing in meaning as new technologies of communication evolve. This chapter is an attempt to rethink the notion of community in the face of the use of the Internet. What remains constant, however, is the notion that communities require interaction and involve people.

With the emergence of media technologies, nations and communities could be imagined around other central popular cultural formations, for instance those of broadcast media and film. Often nations are produced and represented by media and there emerge specific media formations which can be called "national media" because they represent the principal cultural practices of the nation (see, e.g. Elsaesser, 1989; Hay, 1987; Turner, 1988). It can thus be argued that particular communities and nations are symbolically and representationally produced around specific popular cultural practices like those of language and media.

With the growth of CMC, particularly from use of the Internet, a new set of possibilities for community and nation formation have emerged. Unlike the distributed system of mass communication, with a central agency producing the media messages, the computer system could be used as a more "democratic" apparatus where access is broadly distributed and brings with it the option of interaction, offering new possibilities of community formation. For instance, Jones (1995) and Baym (1995) have argued that the new CMC technologies have produced the opportunity and the possibility for the creation of electronic communities where a set of shared practices help to produce the conditions that are similar to traditional communities outside of the realm of computers and virtual spaces defined by the "bit"-based technology of computers (see, e.g., the work of Negroponte, 1995).

To think of community in the electronic age, the construct of commonality becomes central because the technology has now provided the ability to communicate across the boundaries and limitations that the traditional community imposed. Carey (1989) pointed out a fundamental perspective that addresses the issue: "Communication under a ritual view is the sacred ceremony that draws persons together in fellowship and commonality" (p. 7). It is precisely this question of commonality and fellowship that becomes the critical issue in the context of this analysis. Indeed, what produces community in the era of the Internet are the shared systems of culture, language, and beliefs that are spread across large distances and consequently the opportunities for community formation *vis-à-vis* the Internet have broadened in scope and possibilities.

This broadening of the horizons has happened in the last couple of decades, which have seen significant steps in the development of CMC in the production of interpersonal and group relationships; this period has also witnessed the emergence of new social blocs whose communal, tribal, and national roots have been disrupted by voluntary and involuntary migration and immigration, with the consequent production of atomized individuals who find themselves spatially removed from the people with whom they have been historically affiliated. The movement of people across geographic borders and the emergence of diasporic immigrant communities across the globe, particularly in Western Europe and America, have now produced a large group of people whose places of origin are far removed from their current location. Instances of such groups abound as Census in America reports the increasing presence of immigrants and permanent residents.[3] These are people who are also playing a pivotal role in the culture, politics, and economics of the West. Along with this development has come increasing tension about the presence of such immigrants, as evidenced in the enactment of laws that curb the freedom of immigrants, exemplified in the 1994 passage of Proposition 187b in California, which denies access to public service for specific classes of immigrants.

Immigrants are usually not geographically close to each other (barring the instances of "Korea-towns," "little-Indias," and other groupings of sociologically and ethnically similar people in large urban areas of the West). Unlike the earlier immigrants who set up home in the boroughs of New York and neighborhoods of Chicago, producing Italian, Polish, and other ethnic enclaves in metropolitan areas, with a shared language and often shared common work-areas, the new immigrants, particularly the well-educated, professional Asian immigrants, do not share the same geographic spaces. They are often scattered across the Western hemisphere, working in similar professions but spatially distanced from each other. This has produced an increasing need for alternative means of community formation, and I believe that one of the many ways in which such groups are being formed is with the use of electronic communication systems.[4] This is more and more evident in the growth of electronic "newsgroups" which are earmarked for specific nationalities and communities within nations. I will elaborate later, but suffice to say these diasporic people, geographically displaced and distributed across large areas, are gaining access to CMC technologies and are increasingly using these technologies to re-create a sense of virtual community through a rediscovery of their commonality. Through this process, new images of community and nation are emerging by the discursive activity of creating and exchanging messages on electronic bulletin boards.[5]

The conditions of existence of the diasporic individuals and their need to form community cannot be understood in traditional terms where spatial proximity was a necessity. It is only when one can move the discussion of community to the more abstract level of shared practices and experiences such as those of language and media that it is possible to begin to understand how a shared system of communication such as CMC, with its shared language and systems of meaning, can be used to produce communities that do not need geographic closeness. This is precisely why the construct of the "imagined" community becomes powerful in thinking of the communities being formed in the electronic forum. The electronic communities produced by the diasporic people are indeed imagined connections that are articulated over the medium of the Internet, where the only tangible connection with the community is through the computer, a tool to image and imagine the group affiliation.

Internet Communities: Towards Finding Defining Characteristics

The computer-aided communication system that is now widely available has been labeled several different ways. However, as an emergent cultural formation, it has not been described in any detailed and standardized manner. "Internet" is a term that has been used as an umbrella for the various forms of this technology (see, e.g., Badgett & Sandler, 1993; Braun, 1994; Glistner, 1993; Krol, 1992; LaQuey, 1993; see also the work of Jones, 1995; Rheingold, 1993). The term "Internet" has become a generic label that refers to the electronic system and space where many people can present their ideas to produce a new computer "reality" which is the sum of the various opinions, ideas, practices, and ideologies represented by the texts that make up the bulk of bulletin board "postings."[6]

As suggested by the term "posting," Internet information is primarily textual, although increasingly there is a movement towards the use of images and sound to supplement text-based information. The user of the interactive component of the Internet is consequently immersed in a discursive space and is bombarded with a barrage of texts that are constantly being produced by thousands of other users. Since the Internet user is empowered to play an active role in the production of the discursive community, identity and community are formed around the discourses that are shared by members inhabiting the cross-national virtual space of the computer and Internet. The texts exchanged on the Internet are the artifacts which hold the Internet communities together as well as indicators of the direction in which the community is headed. Identities within the community are produced primarily by the way in which the participants insert themselves into the discourse. Consequently the textual nature of the Internet communities is its first distinctiveness.

This textuality of CMC has also attracted a large amount of research attention. However, most of the concerns have been with the way in which the text is used to produce messages, such as the use of "emoticons," "flaming," "spamming,"[7] and other characteristics of the discourse specific to the electronic medium. Part of the reason for the involvement with the characteristics of the text has arisen out of the focus on the "interpersonal" aspects of CMC. The effort has been towards understanding how dyadic communication proceeds in the scenario of the computer, but when considered as a discursive arena with multiple voices, it is important to move beyond the question of the dyad or the small group and tackle the question of the community as a large collection of users of the Internet. On the other hand, the arguments about "pseudo-community" that have been proposed by Beniger (1987) and Peck (1987) question the authenticity of the community being produced solely by electronic texts. The question of authenticity is connected with the interpersonal/impersonal debate in which the textual form of the Internet is criticized for lacking the "touch" that traditional communities would share. However, this argument presupposes a fundamental proximity of space that Rheingold (1993) denies, insisting that "virtual communities" are free of the constraints of place and space and are able to emerge as global communities separated only by time zones. There are thus a variety of ways of thinking of the significance of textuality. However, what remains true is the overwhelming textual dependence of the Internet.

Another defining characteristic of the medium is its ephemerality. It is a constantly shifting space where specific texts remain available for a limited period of time. Consequently the image that is produced by these texts is non-permanent.[8] Therefore, to become a member of the community one has to maintain an element of continuity, and access the boards and newsgroups on a regular basis to follow the discourse. Rheingold's (1993) discussion of the WELL also presupposes this continuity because only in that continuity does the community develop. While it is possible to preserve the continuity in a digital fashion, and it is also possible for a new entrant to a newsgroup to call up that stored information, that is a rare occurrence and can be compared to the nearly impossible task of attempting to learn the history of a geographical neighborhood by trying to access all the conversations the neighbors might have had since the neighborhood was formed. Consequently the images of the community are produced through the ongoing interaction that is possible on the Internet.

The image produced by the texts exchanged in the electronic community is thus unstable and predicated upon prior knowledge. Since messages are categorized by theme, the arguments proposed in the messages become relatively incomplete unless the user is able to draw upon the memory of earlier texts that shape any particular topical discussion. This is a fundamental characteristic of any dialogic process, where only in the exchange of texts does an argument or an image evolve. This can be constructed in terms of Bakhtin (1981) and Volosinov's (1973) argument that the dialogic nature of text can either be open or closed. In the context of the Internet the discourse is indeed open and, as argued by Bakhtin/Volosinov, dialogue is generative and continuous as the textual utterances on the Internet necessarily anticipate other utterances, and it is in the exchange that specific images and positions appear.

Next, the question of agency and intentionality becomes more problematic here than, for instance, in the case of television. Even though there have been changes in the way the audience of media could be studied (see, e.g., the 1980 work of Hall on encoding and decoding of media texts, and the 1988 article by Allor on rethinking the site of the audience), the Internet poses a different situation because there is no Internet audience who is also not empowered to become an agent to mold the space as he or she wishes. In this case the notion of "using" a text becomes particularly powerful because the audience can indeed take any text on the public sphere of the Internet and "respond" to it or "rewrite" it in a new way where the new text immediately becomes a part of the discursive space accessible to everyone. Consequently I prefer to use the term "user-audience" to capture the dual role of the Internet participant (see de Certeau, 1984, for a discussion of "use" of texts).

This ability to produce texts and become a part of the discourse has often been referred to as the "interactive" nature of the Internet. Additionally, the issue of interactivity has been used to construct the similarities between the Internet and traditional face-to-face modes of communication.[9] Some authors have questioned the need to find the congruences between face-to-face situations and the electronic contexts, arguing that the face-to-face condition need not be considered primary or standard. This is particularly true in the context of the construction of national images since traditional face-to-face community-building simply did not provide the opportunity for the level of discourse and the proliferation of texts necessary to produce a national image that the spatially displaced electronic community provides. I therefore believe that in the context of national image production the electronic community needs to be compared with traditional media of mass communication. Indeed the Internet's text-based system provides the "high touch" that is lacking in the mass-mediated situation, as well as developing the *Gemeinschaft* associated with the face-to-face situation. To me the key is the empowerment that the Internet provides across a much larger forum than the face-to-face situation can provide. The user-audience can much more decisively determine how specific images will be produced at any moment either by posting responses or by posting original texts to produce new images.

The Internet Communities and Nations

The collective thinking that is possible on the Internet happens in a virtual space that is accessible to anyone with a computer, a modem, and an "account" on a computer system that is networked. There are minimal technological barriers to using this entire unlimited virtual space to send a message. However, the user-audiences of this space have attempted to contain the potential anarchy of unlimited postings by artificially sub-dividing the space into many spaces which, in the Internet vocabulary, are called "subgroups."

For the purpose of this analysis I focus on the subdivisions within the "soc.culture" Usenet group. There are numerous subgroups within the hierarchy of "soc.culture." These represent nations, communities, tribes, cultures, and ways of life from Afghanistan to Zimbabwe. The nationality of a subgroup is indicated by a third element to the name. There are thus groups such as soc.culture.*indian*, soc.culture.*korean*, etc. For the purpose of this analysis, the Indian subgroups are selected for critical review. However, the analysis considers other subgroups that also play a role in producing the national image. Currently there are a large number of subgroups across which cross-posting occurs to produce images of India and the subcontinent. These are subcategories of the general Indian sub-groups, but this analysis will also make reference to other groups, particu-larly soc.culture.bengali, soc.culture.pakistani, and soc.culture.bangladesh, since the image is the product of discourses that occur across all these groups.

Looking for India on the Internet

For the purpose of this study a listing of all the postings on March 25, 1995 was obtained from the soc.culture.indian (sci) group. A total of 1,287 postings were identified. Subsequently the newsgroups were observed on a random basis to explore emergent issues that appear in the virtual space. The identification of the large number of postings on a specific day works as a "freeze frame" of the thousands of postings that appear on the bulletin board and disappear as they are read and responded to, while the regular visits represent the way in which the community grows or deals with the issues that are important to their members. These postings represented members of the community who are actively participating in producing discourse by reading and responding to the texts that appear on the Internet space. However, there is a larger group of users who are only reading the posts and not necessarily adding geographic space where they are attempting to negotiate their dual identity as an immigrant and as a member of a place of origin, an amalgam which now becomes discursively produced in their postings. These users enter into an exchange of ideas and opinions which collectively represent their new identities in the West while also producing their own images of the West and India.

These images are produced within a second thematic area that can be called *national critical discourse*. These are postings that address the issue of religion, and the tensions around the practices of religion that produce the contemporary national identity of India and its relation with other nations of the world. Postings with subject headings such as "BURN KORAN IF BOY DIES" and "STOP BASHING OUR PRIESTS" attempt to produce an image of India rooted in a rediscovered allegiance to the Hindu religion. The theme is developed through a process of exchange. The themes also mutate as new postings appear, so what could start as a discussion about religion could easily transform into a discussion about politics, culture, and language. For instance, the following exchange responded to recent regional polls and the victory of a self-professed Hindu party in a Western state of India (Maharashtra):

> *On March 25, 1995 "kulbir" wrote:*
> The new premier of Maharashtra, a Western Hindustani province belongs to Shiv Sena whose head is Mr. Bal Thakre. Mr. Thakre is a controversial charismatic right wing leader of Hindus. He is on record saying that if he becomes the PM of Hindustan he will give Muslims 48 hours to leave India.
> *To this, "Dr. Jai Maharaj" responded on March 26, 1995 with the following:*
> Is it possible for you to substantiate your claim above with a reference to a published source?
> *On the same day "Rohan Oberoi" quoted both the above posters and wrote:*
> I can give reference for this one. The interview was published in TIME, January 25, 1993. Asked "But Muslims are beginning to flee Bombay," Thakre replied "If they are going, let them go. If they are not going, kick them out." Told that "Muslims are beginning to feel like Jews in Nazi Germany," he replied, "Have they behaved like the Jews in Nazi Germany? If so, there is nothing wrong if they are treated as Jews were in Nazi Germany."
> This is from memory, so I may have the wording wrong here and there, but you're welcome to look up the interview.

This exchange illustrates several aspects of the way in which opinions are developed and disseminated on sci as claims are made, refuted, and substantiated by members of the network. Interestingly, the initial claim made by "kulbir" is later substantiated not by the same person but by a different member of the community who offers the citation from the popular news magazine. In addition, the entire exchange produces a polarization in the community as there are clearly two schools of thought concerning this politician and consequently the way in which India can be imagined on the network. Moreover, all three of the posters are outside of India and are using the sci space not for any specific political activism but only as a forum where conflicting opinions can be aired, and through such discourse a national image can be produced. This exchange also highlights the textuality of the Internet, its constantly shifting foci of discussions, and the empowerment of the user-audiences, all of which are the unique characteristics of the network.

Other subject headings also produce similar polarizations and national images. While the above exchange was going on, members of the sci group were also participating in discussions of another topic area of critical national importance. Given the early 1995 victory of the party led by the politician referred to above, the other theme also dealt with the issue of religion, culture, and politics. The connection between themes, worldviews, and authors become apparent in the following exchange between "Jai Maharaj" and a set of other participants. The theme of this exchange is the debate that has erupted in India over the renaming of the commercial center of Bombay (the capital city of the state of Maharashtra) to its pre-British name of Mumbai. The following exchange lays out the connections that are being drawn between this event and other themes that are popular on sci:

On March 25, 1995 "Krishanan" posted the following:
I realize that the Shiv Sena is changing the name because it the name BOMBAY was christened by foreigners. But the implications are too expensive. All the airlines have to change the name from Bombay to Mumbai. . . . And all of this for what, it is not going to benefit anybody for changing the name, bcoz the British do not feel slighted by this act, except it might just elicit a few laughs at this jingoistic and brash act.
In response "Dr. Jai Maharaj" wrote:
Send the bill to London. Also, enclose a demand for the return of the Koh-i-noor diamond, all other stolen riches, and just compensation to all victims and their descendants for the British atrocities on the people of Bharat and south Asia.
The piece is signed off with the Hindu greeting "Om Shanti," which translates to "Hail Peace."

This exchange demonstrates the way in which particular posters align themselves with specific images of India. Maharaj claims that India is better called "Bharat," the ancient Hindu name for the geographic space, while the other poster offers a more pragmatic analysis of the consequences of the change of name.

Connected with this polarization is the way in which the Indian national image is juxtaposed with its relationship to Pakistan. Given the strong Hindu-centric tendencies seen in the newsgroup, and the cross-posting that continues constantly, exchanges such as the following become common-place and reproduce the antagonism between the nations:

On April 3, 1995 A member of the Pakistani newsgroups responded with the following to an earlier cross-post:
You damned Sikhs/Hindus you are right, you do not level up to Pakistanis. So do not bother comparing your lowly selves to us.

is flawed and unproductive. Connected with the Hindu base are associated concerns about the role of women in Indian society, where, too, there is continuing debate over the appropriate "place" for women in India and their specific insertion in the social fabric.

Also connected with this religious and nationalistic image is the strong antagonism that is expressed towards Pakistan and Bangladesh. Indeed, it would appear that many members of the group would just as well "nuke" Pakistan and remove it from the face of the earth. When such messages are cross-posted in the Pakistani newsgroups there is certainly a groundswell of reactions and the virtual conflict becomes even more pronounced. This image of the struggle is manifest in a variety of contexts that deal with the issues in Kashmir, terrorism in Punjab, the general Hindu revival, and anti-Islamic feelings in India.

Connected with this image is a picture of internal dissent that is not only manifest in the debates about politics in India but is also represented in the number of subgroups that have emerged out of the sci parent group. The fact that there are separate groups for Tamils, Bengalis, and Punjabis becomes a representation of the irreconcilable differences that exist between the "tribes" within India. The notion of a "tribe" on the Internet has been suggested by Rheingold (1993), who considers the various parts of the WELL as tribes, while as a post-national formation the concept of the ethnic tribes has been suggested by Appadurai (1993), who argues that there is an increasing emergence of the trope of the tribe as media, such as the Internet, are being mobilized by the diasporic communities to rediscover their fundamental affiliations and allegiances. It is this tendency that is represented on the Net as well, but now a large number of people can obtain this image by following the discourses on the Net.

Finally, the network image of India is produced by the discourses of a limited set of people who have taken the initiative to wield their electronic strength, and it is these voices that are heard over and over again as they attempt to establish a particular dominant image of India. There has been a certain degree of debate about the identity of these users as well. As illustrated in the earlier examples, in the period considered here, perhaps one of the most vocal members of sci has been the character called "Dr Jai Maharaj." This user had been cross-posting in a variety of newsgroups and maintains a strong Hindu/Indian stance that supports the creation of a Hindu state and the resurrection of "Bharat," a historical name associated with a re-imaging of the subcontinent around its Hindu orientation. His posts have also included arguments about the need for vegetarianism and the connection between vegetarianism and Hinduism. He became known primarily because of his rampant cross-posting, which angered members of newsgroups who felt that their spaces were being violated by a person with whom they felt no need to communicate. This process has led to a large degree of animosity towards the poster and a consequent curiosity about his or her origins.[10] The name would suggest an Indian of Hindu origin but that itself is debatable, as the following exchanges would show:

In response to the question: "Who is Jai Maharaj?" a user wrote the following on March 20, 1995:
You have asked the $64,000 question. I have watched and sometimes posted in ACH [alt.culture.hawaii] for about 2 months. Jai has never responded to any questions regarding his background. The closest information comes from the ACH Lynch Mob. From what I can gather the Lynch Mob was a bunch of people who were becoming iirateat [*sic*] Jai"s constant cross posting of articles into unrelated newsgroups [spamming]. When these people became vocal, he called them a Lynch Mob.

Well maybe you will succeed where many have failed in answering the question "What is Jai Maharaj?"

Good Luck"

Ken

This note shows how one user can generate confusion and interest and create specific images of the people he represents. This is the way in which images on the Internet begin to form and emerge. Needless to say, with time, sci users recognized that the poster was unreliable and often abusive. However, an outsider entering sci and encountering the postings of Maharaj might perceive a specific image of India.

Based on these postings it is possible to claim that the image of India that emerges on the Internet through the various postings and cross-postings arises from issues that are predominantly negative and produce a particularly dismal picture of divisions and differences, ones that are now being translated to the virtual space of international electronic networks. Needless to say, some of the discourse can be ignored as trivial drivel between people who are engaging in unproductive and abusive arguments. Yet, it is through this discourse that the diasporic community is reimagining itself as well as presenting an outside "face." Clearly these examples, and continuing responses to cross-posting, show that the Indian "face" that is being presented is being despised by many of the users of the Net. Yet the ones who are disgusted with the divisionary image of India are not necessarily the ones who can offer an alternative voice of unity or sobriety. The only argument has appeared in the form of further inflammatory remarks, as illustrated earlier where the members of other forums are being equally bigoted in "screaming" out at the Indians and asking them to keep their troubles to themselves without "polluting" various news-groups. This is a matter of concern because this can ultimately hurt the way the Indian communities in the West want to create a collective memory of themselves in the space of the Internet.

Significance of the Image

Groups such as sci emerge as electronic communities where many of the traditional aspects of community are reproduced in a textual format. Thus when a user posts about his or her college affiliation and attempts to find an old acquaintance on the Internet the fundamental communal assumptions of a common fraternity are mobilized. Moreover, when such a poster gets a response from a member of the group new connections and networks are produced. The national newsgroups become particularly important in this respect since the electronic community is produced in the same way that Anderson's imagined community becomes a nation. The "imagination" that binds the members of the electronic group is the common memory of the same putative place of origin from which most of the posters came. The sense of community is based on an original home where everyone belonged, as well as a sense of a new space where the question of belonging is always problematized. Since the original home is now inaccessible, the Internet space is coopted to find the same companionship that was available in that original place of residence.

However, if the postings were restricted to the space of sci alone some of this purpose would be lost. The electronic system offers the opportunity to cast a large "Net" and this is done through the process of cross-posting. Yet it is this mechanism that also allows for the construction of an electronic national image that is available widely and easily. Consequently, irresponsible postings, and postings that are often sent to incite attack, not only fuel debate but also lead to the production of the national image. Here the metonymy between the organization of the Internet space and the way ethnicity is spatially organized becomes remarkable. The fact that the diasporic Indians now occupy a new space—in America and Western Europe—demands the production of a specific "face." This is the product of a variety of everyday practices from the performance of religious rituals to the Independence Day parades in New York. Increasingly, as the Internet becomes a part of these practices, the way in which posters send messages to the common and shared spaces of the Internet will determine what "electronic face" that community produces for themselves and for their country of origin.

The reorganization of space and the dissolution of boundaries is one of the more important elements of the virtual communality that the newsgroup produces. With the increasing immigration and emigration of people, who once shared a sense of traditional community with spatial commonality in colleges, workplaces and towns and cities in India, the rediscovery of the commonality on the seamless and virtual space of the Internet becomes an important aspect. Indeed the lack of the "human touch" that has been argued to be one of the drawbacks of the electronic community is restored through the Internet for the immigrants whose spatial orientation has been disrupted. As a matter of fact, for this virtual community, the electronic space is the only common space that they can occupy. Consequently, the traffic of communication on the newsgroup (as in other national newsgroups) is often far larger than in other groups, which often operate as fan clubs, as Snyder (1996) suggests. Thus negotiated here is the lost space of a nation, community, or tribe which is being re-created and reinvented on the other Internet space. Therefore, for the immigrant newsgroups the question of space is critical and the loss of geographic proximity is the *raison d'être* for the mobilization of the Internet space.

Another unique feature is drawn from this particular face that is produced by an electronic community such as sci. Here the texts and discourses that make up the substance of the community become representations of a range of deep structural contradictions that become a defining characteristic of the country being imaged. The image of a country can be thought of in two ways. One is the public image that is produced by organized sources such as national media, international news flow, and other mediated forums where a monolithic image is constructed for specific political and ideological purposes. On the other hand, there are the non-naturalized images that are shared by the people most involved with the consequences of the image. These are the immigrants who have to constantly negotiate their existence based on the public memory of the country they come from. The electronic medium now offers an opportunity to develop discourses that provide this internally contradictory democratically produced image that is open for debate and reimaging as new debates emerge on the Internet. This becomes particularly true for India and the sci group, which is constantly concerned with the contradictions that mark contemporary India. Consequently, the large range of discussions about the merits of Hinduism, the problems with Pakistan, and the support or criticism of the newly emerging Hindu party in India all become manifestations and concretizations of the fundamental contradictions between the different social, cultural, and political blocs that make up post-Independence India. This post-colonial national formation is the product of the people who make up the electronic community, and given the wide range of opinions and worldviews proposed on the Internet, the image of India that is produced on sci for its users is replete with the contradictions that are a mainstay of everyday life in the South Asian country. While the community here does not have any geographic connections with the national space, all the cultural, religious, and political baggage carried by the members of the electronic community become evident in the discussions on the Internet space which provides a relatively "safer" environment for the debates and arguments than the riot-torn streets of Bombay. The struggle that is commonplace in India now becomes a struggle over meaning in the space of the Internet, albeit in languages and styles that are often bigoted, suggestive of violence and sometimes low-level harangues.

Finally, no particularly new directions of thinking that would provide alternatives to the traditional structural contradictions are emerging on the Internet space. For instance, in the exchange cited earlier, Jai Maharaj wants the Bombay name-change proposition to be sent to London. This is yet another throwback to the colonial past and the continuing struggles over identity in a post-colonial era. In this manner, and through similar such exchanges, sci is becoming a site for the reproduction of the conventional struggles, issues, and contradictions that have been a natural part of India for too long. All other mediated images of India have also reproduced the opposition between the Hindus and Muslims, the higher and lower castes, and people of different languages as the primary defining characteristics of the country and the Internet space has to a large degree circulated the same image. This becomes a reconfirmation of the fact that the users of the Internet are indeed products of an ideological system where they have been subjected to accepting certain aspects of India as fundamental and "natural" without having the ideological option of questioning or challenging their assumptions. Consequently, a user who once made an argument about the precariousness of the Indian Republic as a union of various states was quieted quickly as that position was found to be far too "unnatural" and potentially disruptive.

This tendency toward segmentation is balanced only by the precariousness of the immigrant identity, in as much as most members of the community need to negotiate their existence in a society where they feel marginalized. This paradoxical phenomenon is evident in the postings that tend to bind the community together around a sense of national pride and a challenging of the mainstream Western way of depicting India. Consequently, when users question headline stories and the practices of the media industry, not only does an image of their original country emerge but their user identity as immigrants is also being exposed and discussed. These discussions often serve as the glue that holds the community together in the electronic space as the members continue to discuss the issues that divide them around their differential images of India.

Conclusion

There are two forces at work that implicate the dynamics of the way a nation can be imaged in Internet space. On the one hand there are the centralizing tendencies through which members of the virtual community use the electronic space to develop a certain fraternity around the place of origin and their identities in the New World. Because the Internet space is divided as it is, any community can feel cohesive by the fact that they are distinct from other electronic groups. Consequently the sci group members can feel a sense of community in knowing that they all have a common place of origin in India, and thus their legitimacy and claim to the sci group. Along with that legitimacy comes the feeling of distinctiveness from other groups such as soc.culture.pakistan or any of the various other national discussion groups on the Internet. While cross-posting is common, it is recognized as an aberrant phenomenon, and the fact that it invites wrath and flaming is a further underscoring of the fact that the members of the groups do indeed feel a centralizing and "parochial" force where the intrusions of cross-posting are accepted but unloved.

On the other hand there is a strong segmenting force that constantly tests the glue that holds the community together—its place of origin. The centrifugal forces generated by the variety of discourses that image India always expose the differences between the members of the community and can often lead to the disruption of the community. This is most evident in the way in which the space is constantly carved up into smaller slices as specific "tribes" demand their own space and forum. Thus the creation of groups which have an additional defining characteristic such as Indian-American, Indian-Bengali, and so forth. However, such segmentation does not undermine the fundamental centralizing forces, because very often the users of these subgroups would also pay attention to the "parent" group (although there is no technical hierarchical organization of the groups). This attention is manifest in reading the articles on sci and posting articles to sci as well as the subgroup that they feel closer to. Ultimately what the centralizing and the segmenting forces accomplish is the production of a large set of debates and discussions that not only help to create the image of India but also question and reflect on the segmentation that continues for the Indian network groups.

Such dialogue is possible because the space cannot be coopted by any particular point of view. The power and the uniqueness of the dynamics of the electronic community lie precisely in the absence of restrictions and controls on anyone's voice. This is indeed a forum where everyone who is able to access the space is also able to speak within the space. Everyone has a "voice" in this space. This has far-reaching consequences, particularly in the way the space can be utilized to produce national images. In other kinds of traditional public spaces, such as those created by broadcast media or film, the question of empowerment becomes much more diffuse than in the case of the Internet. The arguments of hegemony and the existence of a dominant ideology that serves the needs of the leading social bloc become particularly generative in thinking of the ways in which mediated national images are produced, because very often the centralizing tendencies of media texts ignore the segmenting tendencies of an increasingly diversified audience. For instance, it has been argued that television has played a focal and centripetal role in the resurgence of Hindu fundamentalism in India (Mitra, 1993), but it becomes much more difficult to propose the same argument in the case of the Internet since it is much more difficult to locate the dominant in the virtual space.

The Internet space is indeed a cacophony of voices, all of whom feel empowered, and the traditional definition of dominance becomes nearly inapplicable to this community. Gramsci's fundamental proposition that hegemony is produced by gaining consent of the masses often provides the backbone for the arguments about media dominance (see, for instance, the vast literature on media and critical/cultural studies). However, using the same notion of hegemony, it becomes clear that the question of gaining consent becomes unimportant in the electronic space because the traditional centers disappear on the Internet. Here power of any nature, be it coercive or non-coercive, is only manifest in the texts that are produced by its users.[11] This is a space where power is manifest in discursive capital, and, given the varieties of ideological positions that find voice on the electronic space, there is no single dominant ideology that can be identified.

This, too, is the primary strength of the Internet space, because it provides a forum where there is no ideological closure, which accompanies most centralizing forces. As evidenced in the case of the debate over the naming of Bombay, or the fate of the Muslims in India, the debate never ends because no single argument appears to be convincing and persuasive enough to attract consent from all members of the Net. And this multiplicity of voices is only possible because of the way the Internet space is organized, with minor checks and balances, and with no tangible "control" on how the space is utilized.[12] While in some respects this could have negative outcomes, in the case of imaging a nation this "freedom" certainly provides for ongoing and necessary debate. No grand narratives about India emerge on the Internet space. Unlike broadcast media, no one is in "control" of the space and the images of the nation that evolve are constantly metamorphosing. The notion of permanence of image is subverted by the ongoing discourses on the space and nationhood and nationalism become constantly contested and discursively produced. Moreover, in most public discourse there is a need to find closure because, as in movies, television, and other forms of mass media, there is always a point of view that is preferred and is more "natural." Given the fact that such mass media are produced by groups with specific interests, there is some ideological work to be done and the hegemonic tendency is to produce one particular closure over others. As my work on Indian television (Mitra, 1993) has demonstrated, the Indian state-owned television system had a particular Hindu image that it was trying to portray through an array of texts. In a similar fashion it is possible to identify a specific colonial/oriental/neo-colonial image that has been produced in literary texts and movies of the West (see, e.g., Mitra, 1996; Said, 1993). However, these are organized sources and far different in character from the discourses on the Internet, where the nature of the texts does not require closure. Narrative analysis of literature, movie, and television presupposes the notion of narrative closure, which is tied to, and implicated by, ideological closure, but the ongoing heteroglossic discourse of the Internet neither requires nor produces such closure because it is an ongoing process.

My approach to the Internet emphasizes the textuality of the system of messages that are exchanged. These are texts produced by the users, who are constantly accentuating the texts with their ideologies and worldviews. This calls for a theoretical foundation that sees the process of language as non-singular and non-monolithic. Bakhtin/Volosinov provide this argument and also go on to suggest that language is indeed ideological. Consequently the way the image of the nation and the identity scripts are produced by these texts needs to be examined in terms of their ideological implications. While this analysis is a step in that direction, plenty of research still needs to be done with these texts to arrive at convincing images of nations that are obtained from them.

Foucault argues the same in saying that the "social" is produced in the network of discourses and discursive practices, and the Internet messages become an example of the phenomenon where heteroglossic language constantly produces the Internet version of the social. However, Foucault becomes problematic in relation to the Internet, since it is difficult to make the connections between power and discourse that he would want to draw. Indeed, as exposed in this analysis, the very nature of the Internet precludes any discussion of power since there is no specific repressive power that sets boundaries, or productive power that produces any grand narrative or preferred discourse. The only form of control lies in the boundaries that are produced by the discourse and the members who produce the discourse. In Foucault's thinking these can be considered to be the only form of control of discourse, as in his words:

> There is a raefication, [*sic*] this time, of the speaking subjects; none shall enter the order of discourse if he does not satisfy certain requirements or if he is not, from the outset, qualified to do so. To be more precise: not all regions of discourse are equally open and penetrable; some of them are largely forbidden (they are differentiated and differentiating), while others seems to be almost open to all winds and put at the disposal of every speaking subject, without prior restrictions. (Foucault, 1989, p. 221)

This to a large degree captures the situation with the Internet, where the forces of inclusion constantly struggle with the forces which throw open the virtual discursive space to "every speaking subject without prior restrictions," except in the form of creation of subspaces.

Yet because of the lack of restrictions and the particularly "fluid" nature of the system there arise two additional concerns. First, the image of a nation that is produced is indeed transient and ephemeral. True to its postmodern form, the discourses constantly regress and no center emerges that is constant and permanent. While permanence of an image is a strongly debated issue within postmodern scholarship, the Internet poses a new condition since every single posting changes the image to some degree and this change is a continuing process since the postings never stop. Even as this chapter is being written, and when ultimately it is read, the Indian image on the Internet will have changed somewhat. However, the emphasis is really on the "somewhat," because just as political and cultural changes do not occur rapidly, the general image on the Internet does not change very quickly. What does alter rapidly is the nature of the discourse on which the image is based. New and fresh voices appear much more easily and expediently than in any other form of mediated communication. This, too, sets the system apart from other forms of communication. This uniqueness is certainly connected with the empowerment that the Internet provides, and the users can perhaps feel that their single contribution, while not "singular," is a significant part of the metamorphosing image.

The second issue connected with the process of metamorphosis is the problematization of the research of the Internet text. When approached from the perspective of content and theme, as in this case, it is customary in other forms of media research that an "end" of the text is clearly defined (barring the case of soap operas, this is true for most television program episodes and certainly true for cinema). This closure provides an anchor for the analysis. Additionally, a reading of the closure provides insights into the ideological, cultural, and political arguments implicating a particular narrative. Moreover, the closure in the text provides a certain degree of finality to the analysis as well. Consequently, independent of the fact of how a text is analyzed, it is expected that any particular analysis will provide a unique perspective on the text, while the text remains static and unchanging. In the case of Internet texts this fundamental assumption simply does not hold true. At best it is possible to identify a period in time and obtain a snap-shot of the image being produced and circulated. That conclusion is neither binding nor exhaustive since, ever-metamorphosing and ever-growing, the "nature of the Internet beast" continues to change every minute (literally), undermining any claims of authenticity that researchers can have of their reading of the network discourse. Researchers need to be aware of this, and thus be cautious and prepared to accept the fact that the image is indeed transitional and is bound to change with time and the appearance of new community members. Consequently, in this space every textual utterance is open to challenge and questioning and ultimately no dominant, unquestioned national image emerges because the very nature of the Internet space does not allow for permanence of images.

Notes

1. The concept of the "nation" has been contested from Deutsch and Foltz's (1966) notion of the nation as a geographic construction, to Gramsci's (1971) idea of the nation as civil society to Anderson's (1983) proposition of nations as imagined communities. More recently the issue of the nation has been debated by other authors, such as Appadurai (1993) and Buscombe (1993), who have argued for the erosion of the nation-state and the emergence of post-nations that do not have well-defined and naturalized boundaries.

2. Here the notion of residual and emergent is a reference to Raymond Williams' (1961) proposition that at any moment in time there are in all cultures elements that are reminiscent of the history of the culture while there also are elements that are emerging as new elements in the culture. This is important to the argument proposed in this chapter, because the key struggle discussed here is between the residual constructs of nation as geographical entities and the emergent proposition that nations can be constructed around emergent elements of culture—in this case electronic communication systems.

3. The September 25, 1995 issue of *US News and World Report* reports a steady growth, from a little over 4 percent in 1970 to a little over 8 percent in 1994, of foreign-born residents as a share of the US population.

4. Other forms of community formation include the emergence of ethnic media such as Chinese television channels, Indian newspapers, and ethnic community centers and schools.

5. The issue of diaspora and the emergence of diasporic communities has now been discussed and debated from several perspectives. Some of the critical discussions and examples of community formation by diasporic people have appeared in *Public Culture*. There have

been discussions about the Cuban diaspora (Campa, 1994), the production and implications of the Korean community in America (Palumbo-Liu, 1994), and fundamental discussions of the new diasporic condition (Appadurai, 1993). These discussions point out that immigrant and displaced communities are constantly struggling to produce new identities and are using different means to achieve this; I argue that the electronic communication systems offer such an opportunity.

6. There are a large number of terms that are used to describe various aspects of this system. However, fundamentally they all refer to various manifestations of the same phenomenon—the ability to communicate with others using the computer. Consequently I do not engage in the discussion of the various networks available or the multiple "browsing" systems available to look at the networks such as "Usenet," and the "World Wide Web." For the purposes of this chapter, the technology will primarily be referred to as the "Internet."

7. Terms such as "flaming" have become popular in response to the need to give names to the various kinds of textual elements that started to appear on the Net. For example, "flaming" refers to the process where users resort to highly inflammable language exchanged between individuals for no apparent reason. Kiesler, Siegel, & McGuire (1984) expressed it as "emotional expression of opinion and feeling which occurs more frequently on the computer than in other communication settings." Similarly the use of type written symbols used to mimic the expression of the human face have been called "emoticons" (Dery, 1993) and "spamming" refers to the process of cross-posting across a large number of newsgroups.

8. Researchers such as Negroponte (1995) would argue differently, claiming that the "digital" nature of the messages makes them permanent and that it is possible to access the past messages with relative ease. However, while that could be the case for the researcher, it is relatively unlikely that the user of the Internet who simply wants to participate in virtual community discussion would be interested in scrolling through thousands of past messages that are preserved by the system. Indeed this is reflected in the way in which the news browser provided by Netscape presents the information with the "Earlier" articles being kept invisible unless the user asks for them.

9. There has been a significant amount of work undertaken examining the relationships between CMC and the face-to-face situation in the interpersonal and group settings. Walther (1992, 1993, 1994) and Walther & Burgoon (1992) explore the area of interpersonal communication through computers, whereas Poole & DeSanctis (1987) explore the area of group communication over the computer medium. However, the Internet poses a new challenge, possessing the characteristics of both interpersonal and group communication, but also displaying characteristics of mass communication, where the audience size is enormous and the source of the message is diverse.

10. This is perhaps one of the most powerful aspects of Internet communication: the identity of the poster can be successfully hidden from public scrutiny. It is often impossible to recognize gender, national origin, and ethnicity if the poster chooses to use a well-hidden pseudo-name. To a large degree Dr Maharaj has been successful in doing that.

11. The way in which power is exercised is through the process of "flaming," where the errant voices are "burnt out" and subdued and quieted. Yet that works only because the errant members choose to keep quiet and not due to any other reasons (see, e.g., the work of Siegel, Dubrovsky, Kiesler, & McGuire, 1986).

12. The only control is exercised by system administrators and network moderators who can review articles before they are posted. However, groups such as sci are often unmoderated, thus eliminating even this minimal control. Only when an exchange might violate the "netiquette" of language and decorum could it be brought to the attention of the system administrator of the poster's computer, leading to some repercussions to the user.

References

Allor, M. (1988). Relocating the site of the audience. *Critical Studies in Mass Communication, 5*, 217–233.

Althusser, L. (1971). *Lenin and philosophy and other essays.* New York: Monthly Review Press.

Althusser, L. (1986). Ideology and ideological state apparatuses. In G. Hanhardt (Ed.), *Video culture* (pp. 56–95). Rochester, NY: Visual Studies Workshop, Inc.

Anderson, B. (1983). *Imagined communities: Reflections on the origins and spread of nationalism.* London: Verso.

Appadurai, A. (1993). Patriotism and its futures. *Public Culture, 5,* 411–429.

Badgett, T., & Sandler, C. (1993). *Welcome to Internet: From mystery to mastery.* New York: MIS Press.

Bakhtin, M.M. (1981). *The dialogic imagination: Four essays* (M. Hoquist & C. Emerson, Trans.). Austin: University of Texas Press.

Baron, N.S. (1984). Computer-mediated communication as a force in language change. *Visible Language, 18*(2), 118–141.

Baym, N.K. (1995). The emergence of community in computer-mediated communication. In S.G. Jones (Ed.), *CyberSociety: Computer-mediated communication and communtiy* (pp. 138–163). Thousand Oaks, CA: Sage.

Beniger, J. (1987). Personalization of the mass media and the growth of pseudo-community. *Communication Research, 14*(3), 352–371.

Braun, E. (1994). *The Internet directory.* New York: Fawcett Columbine.

Buscombe, E. (1993). Nationhood, culture and media boundaries: Britain. *Quarterly Review of Film and Video, 14*(3), 25–34.

Campa, R. (1994). The Latino diaspora in the United States: Sojourns from a Cuban past. *Public Culture, 13,* 293–319.

Carey, J. (1989). *Communication and culture.* Boston: Unwin-Hyman.

de Certeau, M. (1984). *The practice of everyday life.* Berkeley: University of California Press.

Dery, M. (1993). Flame wars. *South Atlantic Quarterly, 92,* 559–568.

Deutsch, K.W., & Foltz, W.J. (1966). *Nation building.* New York: Atherton Press.

Dubrovsky, V.J., Kiesler, S., & Sethna, B.N. (1991). The equalization phenomenon: Status effects in computer-mediated or face-to-face decision-making groups. *Human–Computer Interaction, 6,* 119–146.

Elsaesser, T. (1989). *New German cinema: A history.* London: British Film Institute.

Foucault, M. (1989). From the "Order of discourse." In P. Rice & P. Waugh (Eds.), *Modern literary theory* (pp. 221–233). New York: Edward Arnold.

Glistner, P. (1993). *The Internet navigator.* New York: John Wiley.

Gramsci, A. (1971). *Selections from the prison notebooks* (Q. Hoare & G.N. Smith, Eds.). New York: International Publishers.

Hall, S. (1980). Encoding/decoding. In S. Hall, D. Hobson, A. Lowe, & P. Willis (Eds.), *Culture, media, language* (pp. 128–139). London: Hutchinson.

Hall, S. (1986). On postmodernism and articulation. *Journal of Communication Enquiry, 10*(2), 45–60.

Hay, J. (1987). *Popular film culture in Fascist Italy.* Bloomington: Indiana University Press.

Hiltz, S.R., Turoff, M., & Johnson, K. (1989). Experiments in group decision making, 3: Disinhibition, deindividuation, and group process in pen name and real name computer conferences. *Decision Support Systems, 5,* 217–232.

Jones, S.G. (1995). Understanding community in the information age. In S.G. Jones (Ed.), *CyberSociety: Computer-mediated communication and community* (pp. 10–35). Thousand Oaks, CA: Sage.

Kiesler, S., Siegel, J., & McGuire, T.W. (1984). Social psychological aspects of computer-mediated communication. *American Psychologist, 39*(10), 1123–1134.

Krol, E. (1992). *The whole Internet.* New York: O'Reilly and Associates.

LaQuey, T. (1993). *The Internet companion.* Reading, MA: Addison-Wesley.

McLaughlin, M.L., Osborne, K.K., & Smith, C.B. (1995). Standards of conduct on Usenet. In S.G. Jones (Ed.), *CyberSociety: Computer-mediated communication and community* (pp. 90–111). Thousand Oaks, CA: Sage.

Mitra, A. (1993). *Television and popular culture in India.* New Delhi: Sage.

Mitra, A. (1996, August). Images of South Asia on film. Paper presented at the Film, Culture, History: International Conference. Aberdeen, Scotland.

Negroponte, N. (1995). *Being digital.* New York: Knopf.

Palumbo-Liu, D. (1994). Los Angeles, Asians, and perverse ventriloquism: On the functions of Asian Americans in recent American imagery. *Public Culture, 13,* 365–385.

Peck, M.S. (1987). *The different drum: Community making and peace.* New York: Simon & Schuster.

Poole, M.S., & DeSanctis, G. (1987). *Group decision making and group decision support systems: A 3-year plan for the GDSS research project.* Working paper, Minneapolis, MIS Research Center, University of Minnesota.

Postman, N. (1993). *Technopoly: The surrender of culture to technology.* New York: Vintage Books.

Rheingold, H. (1993). *The virtual community: Homesteading on the electronic frontier.* Reading, MA: Addison-Wesley.

Rice, R.E. (1984). *The new media: Communication, research and technology.* Beverly Hills, CA: Sage.

Said, E. (1993). *Orientalism.* New York: Vintage Books.

Siegel, J.M., Dubrovsky, V.M., Kiesler, S., & McGuire, T.W. (1986). Group process in computer-mediated communication. *Organizational Behavior and Human Decision Processes, 37,* 157–187.

Smolensky, M.W., Carmody, M.A., & Halcomb, C.G. (1990). The influence of task type, group structure and extraversion on uninhibited speech in computer-mediated communication. *Computers in Human Behavior, 6,* 261–272.

Snyder, J. (1996). Get real. *Internet World, 7*(2), 92–94.

Sproul, L., & Kiesler, S. (1991). *Connections: New ways of working in the networked organization.* Cambridge, MA: MIT Press.

Thompson, P.A., & Ahn, D. (1992). To be or not to be: An exploration of E-prime, copula deletion, and flaming in electronic mail. *ETC: A Review of General Semantics, 49,* 146–197.

Turner, G. (1988). *Film as social practice.* London: Routledge.

Volosinov, V.N. (1973). *Marxism and the philosophy of language* (L. Matejka & I.R. Titunik, Trans.). London: Seminar Press.

Walther, J.B. (1992). Interpersonal effects in computer-mediated interaction: A relational perspective. *Communication Research, 19,* 52–90.

Walther, J.B. (1993). Impression development in computer-mediated interaction. *Western Journal of Communication, 57,* 381–398.

Walther, J.B. (1994). Anticipated ongoing interaction versus channel effects on relational communication in computer-mediated interaction. *Human Communication Research, 20,* 473–501.

Walther, J.B., & Burgoon, J.K. (1992). Relational communication in computer-mediated interaction. *Human Communication Research, 19,* 50–88.

Williams, R. (1961). *Marxism and literature.* Oxford: Oxford University Press.

4

Structural Relations, Electronic Media, and Social Change: The Public Electronic Network and the Homeless

Joseph Schmitz

> *I have been living on the streets in Santa Monica for one year. . . . To tell you the truth, PEN is indispensable in my life at the moment, I don't know what I would do without it . . . it does keep my brain alive . . . it has been an enlightening experience to be able to communicate with so many intelligent people, from the city attorney, Bob Myers, to a professor of psychology, Michele Wittig.*
>
> — David Morgan, 1989, then homeless, in a letter to the author

David Morgan's letter to me was written on Santa Monica's Public Electronic Network (PEN) about seven months after the network was unveiled in February 1989. As the first city government-sponsored, interactive electronic communication system in the United States, PEN was expressly designed to extend this new medium to *all* residents, including homeless persons like Mr Morgan.

PEN consisted of a host computer, ports that connected users via telephone modem links, and computer software that provided users with three different types of services. First, PEN displayed bulletin board text posted by the city. This "read only" text included keyword-searchable information about government and social services designed to meet residents' needs. Second, users could send electronic mail to other residents and to city officials. Third, PEN users could join electronic conferences with other PEN users. These PEN conferences addressed broad topics that included more specific topics arrayed in sub-conferences or "items." While this chapter centers on the Homeless conference and the efforts to change Santa Monica that were prominent in that conference, PEN's Planning (land-use), Education, and Politics conferences also featured PEN entries that advocated systemic changes in Santa Monica's social and economic structures.

When it was created, Santa Monica's PEN system had six main objectives:

- to provide electronic access to public information;
- to aid delivery of city services;

- to enhance communication among residents;
- to enhance Santa Monica's sense of community through electronic conferences among residents;
- to diffuse knowledge of, and access to, the new communication technology;
- to facilitate an equitable distribution of communication resources to the "have nots."

This analysis is based on my role as a participant-observer during the creation and operation of the PEN system. Starting in 1986, I participated extensively in the design and implementation of PEN and consulted with PEN's manager during its early years. During the past ten years, in addition to being a frequent PEN user, I also helped design and conduct three empirical surveys of Santa Monica residents regarding potential and actual PEN usage. The third source of data is the Homeless conference, a collectively authored text exceeding 20,000 entries. The Homeless text cited comes from a convenience sample of over 3,000 entries that I downloaded in large blocks from the almost 7,000 entries that I read while logged on PEN. This text represents the types of discourse on PEN, discourse that ranged from information sharing, project planning, and coordination, through personal and political discussions, to ideological railing and the exchange of personal insults. As time progressed, the PEN text became increasingly uncivil. The lessened civility in the Homeless conference mirrors similar changes in much of PEN, although several conferences, often the few moderated ones, remained more civil.

Social Structure and Social Change

As new communication technology is introduced, we should closely examine its effects upon existing social structures and processes. What is likely to change? How are diverse stakeholders affected? To address these questions I focus on the issue of homelessness because homelessness reflects fundamental power relations, conflict, and structural change in Santa Monica and in other contemporary communities. My analysis is grounded in a symbolic interactionist perspective, one influenced by the Chicago School of Sociology, and one aware that the symbolic environment we create for each other as we interact profoundly shapes our personae, beliefs, and consequent actions. These interaction patterns become important to the extent our symbolic environment depends on the persons with whom we interact. Before I discuss the consequences of Santa Monica's PEN system, I want to consider "community" in more abstract terms. Here, the Chicago School of Sociology and the theory of George Simmel offer useful insights.

Simmel provided an important root of the Chicago School of Sociology and underpins much American contemporary sociology and social psychology (Rogers, 1994; Scott, 1992). In *The Web of Group-Affiliations* (Simmel, 1922/1955) he argued that the pattern of group interactions shapes the interests and the personae of individuals. When, as in traditional societies, individuals form groups that are typically arranged in concentric arrays, these groups "produce" clusters of relatively homogeneous individuals. Similar individuals are clustered in stable groups that share a common occupation, religion, and social class. So in the traditional social orders, used by Simmel as one ideal type, the folk-saying "birds of a feather, flock together" often held true. Traditional societies, comprised of basic units such as manor, guild, and village, had hierarchical social structures that more wholly contain individuals and possessed great authority over them (Coleman, 1974).

Conversely, when groups intersect and cross-cut in the multiplex ways more common to modern societies, more heterogeneous clusters of individuals resulted. While class and occupational differences still existed, interpersonal interaction patterns more often crossed these gaps. Scott (1992) notes "a vastly increased variety of social spaces is created, and no two individuals are as likely to share the same social location or to hold the same social identity" (p. 152). Scott argues that this increased cross-cutting of groups facilitates an emergence of individualism and of special purpose groups. These changed interaction patterns comprise a greatly expanded and integrated matrix of interpersonal relations and profoundly alter our symbolic environments.

Further, in modern societies, our *assumptions* about others differ. To the extent Simmel's representation of traditional societies is accurate, persons quite correctly assumed that the others they usually dealt with were much like themselves. In contemporary societies this assumption no longer holds. Others may differ in both predictable and unpredictable ways. So one legacy of Simmel is the insight that modern social orders contain: (1) more diverse sets of interacting persons, and (2) a greater awareness of our differences.

Before we assess how electronic communication media can serve the disadvantaged, we should examine the structural relations among and between elites and non-elites. Just as Simmel offers insights about how we come to differ, Blau illuminates the structural consequences of those differences. Blau (1974, 1977) argued that society still remains structured to cluster homophilous individuals, conceptually defined as "the degree to which pairs of individuals who interact are similar in certain attributes, such as beliefs, education, social status, and the like" (Rogers, 1983, p. 18). The intersection of groups with consequent links among hetrophilous (different) persons that Simmel held to be a characteristic of modern societies is not complete. Persons remain grouped according to nominal parameters (e.g. gender, racial identification, religion, and residential locale) and graduated parameters, such as wealth, education, and power. Like Simmel (1922/1955), Blau noted that social relations were more frequent among similar, clustered persons. And like Simmel, Mead (1934), and more contemporary social interactionists (e.g. Wood, 1992) or social constructionists (e.g. Berger & Luckmann, 1966), Blau argued that the structure of personal interactions shapes our assumptions, beliefs, and our personae.

At the micro-level, clusters based on social, workplace, and residential boundaries aggregate persons with similar characteristics, for example those with similar interaction patterns and common socio-economic, ethnic, and cultural ties to bind them. But, on the macro-level, Blau (1974) asserted that the relatively infrequent associations among heterophilous individuals are vital because these interactions serve to integrate diverse elements of a society. For social systems to avoid rigid social structures that resist evolutionary changes and feature large inequalities, ties that cross socio-economic strata are critical. So, paradoxically, our similarities bind us within relatively homogeneous groups, while our social systems depend on what Granovetter (1973) terms "weak links" that connect us across our differences.

Empirical social network research has often found that while social ties are most dense within homophilous groups, they frequently cross cultural and socio-economic boundaries. These links among diverse persons can serve important functions: to find employment (Granovetter, 1973), to facilitate local development (Granovetter, 1982; Rogers & Kincaid, 1981), and to serve as conduits for emotional and material support (Wellman, Carrington, & Hall, 1988). Cross-group linkages are important levers for change because they often reflect patterns of dependencies among different groups and can thus facilitate an exchange of resources and information across groups and persons. For example, Erickson (1996) found that a diverse personal network conferred substantial advantages in one's leisure, employment, and knowledge that were independent of social class.

Yet because we often interact with similar others, efforts to create structural social change may become stymied within homophilous groups (Rogers, 1983). And the "have-nots" are at great disadvantage because they lack influence to change policies crafted by elites. When decision-makers are insulated from non-elites, successful change agents must bridge the socio-economic and cultural gulfs that Blau described. For structural change to take place, dissimilar groups must exchange information, resources, and influence. They must also change the terms of their relations. Still, if dissimilar stakeholders form dependencies based upon new exchange relationships, new patterns of cooperation and competition may become institutionalized.

Change agents must also maintain ties with their constituencies. To facilitate structural change, relations must be maintained both with constituents who desire change and with elites who may seek to maintain the status quo. So communication technology that fosters links within *and* across different groups may help to restructure relational patterns within a community, and, in so doing, alter the ways a society views itself.

Communication Media Characteristics and Community Change

A danger when assessing the potential of electronic communication media to change communities is to uncritically accept assumptions of technical determinism. While tempting to attribute changed communication outcomes to changes in communication media characteristics, such a causal linkage both unduly simplifies a complex social environment and finesses the issue of how we come to change. Because our communication media are embodied in our social systems, they must inevitably reflect them. Media systems are conceived, enacted, and given meaning by the social context that surrounds them. So the "hard" technical characteristics cannot dictate how a technology will be used. For example, the same basic technology may be used to provide commodified phone sex, or, alternatively, may constitute a corporate voice mail system. These vastly different communication systems vary not in their technology, rather, they have different goals and symbolic meanings attached to them.

An important issue, closely linked to technological determinism, is the nature of social change and the limits of rationality. Ortner (1984) offered a compelling rationale for processes of social change when, drawing from Sahlins, she said that:

> change comes about when traditional strategies which assume traditional patterns of relations . . . are deployed in relation to novel phenomena which do not respond to these strategies in traditional ways. . . . Change is failed reproduction. (pp. 155–156)

This view, while granting importance to active supporters of the status quo, emphasized that because we are all enculturated, we each "embody the system as well as live within it" (Ortner, 1984, p. 156). The symbolic interpretations we develop in the past shape our future expectations of innovations. Yet even as we conceive of the new using familiar cognitive templates, novel elements spur revisions in our practices, often in ways we fail to anticipate.

Technical Bases for Change

Yet although technical systems are grounded in our social systems, the new technologies themselves can offer opportunity for structural change. Two technically deterministic arguments that follow demonstrate how electronic media may modify social interaction patterns and thus bridge the social gaps that Blau described. Still, we should be mindful of the previous reservations with regard to unbridled technological determinism.

The first argument stresses the unique suitability of electronic media to span gulfs separating persons and groups. These boundaries may be (1) spatial, (2) temporal, (3) perceptual, or (4) psychological—and their reduction can thereby lessen cultural and socio-economic distances within a community. So, electronic communication systems have great technical *potential* to enable geographically separated, socially heterophilous users to exchange information asynchronously and bridge the boundaries described earlier.

The second argument compares electronic media with traditional face-to-face interaction and finds that electronic media have a "cues filtered out" aspect (Culnan & Markus, 1987). This paucity of electronic cues is held to obscure the social categories we use to shape our patterns of affiliations. Because these cues are not available to screen out "undesirables," we may gain opportunities to form new electronic groups that are more heterophilous than traditional groups. To the extent that homed people hold negative, perhaps inaccurate stereotypes of the homeless, electronic media can obscure many stigmata associated with the homeless. Here, the *absence* of face-to-face cues restricts information that might prejudice us and thus facilitates interaction across greater socio-economic differences.

For those who would use electronic media to foster change, their potential seems great. Because these media more easily transcend space, class, and cultural constraints, organizers can "broadcast" to many. Conversely, these media may concurrently facilitate "narrowcasting" to sympathetic others via special interest groups or electronic back-channels. But potential restructuring outcomes are realizable only if access to these media is given to (1) change agents, (2) "target" populations, and (3) a critical mass of community members.

But arguments that electronic media create more level playing fields and thereby enhance interaction and persuasion across socio-economic strata remain largely uninformed by data. At least three counter-arguments exist. First, much social science literature and common folklore suggests that influence is most successfully accomplished through interpersonal interaction (e.g. Bandura, 1986; Reardon, 1987). Second, claims of effectiveness often rest upon the "cues filtered out" nature of these media—and on related claims that these media are more democratic and egalitarian (e.g. Kiesler, Siegel, & McGuire, 1984). More recent empirical studies find that predicted equality in participation/influence is not reflected in actual usage patterns of "real" individuals in electronic networks (Schmitz & Fulk, 1991; Valacich, Paranka, George, & Nunamaker, 1993).

Third, we must temper egalitarian assumptions embedded in the metaphor of a level electronic playing field. Electronic media typically demand skillful verbal and word processing abilities. Consider David Morgan's words that introduced this chapter. Mr Morgan's linguistic skills strongly enhanced his self-presentation. Even for those less gifted, English fluency, basic writing skills, and keyboarding skills become more critical when using electronic media (Schmitz & Fulk, 1991). So although physical appearance, dress, and other status cues recede, educational competencies and linguistic skills increase in importance. Computer-communication media are not neutral with regard to culture, education, and socio-economic class. And electronic persons are not more "equal" than proximate individuals, we just use different criteria to rate them.

PEN Origins, the Enfranchisement Imperative, and the PEN Action Group

PEN rested upon a broad base of technical experience with a municipal electronic mail system, developed in 1984 by Ken Phillips, Director of the Information System Division for the City of Santa Monica. I met Phillips through an earlier study of Santa Monica's innovative e-mail system. After that study was completed (Schmitz, 1987), Phillips asked me to survey Santa Monica residents about their hypothetical reactions to being "electronically linked to city hall."

The feasibility survey found that Santa Monica residents liked a listing of electronic communication options. Residents favored information-seeking activities like electronic library access or city services information more than they wanted to communicate electronically with city hall or with each other (Schmitz, 1988). Computer and modem ownership was then widespread in Santa Monica, 33 percent and 11 percent respectively. Most importantly, the survey: (1) documented public support for the "Citizens' Electronic Network Pilot Project;" (2) let Phillips "test the waters" before he committed large resources then needed to create such a system; and (3) legitimated Phillips' subsequent efforts to create PEN.

Even so, it was clear that any new system would disproportionately benefit elites unless steps were taken to extend access to less fortunate Santa Monica residents. And in 1987, except for the French Minitel, no models existed upon which to base PEN. Although a few organizations had adopted e-mail and electronic bulletin boards were becoming commonplace, no local governments offered electronic communication to residents. So although this *technology* was "old hat" in 1987, its use to meet community networking needs was novel, in exactly the sense described earlier by Ortner (1984).

The Enfranchisement Imperative

That Santa Monica would first create a distinctive system like PEN was not happenstance. At least four factors contributed to PEN's Santa Monica origin: (1) Santa Monica was quite affluent; (2) it had obtained experience with a similar and successful innovation from the municipal e-mail system; (3) Phillips, as PEN's institutional champion, provided access to critical resources; and (4) Santa Monica historically had valued political participation by *all* stakeholders. This tradition of enfranchisement, labeled "middle-class radicalism" by Kann (1986), echoed through interviews with political leaders and municipal decision-makers of this city, which had been called "The People's Republic of Santa Monica" (Guthrie, 1988).

PEN's designers believed that to ensure their project's success they must provide access to disadvantaged persons, particularly young, old, and poor residents. Phillips and Schmitz (1988) argued in a policy paper that "equitable access for all SM residents is fundamental for the project's long term success" and proposed that public terminals and system training be available at libraries, municipal buildings, and public schools. This view reflected a local political consensus that taxpayers' funds should most serve the interests of the needy. We knew from the academic literature that both access to and benefits from information technology favored elites (e.g. Dutton, Rogers, & Jun, 1987; Rogers, 1983), and felt constrained to remedy these disparities.

Because Santa Monica's PEN project was linked closely to the Annenberg School of Communication, many scholarly accounts describe its origins and consequences (see Guthrie & Dutton, 1992; O'Sullivan, 1995; Rogers, Collins-Jarvis, & Schmitz, 1994; Schmitz, Rogers, Phillips, & Paschal, 1995; Wittig & Schmitz, 1996). A point obscured in these accounts is that PEN's designers were not particularly concerned about how PEN might affect the homeless *per se*. Although homelessness was a serious problem in Santa Monica by 1987, it did not drive efforts to enfranchise "have-nots" via PEN, largely because during PEN's development, PEN's designers conceived of disadvantaged persons using demographic criteria such as ethnicity, age, or perhaps income—but not homelessness. I suspect, with chagrin, that we viewed homeless persons much like the stereotypical panhandlers and substance abusers so common in media representations and so visible on Santa Monica's streets.

Although residents' support for an electronic conferencing feature was at best mildly enthusiastic, as shown by the feasibility survey results, Phillips wanted to build "an electronic town square." He sold the PEN system to the City Council using a metaphor of an electronic city hall that featured areas for all to meet and discuss common issues. Still, when PEN was first unveiled in February 1989, except for a conference to help users to operate PEN, only one mega conference, "Ideas," was provided.

The PEN Action Group

As more city residents adopted PEN, discrete conferences were created, each containing additional distinct items or topics. By April 1989, the Homeless conference provided an electronic meeting place for what later became the PEN Action Group. This group, grounded in a social activist tradition reminiscent of the early 1970s, was formed in response to Michele Wittig's "Invitation to BRAINSTORM Ideas for PEN Action . . . to consider mechanisms for directing PENtalk into PENaction" (Wittig, 1989).

The PEN Action Group used the Homeless conference and PEN's e-mail to help develop plans and coordinate activities. The group included several (then) homeless men, among them, David Morgan and Donald Paschal. Soon the PEN Action Group met in person and on-line as they developed the SHWASHLOCK (SHowers, WASHers, LOCKers) program for the homeless. Later they successfully lobbied Santa Monica's City Council for $150,000 to fund their program.

A central argument for funding used by the PEN Action Group was their accurate claim that homeless persons had played a direct role in SHWASHLOCK's creation (Wittig, personal communication, June 1993). This claim both legitimized SHWASHLOCK just as it challenged common stereotypes of the homeless as incompetent, substance-abusing panhandlers. These positive characterizations of the homeless were bolstered by thoughtful PEN entries by homeless authors. The Homeless conference had become an important venue with participants that included four City Council Members and a political leader's spouse who was influential in her own right.

PEN Use, Public Terminals, and Homeless Users   After the first year of operation, almost 2,000 persons had registered to use PEN, but only a small percentage of these were frequent or intensive users (Guthrie et al., 1990). Because many PEN users lacked the hardware to access the network, almost 20 percent of all logons originated from public terminals during its first year of operation. Public terminal usage increased to 27 percent of logons during PEN's second year of operation as more individuals who lacked personal access to a computer and modem adopted the network. The 1990 PEN survey also found that public terminals provided *primary* access for more than 15 percent of the respondents. This level of public terminal usage suggests that they provided access for many of the disadvantaged persons whom PEN's designers had hoped to reach.

Public terminals, often located in libraries, were intensively used by a few homeless persons. For them, city libraries served as temporary quarters, surrogate homes that closed at 10 p.m. each evening. Even so, with PEN's advent, these homeless now had their own "virtual" addresses. This development was important because the homeless could now, for the first time, gain access to a reliable, even prestigious, "place" where they could be reached and they could easily contact others who used PEN. Perhaps most important, they could now interact on a far more equal basis with other Santa Monica residents. For example:

> The part I hate most is that we without shelter are looked on with disdain, fear, loathing, pity, and hatred. This difference makes "normal" contact with other humans almost impossible. . . . In the minds of many, people who are different must be avoided. This is why Santa Monica's PEN system is so special to me. . . . To me, the most remarkable thing about the PEN community is that a City Council member and a pauper can coexist, albeit not always in perfect harmony, but on an equal basis. I have met, become friends with, or perhaps adversaries with, people I would otherwise not know—even if I were homed. (Donald Paschal in Schmitz et al., 1995)

The Homeless Conference Text

The Homeless conference consisted of several related, unmoderated conferences that first started during April 1989 and continued until February 1993, when the City of Santa Monica changed the PEN format considerably. These conferences included the Homeless conference and three other "minor" conferences that totaled over 20,000 entries (Mayall, 1995). They included the Homeless conference, the Homeless Resource Directory, the SHWASHLOCK Event Planning conference, and the Task Force On Homelessness Staff Report. While each conference featured a theoretically distinct topic, PEN text is typified by frequent topic shifts and "off thread" comments in all but the (read only) Staff Report. This ebb and shift of both topic and tone reflects the diverse styles, personal agendas, and changing moods of PEN authors.

Some of the first Homeless entries chronicled an electronic gathering of homeless persons, the sporadically homed, and "elite" Santa Monica residents. Other early entries provided information useful to the homeless and to those who wanted to help them. Note the entry by Ken Genser, then Mayor of Santa Monica, and his concern with placing the Homeless item in the Crimewatch conference. This placement changed later as "Homeless" became a separate conference. Note also the direct exchange between "Bill," a social worker and David Morgan, then homeless. Throughout this section my clarifying comments are italicized within square brackets.

2:1) "Jim"   24-APR-89 15:58
I was homeless for three months last year when the person who was house sitting my apartment refused to vacate. Fortunately I had friends and was able to rotate between abodes until I got my home back. Nevertheless it was a frightening experience and I can afford an occasional quarter for the less fortunate. I think it's critical that we come up with a permanent solution to this problem immediately.

2:2) Ken Genser [*Mayor of Santa Monica*]   24-APR-89 16:10
I am glad that there is a discussion item about homelessness, but I feel very uncomfortable about it being in the Crimewatch conference. The implication is that somehow it is criminal to be homeless, or that most homeless people commit crimes.

3:3) Buria [*wife of a former Santa Monica Mayor*]   18-OCT-89 8:35
"Jim," how are you holding up? I did not know about the situation in your building. . . . Personally I think that the homeless people have been used long enough for too much in this city, and I am tired of the homeless issue being manipulated to death.

3:19) Donald Paschal [*homeless man*]   23-OCT-89 14:47
Update: The number to Turning Point has been changed. . .they do not know what the new number is. . .please check out and update.   P.A.T.H. is all filled-up.
Is there somewhere else OTHER THAN the Bible Tabernacle where one can get a nights rest?

4:2) Buria   12-FEB-90 16:44
Joanne, the custodians can work at 6 am, the homeless can be allowed to sleep in an enclosed facility, auditorium, etc. from 10 pm to 6 am. Homeless can be hired to help the custodians to clean up, this is a good source for a days job.

4:16) David Morgan [*to "Bill," a social worker*]   13-FEB-90 18:33
. . . "Bill," you lost my vote when you said "we can then 'police' the areas we
don't want them in, such as the high traffic tourist areas, etc" I am not for
herding human beings into an area, or out of an area. I know this will be a novel
statement, but there are drunks living in houses in Santa Monica, and there are
homeless people living in Santa Monica who don't touch alcohol or drugs.
Homeless people are not a disease, and many more people could be on the
street shortly, if there is a big cut-back in defense spending. I am not in favor of
segregation, period.

4:18) "Bill" [*the social worker addressed by David Morgan*]   13-FEB-90 19:27
re 4:16 David. . .touche'. P.S. David, allow me to make myself clear as I just
received some E-MAIL regarding my "policing" statement. I am "attacking" this
problem from the mindset of those people who view the homeless the way
people like "Chris" [*a more conservative, former Santa Monica Mayor*] does.
Unless we can show them the *errors* of their stands, we will—as a community—remain deadlocked on this issue. Slowly, but surely, we are becoming a
more compassionate society. . .but not fast enough for my tastes. At any rate,
sometimes, a little "devil advocacy" goes a long way.

Note how the PEN text features elites conversing directly with the
homeless about issues important to both. While these entries are atypical
because they do not include much of the mundane "chat" common to many
PEN entries of this time, they do reflect the tone and content of the early
Homeless conference. They also show a shared commitment to supply
information and act in concert to aid the homeless. Private e-mail was used
to supplement public conference messages. Sometimes friends would
censure each other privately but refrain from public comment on an entry.
Other times persons might critically respond with a public comment about
a previous entry but privately send a conciliatory message (interviews with
Michele Wittig, June 1993, 1994, and two Santa Monica City Council
Members, 1995). Lastly, David Morgan was quite prophetic; unemployment in the Southern California would exceed 10 percent within a year.

During this early time period, the "SHWASHLOCK Planning conference" provided an electronic home for PEN Action Group efforts. The next
entry demonstrates how PEN was used to bridge physical, organizational,
and social distances. The SHWASHLOCK Planning conference contained
much "spill over" from the Homeless conference; both conferences shared a
common readership and many authors posted interchangeably in either
conference.

7:476) Michele Wittig   07-SEP-90 19:12
The following PENners have volunteered to be JOB Bank liaisons:
    Liaison with Information Systems Department: Michael
    Liaison with OPCC Drop-in Center: Alice and James
    Liaison with the Homelessness Task Force: Joanne & Michele
    Liaison with Convention & Visitor's Bureau: Bruria & Michele
    Liaison with Snyder Co: Kevin
    Sub-committee on computer training: Kathy, Joanne, & Carol
Don's [*Paschal*] idea has blossomed!
Thanks everyone for taking on these tasks. Copy Kevin on your progress.

By 1991, Southern California was gripped by a serious, prolonged recession. Both the homeless "problem" and illegal migration had become more visible and both issues were politicized as available resources for social services dwindled while the resources necessary to meet these needs increased. The PEN Homeless conference, although it continued to focus on the concerns of the homeless, reflected these added stresses. I believe this less munificent community environment increased the level of hostility and was mirrored in the PEN discourse. We can begin to see a shift from a dialogue among persons with shared goals about mutual concerns to a series of adversarial monologues that talk past each other.

16:13) Michele Wittig   14-JAN-92 11:46
Re: SHWASHLOCK. I visited Memorial Park last Saturday and made some inquiries about the availability of early morning showers. . . . Users of the showers report that they open sometime between 7 and 9am, depending on when the staff gets them cleaned after arriving for work. I think that's the best we can hope for at the moment. The City has shown a willingness to accommodate our request for early-opening without major additional staff salary outlay. . . . The laundry voucher program is going well, and continues to be supported by the money raised in the July, 1990 PEN Action Group fundraiser. . . . Our team of two mature CSUN interns has experience, a videotape, and are willing to speak to business groups. Still hope to set a date with the Main Street Merchants, "Jim," E-mail me if you're still interested.

16:16) "Les"   14-JAN-92 18:24
..........I have received a first hand report that one of the TRANSIENT feeding locations is inside
..........the Senior Citizen center located in Palisades Park.
..........In light of the fact that there is NO screening program to identify who the criminals are
..........Seniors will be in more jeopardy than ever before.
..........Perhaps the Senior Center will be renamed the TRANSIENT Center?
..........Apparently our City Council is more concerned about continuing the indiscriminate
..........feeding of transients than they are about public safety of Senior Citizens.
..........It would be a different matter if the people who came to dinner were merely homeless.

16:24) Donald Paschal   15-JAN-92 9:44
This is only clarification. . .there does seem to be a dinner being served at the senior center—. . . .however this "feeding" (I love it when humans are reduced to the state of animals in a zoo. . .) seems to be occurring after hours, so the safety factor seems to be more specious than not.

16:29) "Les"   15-JAN-92 10:21
..........What is very curious is why the NAACP and others have not [sic]
..........have not expressed outrage at the RACIST and HATEFUL threats
..........which were posted on Item 15, Response #833? Why is it
..........alright for a "HOMELESS" person to post OBSCENITY, SLANDER
..........and RACIST THREATS, and be defended by prominent PEN Regulars?
..........As for the cowardly persons who send anonymous FAXes, that
..........is something I have NEVER been accused of. I do not FEAR to

...........put my name on anything that I write. I do suspect though,
...........there are many, many, silent onlookers who are afraid to
...........participate because of the threats, obscenity and ridicule.

16:30) Donald Paschal [*in response to the preceding entry*]   15-JAN-92 10:38
re 29/point #2)I will take your word that you did not send the fax. I must say that
you have put your views on the line. . .even though I strongly disagree.
However, fear of attack should not stifle debate. Besides, "Les", you are not the
only person on PEN who has expressed these views.

While the Homeless conference still featured dialogue among diverse
individuals, the overall tone became much more harsh. More strident
entries, rife with personal attacks, increasingly typified many PEN postings
during 1992. This hostility led many PEN regulars to become disenchanted
with the network; some of the City Council Members who were early PEN
regulars no longer posted entries and many curtailed their PEN reading.

16:133) "Dan"   23-JAN-92 12:31
I am homeless. I sent the city attorney messages about strengthening law or
ordinance on drunkeness, [*sic*] panhandling, other intrusive behavior—as a way
of avoiding discrimination against the homeless. He did not hardly respond but
to say no "strengthening" was needed; the laws were "adequate". . . . I can say
that enforcement in the parks is lax, and in two steps: The rangers, who are not
so well trained. And the police, who arrive too long after an incident of violence,
intrusion, drunkeness, [*sic*] etc. . . . This enforcement seems to BE THE CENTRAL
ISSUE. . . .

16:134) "Reg"   23-JAN-92 13:18
Say Jews can not sleep in the park, see what happens. Say Japs can not sleep in
the park, see what happens. But say homeless Vets can not sleep in the park, no
big deal right?

16:137) City Attorney– [*Then Robert Myers*]   23-JAN-92 13:53
Mr. ["Dan"]: As I informed you, I believe that existing laws are adequate to deal
with anti-social conduct. Your concerns will not be addressed by additional
laws.

16:138) "Susan"   23-JAN-92 14:28
What we have here is a failure to enforce.

16:139) "Dick"   23-JAN-92 15:32
"Reg," what they are trying to say is that it isn't ok for anyone to camp in the
parks. It isn't what they are for, and it prevents many people from using the parks
for what they are for.

16:141) "Dan"   23-JAN-92 15:53
City Attorney: You were supposed to at least address the subject of enforcement
problems also. Two times at least you have failed to make any such distinction
in your responses. Is this just an oversight?

16:143) "Geraldine"   23-JAN-92 18:25
In so far as enforcement is the responsibility of the SMPD, it is not the
responsibility of the City Attorney's Office, "Dan".

16:147) "Les" [*in response to the preceding entry*]   23-JAN-92 21:20
.......""Geraldine" (Per YOUR entry: Planning Item 9:757)
.......As a FOREIGN NATIONAL who has lived in the U.S. 18 yrs on a "temporary work permit"
........who oversees the LARGEST POVERTY "non-profit" in Santa Monica (over $20 million)
.......would you tell us if you oppose an ordinance to prohibit encampment in Santa Monica's
.......parks?

16:149) "Ellen"   23-JAN-92 22:32
What's wrong with this question?

16:150) "Richard"   23-JAN-92 22:41
The questioner.

16:153) "Alice"   23-JAN-92 23:20
All this talk about the CA [*City Attorney*] not "following orders" reminds me of those "good Germans" who, after World War II, claimed they were only "following orders."

As the 1992 elections approached, Homeless conference entries became increasingly shrill. Comparison of the February 1992 entries with those of September 1992 revealed fewer entries in the later period and that many of the more prolific September authors were conference newcomers (Schmitz et al., 1995). There was also a decline in "lurkers," persons who read entries but did not post on PEN. The Homeless conference became a forum for political rhetoric and personal invective in which ideological opponents waged electronic contests. At the same time an important political controversy centered on calls to dismiss the City Attorney for refusing to restrict homeless camping in Santa Monica's public parks. The entries that follow show how this controversy was resolved and demonstrate elites' and non-elites' interaction on PEN.

18:482) "Bill"   08-SEP-92 14:17
I will probably be there, but I don't plan to speak. If I remember correctly, since this is an "Item 9," one cannot address it. Of course, public comments are welcomed <sic> at the end. My friends and I feel that this is another "done deal," which means we will probably have to fight this out in court IF the ordinance is accepted as is. I suspect that the City Council will try to fire our City Attorney again tonight and I fear that whether it is tonight or sometime in the future, the majority of the CC will indeed let him go. . . . Sooner or later, our City Attorney will be gone; probably much sooner than later. The last hurrah of irony is that what will be lost is Rent Control, for this is the real issue.

18:483) Donald Paschal   08-SEP-92 14:21
I think homelessness is the real issue. People don't want people around who have nowhere to be.

18:484) Ken Genser [*City Council Member*]   08-SEP-92 15:28
Members of the public are welcome to address the council on "9" items.

18:485) "Bill"   08-SEP-92 15:47
Thanks, Ken & Don, no disagreement here. I just find it quite interesting to note that those against Rent Control are also so very much against those who are homeless. . . .

18:488) Robert [*City Council Member*]   08-SEP-92 19:17
Don't miss tonight's CC Meeting. It is suppose to be an end of summer block buster.

18:489) Donald Paschal   08-SEP-92 19:19
Yes, I am here to see if you are going to fire Bob Myers, as "Bill" has suggested. [*Later that evening the City Council dismissed Robert Myers as City Attorney*]

18:494) "Bill"   09-SEP-92 0:18
I feel badly for Bob Myers. What a sham. Ken and Judy have definitely lost my votes for their re-election. I feel very let down by them. Only Tom showed the courage of conviction.

The previous discussion started about ten hours before the event occurred. While calls for Myer's dismissal had been covered in the local newspaper, knowledge of his impending firing was not then available to the general public, save via PEN. Note the direct exchange between Robert (City Council Member) and Donald Paschal (homeless); consider the dialogue of "Bill" (social worker), Ken Genser (City Council Member), and Donald Paschal. Comparable conversations, unremarkable on PEN, would be wildly atypical in traditional face-to-face interactions.

Increasingly, the Homeless conference offered a venue for adversarial exchanges about the local elections. Partly this reflected pervasive Santa Monica politics. But it also reflected strong concerns of PEN regulars about homelessness, crime, and contrasting views of an ideal community that were increasingly reflected in contentious PEN entries. Additionally, "Loved Quail," a formerly mentally ill, homeless write-in candidate for City Council, campaigned on PEN with few restraints. What had begun as a forum to discuss homeless issues and help homeless persons had become a much different discourse, one with quite different social norms.

18:567) "Phil"   11-SEP-92 7:52
Mayor, I agree with you that it had to be done. But don't for a second say that it wasn't politically expedient. 2 weeks ago, a poll was taken of four names. Genser, Abdo, Pyne, and Greenberg. You and Mayor Pro-Tem Abdo both lost. You fired Bob Myers in a wave of political expediency, and you will rehire him to save your asses in December. You had the opportunity to fire him at every Tuesday's meeting, and yet you waited. I'm surprised you didn't wait until the District Attorney's office got him disbarred for malfeasance in office. But, that's all past now. He'll go get some job with the ACLU, which is basically what he's had for the past decade anyway.

18:586) "Phil" [*addressing the Mayor*]   11-SEP-92 22:12
Ken, you know damn well that SMRR's campaign/political organs were the ones who conducted the polls. And I'm sure not going to tell you who my sources are on that one. But it's okay. You lost, as you will in November. The City of Santa Monica, at least the RESIDENTS of the City are fed up with your leftist, failed

approach to dealing with the homeless. And they want a change, a toughed-up change. Shall I call U-Haul, or will you?

18:637) "Loved Quail" [*Write-in City Council Candidate*]   14-SEP-92 20:52
    Sung To The Tune Of Pride (In The Name Of Love) (Et Tu?)
    Not too late one September Eight
    Cowards darken the homelss night
    The wise won"t miss
    The Serpent's hissssssssssssss
    But you can't cloak what's not right
    In the name of love
    What more in the name of love?
    In the name of love
    What more in the name of love?
Copyright 1992 "Loved Quail" All Rights Reserved
I agree with I think it was "Bill"—John Jalili [*City Manager*], not Bob Myers would best have served the interest of the public generally to have been fired. Burn like Hell, Satan Monika. I'll write you from wherever I go to when the riots resume, coming to an intersection near you. . .
SHoulda practiced policius status interruptus like I told ya. Now it looks like yer screwed.

The entry by "Loved Quail," typical in content, is far more brief than many of his other entries, which comprised multiple screens of text. The sexual innuendoes probably refer to an openly gay City Council candidate. Some of "Loved Quail"'s entries were extremely hostile and profane; most bitterly criticized the City Council, law enforcement agencies, or the mental health profession. Perhaps because of "Loved Quail"'s goads, the Homeless conference soon "featured" entries by several incumbent City Council Members and other candidates who directly responded to "Quail"'s insults with accusations almost as intemperate.

By the end of 1992, the harsh PEN invective had chilled participation; logons declined about 25 percent from the previous year. During January 1993 Ken Phillips confided to me that he would "just as soon shut all the damn conferences down." Phillips' frustration with PEN shortly became moot as he accepted an attractive job at the City/County of Salem, Oregon. By March 1993, Santa Monica changed the conference format to one in which the city pre-screened most entries and limited their length. Although unregulated conferences still existed, they were consolidated at a few specified "locations" and were both harder to find and less useful.

In one respect, the preceding Homeless conference text is not representative. The larger PEN corpus is more repetitive and often seems pointless or banal. Many PEN entries were composed during the evening or late at night, except for those by homeless PENners who logged off when the libraries and community centers closed. Yet, consider the "ideal" standard: face-to-face conversation. Often our face-to-face discourse fails to sparkle, perhaps more so when late at night and particularly if we are impaired by fatigue or drugs, legal or otherwise. Still, in face-to-face conversation we may more easily end a discussion or signal a change in topic. On systems like PEN, a single conversant may continue without immediate social restraint, partly because many cues have been filtered out.

Must our electronic discourse differ markedly from conventional speech? I think not. It seems that if PEN differs markedly, it differs most for those, like the homeless, who are often silenced. And PEN differs not because of its scintillating discourse, but because it offers a venue where the criteria for acceptance center on the cognitive and verbal skills of would-be participants rather than on their physical appearance and interpersonal skills.

PEN Incivility: Antecedents and Consequences

Some of the negative outcomes associated with the later PEN text seem exacerbated by PEN's technology. PEN's software required readers to scroll through each entry in turn. Although adept users could skip around within conferences, this was difficult for many PEN users, including myself. Consequently, overly long and offensive entries chilled participation by many who came to view PEN as having more chaff than wheat.

At the psychological level of analysis, the PEN text provides examples consistent with the psychological disinhibition claimed by some (e.g. Kiesler et al., 1984; Sproull & Kiesler, 1986) to be an inherent consequence of electronic media, which embody lessened social restraints. Although I am leery of the technological determinism these explanations rest upon, the PEN text does show striking examples of relaxed social restraints coupled with consequent norms of incivility. Further, PEN Action Group members surveyed by Wittig & Schmitz (1996) sometimes attributed their own and others' flaming as a consequence of fewer social restraints on PEN.

For me the most important issues involve not the technical effects of this media, but the social antecedents and their consequences. The PEN system itself was a socially constructed artifact that reflected Santa Monica's norms to include diverse, potentially divisive others in a collaborative dialogue. As an early PEN user, I recall the excitement on PEN about the new enterprise we shared. We could now talk with each other about the local (or national) issues of the day. PEN's early tone was mirrored by the goals that initial Homeless conference participants shared. These first users, although a diverse group of individuals, developed a shared agenda, first electronically, and then, for many, in-person.

Why did PEN later become more uncivil? I think these changes were linked partly to declining economic prosperity and partly to more divisive local politics. The corpus of PEN text reflected these tensions in Santa Monica. Several years later, as the Homeless conference text shows, that early gloss had worn off. As system-wide PEN norms became less civil, the Homeless conference also became more contentious. While thoughtful and reflective conversations still took place on PEN, the PEN text was transformed to a discourse quite different from either its first beginnings or what its creators had originally envisioned.

How to create a venue for "ideal" public speech was a big concern during PEN's early development. We struggled with both censorship issues and moderator options. We also considered starting up PEN slowly with carefully selected persons who would model "desirable" norms. While the PEN Users Agreement stipulated that users refrain from obscene or profane speech and asked that they respect others, this agreement was not held to be an enforceable contract. In the end, the demand to "roll the system out" and legal concerns to protect free speech precluded Santa Monica from taking more aggressive steps to firmly establish norms of civility. So modeling "ideal" conferences, moderated conferences, or strict restrictions regarding the length, tone, and content of PEN entries were not really attempted.

Conclusions

Santa Monica's PEN experience offers at least five insights regarding electronic media in local communities. First, because PEN reflects Santa Monica's distinctive social norms, PEN was created in the context of a strong commitment to share political and economic power. The structure and operation of PEN reflect these community norms. The strength of this commitment was demonstrated by the candidacy of "Loved Quail" for City Council Member and the tolerance shown to his election campaign on PEN. Phillips' use of an inclusive town hall metaphor and PEN's provision of public terminals were not accidental but were rooted in Santa Monica's culture. Later, nearby cities would create their own electronic systems, systems that would be guided by quite different metaphors and systems that would operate quite differently—and operate to serve quite different ends (Guthrie & Dutton, 1992).

Second, the desires of Santa Monica elites also shaped the development and operation of PEN. Because these electronic systems, even as they evolve, remain grounded in their host communities, the goals of elites, and of others, remain important. When PEN's discourse became rowdy enough to drive off many users, the value of the system was reduced for all, particularly for those most needy. Here Sahlin's argument, that change occurs when traditional relations confront novel phenomena that do not respond in traditional ways, is clearly illuminated. And we may see how this process can yield consequences that are quite unforgiving, particularly from the perspective of those who would manage structural change.

Third, the PEN case demonstrates that these types of technology do matter. When they are deliberately employed to bridge social distances, the ability to span social and physical gulfs can serve to include those who are often excluded. The inclusion of homeless persons in the PEN Action Group and their prominent role in developing the SHWASHLOCK program would be wildly improbable in groups that originated through the traditional sequence of face-to-face encounters. A core issue is deliberate employment. PEN was a deliberately constructed social creation, comprised of hardware, software, expectations, and governed by belief structures that created a new venue in which diverse residents of Santa Monica could interact. The same technologies might have been used, in a different social environment, to build a non-interactive, kiosk-based information system in support of the local chamber of commerce.

Fourth, these systems are "intensely malleable" by their users. True, the configuration of their hardware may encourage and also constrain how participants will use them, just as system policies may encourage or discourage particular behaviors. Yet, more importantly, once constructed, systems like PEN are literally created and re-created by those who use them. They are therefore dynamic, interactive, and often unscripted systems of meaning that reflect loosely coordinated behaviors by participants. So we can't expect to control their outcomes in any deterministic fashion. At most, for better or worse, we may partly shape outcomes through influencing the meanings that these systems have for their users.

Fifth, a "dark side" of this technology presents serious dilemmas when core values such as free speech, respect for others, and greatly different views of an ideal community come in conflict. Discussions with members of the PEN Action Group often elicited the theme that, for many, their on-line personae fostered conflict in ways that were atypically harsh compared to their face-to-face behavior. Many, probably most, PEN users felt that incivility was the greatest problem that the network faced (Schmitz et al., 1995; Wittig & Schmitz, 1996). Recall that PEN was explicitly designed to build an electronic community that was open to all residents. In an ironic paradox, partly because PEN facilitated discourse among very different persons who "shared" a common electronic space, this added diversity enhanced the potential for conflict. This paradox, congruent with Ortner's (1984) view of change, should put us on notice that the symbolic meanings we hold for systems like PEN are both dynamic and indeterminate:

> that although the actor's intentions are accorded central place in the model, major social change does not for the most part come about as intended consequence of action, however rational action may have been. Change is largely a by-product, an unintended consequence of actions by many persons. To say that society and history are products of human action is true, but only in a certain ironic sense. They are rarely the products the individual actors themselves, set out to make. (p. 156)

PEN was conceived as a grand experiment to see if communication technology could create public electronic forums with space for all and thereby help bind together a community. We explicitly patterned elements of PEN on social network models that were grounded in symbolic interaction and hoped to create a system that would: (1) be compatible with community norms and needs, and (2) change communication patterns to aid those who were disadvantaged. Mostly we hoped PEN would succeed.

The impact of homeless PEN users was, for me, an unanticipated consequence, yet one consistent with the theoretical views that helped to shape PEN.

Also unanticipated was the steady drift towards conflict that came to characterize PEN and would limit its value to Santa Monica. These changes, although consistent with the increased conflict in Santa Monica, appear magnified on PEN. Here the technology seems to foster the ease by which the meaning of PEN changes from a venue for collaboration to a place for conflict. In this respect, Ortner's characterization of change as failed reproduction is particularly apt.

Yet PEN's heightened conflict should not blind us to important outcomes. Interaction among very different persons took place regularly in ways that would be wildly "inappropriate" using conventional media. Without PEN, a counterpart to David Morgan's letter would be almost inconceivable. It is hard to envision a conventional town meeting that would regularly offer the exchanges among local officials, political activists, and the homeless that were commonplace on PEN. Without PEN, the SHWASHLOCK program would also be quite improbable. So PEN demonstrates that community electronic networks *can* facilitate the kinds of structural linkages touted as important by Blau, while it also cautions us as to the limits of our ability to guide social change.

References

Anonymous (1995, June). Unpublished interviews of two Santa Monica City Council members.

Bandura, A. (1986). *Social foundations of thought and action: A social cognitive theory.* Englewood Cliffs, NJ: Prentice Hall.

Berger, P.L., & Luckmann, T. (1966). *The social construction of reality.* New York: Doubleday.

Blau, P.M. (1974). Presidential address: Parameters of social structure. *American Sociological Review, 39,* 615–635.

Blau, P.M. (1977). A macrosocial theory of social structure. *American Journal of Sociology, 83,* 26–54.

Coleman, J.S. (1974). *Power and the structure of a society.* New York: W. W. Norton.

Culnan, M.J., & Markus, M.L. (1987). Information technologies. In F.M. Jablin, L.L. Putnam, K.H. Roberts, & L.W. Porter (Eds.), *Handbook of organizational communication: An interdisciplinary perspective* (pp. 420–443). Newbury Park, CA: Sage.

Dutton, W.H., Rogers, E.M., & Jun, S. (1987). Diffusion and impacts of personal computers. *Communication Research, 14,* 219–250.

Erickson, B.H. (1996). The structure of ignorance. *Connections, 19*(1), 28–38.

Granovetter, M.S. (1973). The strength of weak ties. *American Journal of Sociology, 78,* 1361–1380.

Granovetter, M.S. (1982). The strength of weak ties: A network theory revisited. In P.V. Marsden, & N. Lin (Eds.), *Social structure and network analysis* (pp. 105–130). Beverly Hills, CA: Sage.

Guthrie, K.K. (1988, March). Unpublished interviews of Santa Monica opinion-leaders.

Guthrie, K.K., & Dutton, W.H. (1992). The politics of citizen access technology: The development of public information utilities in four cities. *Policy Studies Journal, 20,* 574–597.

Guthrie, K.K., Schmitz, J., Ryu, D., Harris J., Rogers, E.M., & Dutton, W.H. (1990). *Communication technology and democratic participation: The PEN system in Santa Monica.* Paper presented at the Association for Computing Machinery's Conference on Computers and the Quality of Life, Washington, DC.

Kann, M.E. (1986). *Middle-class radicalism in Santa Monica.* Philadelphia: Temple University Press.

Kiesler, S., Siegel, J., & McGuire, T.W. (1984) Social psychological aspects of computer-mediated communication. *American Psychologist, 39,* 1123–1134.

Mayall, S. (1995, June). Personal communication.

Mead, G.H. (1934). *Mind, self, and society* (C. Morris, Ed.). Chicago: University of Chicago Press.

Morgan, D. (1989, November, 20). Letter to the author.

Ortner, S.B. (1984). Theory in anthropology since the sixties. *Comparative Studies of Society and History, 26*(1) 126–166.

O'Sullivan, P.B. (1995). Computer networks and political participation: Santa Monica's teledemocracy project. *Journal of Applied Communication Research, 23,* 93–105.

Phillips, K. & Schmitz, J. (1988, April). Policy recommendation to the City of Santa Monica.

Reardon, K.K. (1987). *Interpersonal communication: Where minds meet.* Belmont CA: Wadsworth.

Rogers, E.M. (1983). *Diffusion of innovations* (3rd ed.). New York: Free Press.

Rogers, E.M. (1994). *A history of communication study: A biographical approach.* New York: Free Press.

Rogers, E.M., Collins-Jarvis, L., & Schmitz, J. (1994). The PEN Project in Santa Monica: Interactive communication, equality, and political action. *Journal of the American Society for Information Science, 45,* 401–410.

Rogers, E.M., & Kincaid, D.L. (1981). *Communication networks: Toward a new paradigm for research.* New York: Free Press.

Salins, M. (1981). *Historical metaphors and mythical realities: Structure in the early history of the Sandwich Islands Kingdom.* Ann Arbor: University of Michigan Press.

Schmitz, J. (1987, May). *Electronic messaging: System use in local governments.* Paper presented at the International Communication Association, Montreal.

Schmitz, J. (1988, December). *Circuit city: Survey results.* Report to the City of Santa Monica. Santa Monica, CA: Author.

Schmitz, J., & Fulk, J. (1991). Organizational colleagues, media richness, and electronic mail: A test of the social influence model of technology use. *Communication Research, 18,* 487–523.

Schmitz, J., Rogers, E.M., Phillips, K., & Paschal, D. (1995). The Public Electronic Network (PEN) and the homeless in Santa Monica. *Journal of Applied Communication Research, 23,* 26–43.

Scott, W.R. (1992). *Organizations: Rational, natural, and open systems* (3rd ed.). Englewood Cliffs, NJ: Prentice Hall.

Simmel, G. (1955). *The web of group-affiliations* (R. Bendix, Trans.). New York: Free Press. (Original work published 1922)

Sproull, L., & Kiesler, S. (1986). Reducing social context cues: The case of electronic mail. *Management Science, 32,* 1492–1512.

Valacich, J.S., Paranka, D., George, J.F., & Nunamaker, J.F. Jr. (1993). Communication concurrency and the new media. *Communication Research, 20,* 249–276.

Wellman, B., Carrington, P.J., & Hall, A. (1988). Networks as personal communities. In B. Wellman & S.D. Berkowitz (Eds.), *Social structures: A network approach* (pp. 130–184). Cambridge: Cambridge University Press.

Wittig, M. (1989, April). PEN entry calling for the establishment of the PEN Action Group, Santa Monica, CA.

Wittig, M. (1993, June). Personal communication.

Wittig, M. (1993, July). Personal communication.

Wittig, M., & Schmitz, J. (1996). Electronic grassroots organizing. *Journal of Social Issues*, 52(1), 53–69.

Wood, J.T. (1992). *Spinning the symbolic web: Human communication as symbolic interaction*. Norwood NJ: Ablex.

Acknowledgements

While pursuing my doctorate, I lived with my family in Santa Monica, California. There I met Ken Phillips and was captivated by Phillips' vision of an electronic community, and joined in what would become the PEN project. The first two PEN surveys were funded, respectively, by the City of Santa Monica and the University of Southern California. Without Ken Phillips, the PEN system would not exist; Ev Rogers freely gave valuable advice, insight, and institutional support to PEN and to the author. Michele Wittig provided valuable insights about PEN and the PEN Action group; Donald Paschal helped me to better understand what it was like to be homeless in Santa Monica.

5

Why We Argue About Virtual Community: A Case Study of the Phish.Net Fan Community

Nessim Watson

Scholars attempting to prove that a group of people sharing something online are in fact a "community" are regularly challenged by skeptics of every sort; they are usually criticized as naive techno-utopians drawn in by the hype of emerging technologies and the information age. I have argued and continue to argue, based on my two years working as an ethnographer to an online fan community 50,000 strong, that those youth formed a community which created not only individual benefits for participants but also a group strength which enabled them to alter the routines of the record industry and to help launch a new category of music in American culture. That work has caused me to reflect upon the debate over "community," which has grown louder once again with the emergence of computer-mediated communication (CMC) technologies.

Resolving the question of "virtual" communities may require that we move beyond it, to a deeper background, to examine the political and cultural foundation on which we have placed our arguments about communities. Consider the following question: why argue about an online forum being a community or not? Why does such a debate matter? That is not a cynical question. If we can get to the heart of the answer, we may find the tools with which to resolve this seemingly endless "yes-it-is; no-it-isn't" debate. Is there some power to be had in claiming a word like "community"? Might this debate be important in the context of a group's struggle for greater representation in the larger (potentially global) society? More to the point, does *being* a community have something to do with gaining representation in a democratic culture?

The Question of Community

Communication and Community

As often as Internet scholars argue that they have discovered a virtual community, it is also argued that those researchers are uncritical about the notion of community. Their detractors often accuse them of being overly excited to assign "community" as a descriptor for their favorite and newly discovered online-discussion group. Early arguments for the presence of community online perhaps deserved such skepticism. Any attempt to apply a valuable word like "community" to a new set of phenomena should certainly be met with initial skepticism. These arguments have a long social history, and each wave of the conversation has unfolded in an environment of rapid changes to everyday life. The swiftly modernizing technological age of the 1990s has begun the newest wave of this cultural conversation, in which we are again attempting to define and redefine the notion of "community." This conversation is shot through with discussion about whether to recognize online forums as "communities," and the time has now come to add up the arguments and take some stock of what we have collectively argued to and against each other about the question of community. The time has come for us to ask: what *uses* exist in different definitions of the term, and what is it that we wish to inflect upon our understanding of CMC by using a community metaphor in our description of online social spaces?

One way to answer these questions is to begin with the origin of "community" as terminology. The *Random House Dictionary of the English Language* defines "community" as

> 1. a social group of any size whose members reside in a specific locality, share government, and often have a common cultural and historical heritage . . . 3. . . . . group sharing common characteristics or interests and perceived or perceiving itself as distinct in some respect from the larger society within which it exists. (*Random House*, 1987, p. 414)

The above definition contains requirements of shared proximity as well as a degree of common experience and common interests. Spatial or temporal proximity of communicants is almost never a part of CMC over the Internet (with the possible exception of Internet Relay Chat and Multi-User Dimensions). Thus, this definition precludes the recognition of online communities because it does not connect a conception of "community" to its most closely related word, "communication," and stresses instead a being together which could almost be devoid of communication.

As a communication scholar, I understand communication to be at the heart of the geographically based communities described above. As an Internet scholar, I also recognize that to see "community" online *requires* that the word have a basic connection to the definition of communication. The term "community" *is* clearly related to "communication" as both stem from the Latin root *communis*, meaning common. So how do we resolve the dictionary's oversight? To emphasize the connection between the two terms, James Carey (1989) has advocated the use of a "ritual view" of communication to describe "a process through which a shared culture is created, modified, and transformed. . . . A ritual view . . . is directed not toward the extension of messages in space but the maintenance of society over time" (p. 43). This way of understanding communication challenges the traditional "transmission" view of "communication" as "something imparted, interchanged, or transmitted" (*Random House*, 1987, p. 414). Carey's ritual view, preserving the connection of "communication" to "community," is important to include in any argument about the social health of a community. It gets to the question of how well community members are communicating with each other about their shared conditions. Without ongoing communication among its participants, a community dissolves. Communication is therefore vital to communities both online and off.

Communication creates, re-creates, and maintains community on Phish.net and other online discussion forums through the continued interaction of participating members. However, the technological ability to communicate does not in itself create the conditions of community. Community depends not only upon communication and shared interests, but also upon "communion." The term is used most in a discourse of religious ritual, but even in non-religious contexts the term is often chosen to describe a spiritual, emotional, or, as Rheingold (1993b, p. 5) names it, "human" feeling that comes from the communicative coordination of oneself with others and the environment. The event of communion is even implied by the dictionary definition of "community," though it is presented as separate and apart from the earlier definition of community as spatially proximate people. The *Random House* (1987) definition continues:

> . . . 4. interchange or sharing of thoughts or emotions; intimate communication
> . . . 5. the act of sharing, or holding in common; participation . . . (p. 414)

Rheingold's (1993b) definition of "virtual community" (below) reflects *this* understanding of community in the absence of the earlier spatially proximate definition.

> Virtual communities are social aggregations that emerge from the Net when enough people carry on . . . public discussions long enough, *with sufficient human feeling*, to form webs of personal relationships in cyberspace. (p. 5; emphasis mine)

MacDonald (1994a) concludes in her study of a computer-mediated women-only space that "How well the women commune through communication determines the quality of community they experience" (p. 55). Both Rheingold and MacDonald emphasize the importance of communion to notions of computer-mediated communities, but MacDonald has gone further by suggesting that CMC researchers make their thinking explicit by adopting the term "'commune-ity' . . . more than just community, it is community plus communing" (p. 55).

With such a definition, the measuring rod for the question of community hangs on Rheingold's awkward phrase "with sufficient human feeling." Who is to determine when human feeling has become sufficient, the researcher or the researched? Could the researched subjects with their varying degrees of participation online ever agree among themselves as to whether or not there is sufficient human feeling among them? Such a definition is open to easy criticism about the judgement process by which one determines the answer to the community question. However, the fact that we are left with no empirical measuring rod for answering the question need not be a point of anxiety. Judgements are made about all things, and we are certainly capable of making judgements about the claim of cyberspace residents to be a community. We need to continue defining the terms by which we make the judgements. The answer to the question of community comes (if at all) when enough people agree upon the standards by which to judge. Let us therefore focus the argument upon Phish.net as an example of community and then discuss some of the standards for judging virtual aggregations as communities.

The Community Metaphor

Social researchers use a community metaphor to describe something about online interaction which is similar to what we know as a community in the offline world. The primary reason why CMC researchers like Rheingold came up with the community metaphor to originally describe online interaction forums is that it *feels* right. Subjectively, when one looks into a virtual forum, it *feels* like what one knows as a community. One feature which makes a space like Phish.net appear to be a community is the seemingly continuous presence of other people there. One can "tap into" CMC communities for a wealth of prepared information, or to pose a question to a large group of people with diverse backgrounds of knowledge. Rheingold (1993b) has referred to the collectivity of information and knowledge in computer-mediated spaces as an "online brain trust" (p. 13) and as a "computer-assisted groupmind" (p. 111).

But while knowledge capital as a collective good may be one sign of community, the relationship between an individual and other individuals in that space remains devoid of commitment or stake. The medium's technology allows most members of large discussion groups like Phish.net to act as "lurkers," those who read posts but do not post messages themselves, thus remaining effectively invisible to other members of the group. Even the terminology of the medium (e.g. user, information retrieval) indicates the lack of commitment which an individual is required to make to any such space or its other user-inhabitants. Although the continuous presence of others can be easily sensed by lurkers on Phish.net, without interactive communication with the group at large or with any of its members the ability to commune is precluded.

Another aspect of community which hastens the word's metaphorical use in studies of CMC is that the word "community" has been used in anthropology to draw distinctions between groups of people according to the ideas which bind groups together and which define them in relation to other groups of people and ideas. The notion of community as "institutionally distinct groups" is supported by the social organization of the

Usenet bulletin boards into areas of common interest increasingly sub-divided by topic of discussion.

Bakhtin's argument that "as groups develop over time they generate group-specific meanings . . . [eventually evolving] new forms of speech, or genres, unique to that community" (Baym, 1995, p. 151) has been supported by Nancy Baym's study of the processes by which computer-mediated groups create expression through emoticons, abbreviations, and inside jokes. During 1993, fan mail and debate on the Phish.net news-group about the contents of a particular verse of unprinted lyrics elicited three Phish newsletters filled with the band's multiple joke answers to fan letters about the verse (Phish Update, 1993b). During the ensuing tour, the band changed the lyrics of that verse in performance to alternate suggested answers from the publicly answered fan letters.[1] This became an in-joke of particular excitement to Phish.netters, who soon adopted the term "WATSIYEM," an acronym for the commonly asked newbie question "What are they saying in 'You Enjoy Myself'?", to refer to: (1) the period of debate and band response in Phish.net history, considered a successful communication with the band by Phish.net and other Phish fans; (2) the sorts of questions which now identify the asker as a newbie or an outsider. A CMC group's internal development of expressions which can only be understood and/or fully appreciated by members of that group, and which draw distinctions between those who are internal and external to the group, can be taken as an indication that something akin to community as an institutionally distinct group is developing.

However, common interests are the *only* thing generating this process, and other incentives of individual commitment and stake in the group, the markers of "real" community, are still absent. As one skeptical fan remarks: "Take away the music and you don't have much. To be a community we would have to relate to each other more for what we are, not [just] the music we love" (Robson, 1994). CMC technology does provide the ability for individuals to access information from a group-mind, and to participate interactively in CMC spaces with others holding common interests towards a set of internal group norms. But none of these qualities account for the degree of commitment and interdependence which leads to communion in face-to-face interactions. CMC technology does increase our abilities to interact, but is interaction the same phenomenon as the communication from which commune-ity is supposed to arise? Where is the communion?

MacKinnon's 1992 study of Usenet newsgroup postings attempted to contribute another piece to this puzzle by concluding that "the *frequency and regularity* of contributions by a proportion of newsgroup readers further distinguishes this form of social interaction as a more stable and enduring aspect of community" (McLaughlin, Osborne, & Smith, 1995, p. 92; emphasis mine). This measure is too simplistic in the case of Phish.net, however, where there now exists a discussion core of partici-pants who post at least once per day. This core, rather than being a sign of community, seems to be regarded by most netters as a group of excessive posters who do not understand "proper" use of the newsgroup. "98% post just to post . . . and there is always about 5–10 guys who never have anything to say but post about 5 messages a day anyway. Unnerves me" (Sondericker, 1994). It is notable that none of the original 13 Phish.netters were included in a list of the 50 most frequent posters to Phish.net researched by one community statistician (Silverman, 1994). In fact, this analysis found that posts to Phish.net in a six-month period were transmitted from over 3,300 different e-mail addresses. Although the number appears large, it is actually quite a small core of participants within the total community roster of 35,000–50,000 potential posters. Thus, frequent and regular interaction becomes a difficult term to apply to large groups of people such as Phish.net today. In addition, frequent postings do not indicate whether the posters are interacting *with* each other, nor does it guarantee the sincerity of that interaction. If we are to center a notion of community on the term "communion," then we must investigate the issue of sincerity in CMC.

Sincerity of Online Communication

Rheingold notes that in CMC, interaction is conducted by "personae," or identities that may have little correlation to the identity of the person utilizing them online. The medium inherently prevents the interpersonal identification and judgement processes by which we normally evaluate each other in face-to-face interaction. On Phish.net, the experienced user can control nearly all qualities of his/her presentation to an audience already partially described to them by the common interest specified in the bulletin board's title. For some fans, this fact causes them to doubt my use of the term "community": "Even though you may get to know someone rather well over the Net, you have never met the person, and may never get to know him/her on that level. So with that, comes a sense of removal, or lack of complete and serious commitment" (Welsh, 1995). Rheingold (1993a) thus asks about sincerity in CMC:

> are relationships and commitments as we know them even possible in a place where identities are fluid? . . . [where we] deliberately experiment with fracturing traditional notions of identity by living as multiple simultaneous personae in different virtual neighborhoods . . . where people lack the genuine personal commitments to one another that form the bedrock of . . . community. (pp. 60–61)

Yet all individuals present themselves strategically, sometimes truthfully and sometimes not, to others in everyday life regardless of the medium of communication in order to accomplish their short- and long-term goals. CMC allows individuals to execute a greater degree of control over the usually non-controllable features of their appearance, ethnicity, and gender in presentations to others. This could potentially allow a community to form without the mistrust brought on by visual markers of difference such as skin color. However, it will most likely take more than a technology to erase the distinctions which humans have made among themselves in the offline world.

MacDonald (1994a) is skeptical as to whether CMC is "truly blind to the body markers that are so closely tied to social hierarchies such as gender and race?" (p. 3). Her work suggests that social hierarchies (especially of gender) are established even with the supposed effacement of visual body cues. Although social hierarchy formation appears to be a natural human behavior, I believe it need not establish itself among traditionally structured lines. Especially in fan communities, as MacDonald (1994b) noted, hierarchies are often established according to fan knowledge, measures of fandom level or quality, or access to CMC technology (p. 8). Where does this leave sincerity? There is no standard for determining sincerity of communication across all situations. Sincerity then becomes measurable only in a manner specific to its context and by people familiar with that context.

If the markers of race and gender were of the utmost importance to Internet users, then the inability to make judgements on the basis of those missing cues would create challenges to sincere communion with others in the group. On Phish.net race, gender, and sexual orientation are non-issues. Most Phish fans would claim that this is due to the tolerant values of the community. In the context of this online community, missing visual cues are not necessary to the formation of communion. On Phish.net communion becomes possible in the absence of body markers because Phish fans have developed their own cues of importance. Displayed knowledge, repeated presence, and large lists of collected tapes provide the shared markers of community belonging, as do closeness to the band, extensive fan experience, and Internet experience.

But for groups maintained via CMC, like Phish.net, sincerity of communication, even when based upon fan-developed markers of meaning or "codes" (Bacon-Smith, 1992, p. 300), is always compromised by the growth of membership on that medium. The Internet's membership doubled each year from 1988 to 1992 (Cooke and Lehrer, 1993, p. 61), and the sale of modem technology worldwide was estimated in 1995 to increase at a growth rate of at least 17 percent for the next five years (Jackson, 1995, p. 80). For Phish.net participants, the difficulty of achieving the level of communion which a commune-ity metaphor implies stems from the difficulty in sustaining agreement about meaningful markers of group belonging in the face of a rapidly growing population.

Intimacy and Population Growth

This effect of community size upon the sincerity of communion is not new. Criticism regarding this issue was raised by Beniger (Jones, 1995) in his theories about the rise of "pseudo-community" during the nineteenth century's shift "from face-to-face to indirect or symbolic group relations"

(p. 24). Raymond Williams (1976) informs us that following the growth of nation-state bureaucracy in the same period, the word "community" was utilized to draw a distinction between "the more direct, more total and therefore more significant relationships of *community* and the more formal, more abstract and more instrumental relationships of *state*, or of *society* in its modern sense" (p. 76). Thus, rather than considering *sincerity*, it might be more helpful to consider the effect of population growth upon communion quality to be an issue of *intimacy*, the crux of a lot of Phish.net discussions since the intersection of the band's popularity with Phish.net's entry into the Usenet bulletin board service (BBS) system. While some agree with one fan's view that "the net has a great deal to do with the establishment of the Phish community . . . because it is friendly, accepting, and open to different people" (McKechnie, 1994), others cite the intimidation of newbies as evidence that the intimacy of commune-ity has been lost. "Yes, I am a Newbie, and am sometimes overwhelmed by the scene . . . but you do not need to make those of us out there even more uncomfortable by practically stripping us naked for all to see" (Welsh, 1994). The conflict between new and old members which has accompanied the growth of the Internet and Phish's popularity threatens the intimacy which most deeply attracts use of the community metaphor. But this effect of population upon intimacy paradoxically aids as well in illustrating the similar growth dynamics of offline and online groups, hastening the accuracy of the term "community." As one fan nicely summarized:

> There seems to be a cyclical community destroying dynamic at work in which the newcomers act as newcomers must . . . but are treated at times with outright contempt by net regulars, who are understandably reacting to the uncontrolled growth of "our" thing. If the feeling of community cannot be extended to newbies, then it seems that the staying power of the phishnet [*sic*] as community is severely threatened. (Heling, 1994b)

Thus, an individual's perceived degree of intimacy is largely determinant of the individual's support for use of the community metaphor. Another fan explains how a perceived loss of intimacy led to his departure from the Phish.net community:

> Personally, Phish.net got too large for me to handle. . . . I defected to Minarets (the Dave Matthews Band net.) Minarets is currently at about 700 participants. . . . I feel much more a part of a community on Minarets. I miss the info I got about Phish but I am more completely sated in my craving for electronic community. (Morgan, 1995)

Thus, the degree of perceived intimacy in a social group is a determinant of whether or not the community metaphor is a fitting description for Internet communities. Individual fan practices involve varying levels of participation. Therefore the perception of intimacy is dependent upon the individual in question. As with MacDonald's fan community of women, how well an individual from Phish.net is able to commune with others in the community (under increasingly challenging circumstances of population growth) determines the degree of intimacy or quality of commune-ity which that individual experiences through their everyday interactive fan practices via CMC.

To emphasize the importance of intimacy and its dynamics, let me adopt one fan's analogy of Phish.net to

> a gathering at the coffee shop, just sitting around discussing your favorite band or other related topics. . . . Now those [intimate] moments are harder to get to because of the influx of new people who are not used to civil discussion. . . . (Trimpe, 1994)

This coffee shop metaphor is helpful in that it doesn't simply assign blame to an increased population for the loss of intimacy, the conditional factor of the equation is in the actions of those new participants. A crowded coffee shop can be intimate if everyone works together. Similarly, the intimacy of a community on the CMC medium like Phish.net can be preserved if the actions of its members allow such circumstances to be maintained. It is true that Phish.net is one of the largest fan communities on the Internet (excluding the delta of *Star Trek* fan communities), but as this same fan observes as a corollary to his coffee shop analogy: "We tend to stick together a bit more than some other fan scenes" (Trimpe, 1994).

Intimacy is an important feature of community, but not its end. Our understanding of community includes not just the presence of intimacy but the actions which are collectively taken to achieve and to preserve it. The continual internal battles of a growing group of people with different levels of intimacy is a primary characteristic of offline community. The social aggregations online should therefore be measured not simply for group intimacy, but also for the process of attaining and maintaining it.

Communicative Tools for Maintaining Intimacy and Behavioral Norms

Phish.netters simultaneously use both internal and external communication in a three-pronged attempt to declare internal values, firm up the borders of their community against outsiders, and legislate behavior outside of the community according to norms and values established within the community. This combination of community expansion and contraction is made possible through accountability techniques, organization of off-screen actions, attempts to subdivide the community, and an overall increase in the uses of coded discourse to obscure comprehension to those lacking fan knowledge.

Despite the fact that the ability to strategically use personae is an inherent part of CMC, there are also some features of these media which facilitate the accountability of action which use of the community metaphor has lacked thus far. Rheingold (1993b) has discussed the WELL, an early CMC community where the structures of public Internet protocol were first fleshed out by users and computer engineers: "One important social rule was built into the software. . . . Nobody is anonymous. Everybody is required to attach their real user-id to their postings" (p. 49). This feature of the medium exists for all Phish.net posters regardless of whether they post by Usenet or by e-mail. Although some experienced hackers may be able to bypass this structural constraint, the inherent qualities of the medium do provide for enough accountability of action that individual users operate within groups under a consciousness of behavioral norms.

Baym's (1995) study of a Usenet group devoted to discussion of soap operas found that "the heaviest posters . . . were more likely than lighter users to attend to interpersonal alignment of the interaction" (p. 157), demonstrating the awareness of shared norms which exists in some CMC spaces. This awareness comes to new users through time spent listening to others' discussions and from the inevitable first "flame" or personal message from a more experienced member who attempts to inform the user of where they crossed the line of acceptability for that group. One example of a Phish.net flame occurred when a fan posted a review of three shows at New York's Beacon Theater. The post was entitled "Beacon (I was at all three)" and in it the poster admitted gaining entry to the show with the purchase of fake tickets and congratulated those who participated in a rushed illegal entry through the side doors of the theater. The result was an immediate public and private flaming of both the poster and the unidentified fans who rushed the door:

> do you really think that this sort of activity deserves a "congrats". I think not!!! . . . Pushing open doors to get into a show for free is childish, selfish, and risking the entire scene for everyone who paid to enjoy the show—Brendan. (1994)

and

> This doesn't help Phish, the Beacon, or us . . . I am quite unimpressed, & more than a little disappointed. I posted this, 'cause I want everyone to think before they act. What you do, affects everyone!!—James. (1994)

The awareness of one's actions in relation to behavioral norms of the community is stressed in both of these flames. The practice of flaming often appears intimidating to new participants in CMC groups, who often find their mailbox flooded with flames after making a mistake. But studies of conduct standards across Usenet groups find that "conduct-correcting episodes are commonplace, reflecting the self-regulating nature of the network" (McLaughlin et al., 1995, p. 95). The awareness of behavioral norms and the frequency of conduct-policing by other members of Usenet discussion groups strongly implies that sense of community in which individual actions are always executed within the known constraints of a forum, and where accountability for one's actions is a natural deterrent to fully individualized goal-seeking behavior.

The communication of norms to new members is well illustrated by the above flame examples, which succeeded in regulating the behavior of an individual as well as other public readers in the Phish.net community. Within three days of the final show, the following post appeared:

> In case you don't remember my name I am the one who posted about the fake tickets, and the people who broke into the side of the Beacon. I have since been flamed hard by several people. I have seen their points and would like to apologize. I understand why people aren't supportive of the ones who broke into the side of the theater. I didn't realize all of the implications (the association of the actions with the band, etc.), and I was wrong.
> . . .Although it wasn't necessary to flame me so hard, Those of you who did it, have taught me something. I hadn't thought of the larger implications before posting. (Karpenstein, 1994)

This poster has now publicly demonstrated a newly sensed consciousness of the surrounding Phish.net *and* Phish fan community. The possibility thus exists that such a regulatory device might be able to organize a set of norms to direct behavior in the larger Phish fan community which converges on venue sites.

Such a project is often discussed on Phish.net (especially during touring seasons on the East Coast) as naturally within the legislative realm of the online community. This desire to spread norms outside of the community is perhaps more closely connected to fandom, but is facilitated by the fans' use of CMC technology. A common aspect of fandom is the effort of the fan to attain closeness to the source product and producers. Phish.netters, who must be significantly engaged in the feeling of fandom to perform the labor of participation in the community, often feel that they're closer to the source of their fandom than Phish fans outside the community. It is not surprising therefore that Phish.netters have attempted to impose behavioral norms and a regulatory structure both inside *and* outside of their community in an attempt to deal with the rising populations of both sectors. The notion that participants understand a set of internal norms and wish to apply them to others in every social context as simply "norms" hastens the utility of a community metaphor.

Phish.netters have attempted to use the medium as a way to communicate the expected behavioral norms of the audience during concerts. As devoted fans they often feel that others in the audience do not respect the band as much as the denizens of Phish.net. At shows, it is considered a breach of fandom norms to yell requests at inappropriate times such as during the quiet parts of longer songs and during the non-miked *a cappella* performance of the evening. "It, to me, is a sign of extreme disrespect that a crowd would do this. It seems that many are there to 'be entertained' and not to enjoy the artistry of the band" (Rogovin, 1994). Phish.netters at shows are often annoyed at the behavior of other audience members, but they most often voice their complaints on Phish.net rather than at the venue itself.

> Major Complaint: All those a--holes who insisted on yelling and screaming during Amazing Grace. Please, be a bit more considerate. It's not cool, and it

detracts from the enjoyment of 90% of the people who actually want to *hear* this song. The band was also visibly irked, particularly Page, who kept motioning for everyone to shut up. (Gladfelter, 1994)

Note the elements of fan ideology and reasoning in the above statement. Observation of the band's negative emotional reaction during this portion of the show becomes a basis for labeling the audience behavior inadequate. Fans' attempts to observe and to please the band are thus evident. Further, as a member of Phish.net the above fan feels that he is in the majority at shows ("90%") and can therefore legislate the behavior of others. That the fan chose to express this sentiment through Phish.net may be a utilization of media to reach a large audience, but it may also be a sign that this fan was not really in the majority at the show attended, and thus chose to hold this complaint until safely within the Phish.net community again. This form of post has appeared more commonly on Phish.net as the venue size of concerts has increased to accommodate larger audiences.

The feeling of a loss of control as population increases applies to both the Phish.net community and the larger venue's audiences. Even within the community, the above post quickly received a response which was less typical of Phish.net values:

> I always get a kick out of hearing the very loud "SHHHHHHHHHHHH" right when the band tries to do the acapella stuff. . . so I cracked up when some loud drunk in Atlanta started yelling everytime it would get quiet. . . . Get a life if you feel otherwise, besides the acapella stuff doesn't come out on the aud-tapes anyways. . . yawn. . . the show's over anyhow. (STMT, 1994)

Although Phish.net is considered by its members to be a forum for debate (among other things), certain fan values regarding respect for the band and appropriate behavior both on the Net and at shows are not considered to be debatable. Posts such as this which breach the values of fandom upon which the community is based are often either personally flamed or publicly ignored (i.e. not responded to) or both. In the long run, however, such signs of a changing population in both the Phish.net and venue communities are reacted to with an urge to explicate and protect the older values of the Phish.net community. This reaction also sits well within a metaphor of community in which a center is often trying to maintain original community values in the face of a changing and growing population.

The frustration at a loss of control over behavioral norms on Phish.net is often expressed through a language division which describes Phish.netters (or sometimes only old-time Phish.netters) as true fans or true members of the community, while assigning clear outsider status to those which do not conform to the community's normative values. Observe the use of language to draw this distinction in the following post:

> I hate to speak in a negative tone about Phishscene . . . but the time is here that we must address protecting our reputation as a fanbase so as to protect our band

and our ability to see them. In my opinion, the problem . . . is that too HIGH a percentage of people come to shows for the drugs . . . take away the music and they probably wouldn't care. . . . Well, it's these people that we need to do something about, It's these people who scream . . . during a cappella songs, it's these people who kick and punch security guards, it's these people who have no respect for the rest of us . . . or for the band. All I can propose is if you have extras [tickets] for a show, please don't give it to these people, give it to Phish fans. . . . (Bassin, 1994)

For this fan as with the many others who read this post, Phish.net exists even more clearly as a community when it is under attack and forced to define itself against other groups. In the case of Phish.net, not only does a core set of values, norms, and practices exist with enough vigor to warrant a nationalist feeling of protectionism among its members, but that community pride has at times extended into organizational plans for communicating these values throughout the larger venue gatherings of Phish fans.

One fan suggests adding a physical presence for Phish.net at each concert venue which could serve as a source for communication of values from the Phish.net community to fans-at-large:

maybe we need to set up something outside the venue. A booth . . . a service to the general audience . . . a couple of versions of the HPB [*Helping Friendly Book*, see below], and Tour Dates and Info, and Net generated stuff. . . . Could someone talk to someone about supplying garbage bags to distribute? . . . we may be the net, but we do not represent the majority. I believe we are a heavily educated people, and can do some good out there where it really counts. Let's help foster the scene in a positive direction. (Stew, 1994)

The same fan later suggested creating the "Helping Friendly Flyer"[2] for distribution at shows. This flyer was intended to outline for general fans the Phish.net view of appropriate and inappropriate activity, as well as to suggest tips for added safety and to make a plea against littering at the venue. Further, the flyer was to instruct general fans not to support the bootleg CD industry or the growing number of ticket scalpers and to connect these issues with reasons why ticket prices continue to rise. The flyers were first produced locally by fans attending specific shows. They are now produced by the band's management and distributed by Phish.net volunteers attending each show. Thus, Phish.net has organized a communication of community norms to others in the larger Phish fan community gathering at venues. There have also been attempts on Phish.net to communicate to the band's management about problems with too much or too little security at particular venues. Another development to protect the concert-going experience of Phish.netters has been the cooperative organization of "Phish-Info" by both Net fans and the band's management. "Phish-Info" now serves to distribute early information on ticket sale dates and how to avoid paying Ticketmaster service charges.

Thus, as populations have grown, there have been organizational movements in the Phish.net community to protect the values and norms of older fans and to legislate behavior at shows by communicating those values to fans-at-large. Protectionist behavior or community contraction through a declaration of borders thus occurs simultaneously with attempts to outwardly communicate values and norms for the purposes of community expansion.

In addition to a protectionist marking of outsiders with contempt, the Phish.net community has seriously debated a splitting of the newsgroup. The underlying logic of a "netsplit" for some Phish.net participants was that numerous posts on undesired subject matter could be directed to another newsgroup, thus preserving respectively for different fan activity groups the intimacy which facilitated communion. The suggestion of a "netsplit" came primarily from tapers (fans who tape concerts), and from information-gathering fans who found it difficult to sort through an increasing volume of posts for desired material. As one taper suggests:

> not to dis the discussion that occurs . . . [but I] just don't have time to. . . . Many of us are quite into collecting shows or trading tickets . . . and an eventual split would make everyone's netlife more enjoyable. It wouldn't be an inflexible divide, people could read either or both, whatever. (Heling, 1994a)

The most popular suggestion is visibly taper-oriented in that it suggests a "tapes and tickets net" as separate from "rec.music.phish.blithering" (Rioux, 1994). In the end, this proposed netsplit was not enacted. One reason expressed was that grovel-requests for tapes and tickets on one net would invade the discussion net once pleas went unanswered (Rioux, 1994). A second and more intriguing reason worked in opposition to this first reason while invoking a nationalistic pull for unification based on the values of reciprocation which the Phish.net community claims to embody.

> No, this is NOT a good idea. Quite simply, tape and ticket grovelers will go unanswered if they post on the proposed second newsgroup, whereas here if someone (like me) has a tape someone else happens to be groveling for, the groveler will get a response.
> ". . .and so fell the weight that I never can lift,
>   behind us the darkness, between us the rift. . ." (Introne, 1994)

Jenkins (1992, p. 280) has recorded values of reciprocity among media fans, and in the world of Phish fandom the mythology of Gamehenge provides a virtually unquestionable assumption of reciprocity as a value of Phish fandom.[3] Thus, the above fan affirms the values of reciprocity and the sharing of music and information as a rationale for unity within the Phish.net community. To connect his argument explicitly to the mythology of the fictive universe, he ends the above post by quoting and reinterpreting the song "Rift" (originally about problems in a romantic relationship) to suit the context of his argument. His use of codes within the fictive universe to support an argument about unification are further evidence that Phish.net functions as a fan community with its own conventionalized language of recognition signals. The fan's statement thus works on multiple levels to affirm Phish.net values, to prevent further changes within the community, and to limit comprehension of Phish.net discussions to only those fans with enough knowledge of codes to participate.

Other attempts at community contraction and protection from outsiders have included the launching of an unsuccessful private BBS called "DividedSky" (Goodman, 1995), and the establishment of an IRC channel "#phish" or "Phishserv" (Snyder, 1994) devoted to computer-mediated discussions in real-time. Both announcements to Phish.net of such actions stressed that the purpose was to isolate space for the die-hard fans who were craving the intimacy of communion which was more difficult to achieve on the larger newsgroup. Due to the nature of CMC, there is no way to determine whether other subsections of the Phish.net community have become "privatized" as elite enclaves of attempted intimacy. Most recently, Phish.netter Rosemary Macintosh has organized "rosemary-digest," a personally filtered version of the Phish.net digest designed to include only posts matching the "original" intentions of the Phish.net community. Rosemary's goal was not just to isolate "true" Phish.netters but also to encourage more discussion along sanctioned lines. Filtered digests are intended to stimulate sanctioned responses by "true" Phish.netters, and then those responses are posted to the full Phish.net community in an attempt to give "true" fans more speaking power in the community. Although based in purification of the whole community rather than isolation of a pure portion, Rosemary's action speaks to the same struggle of all communities: to maintain core values and intimacy level during population growth. The community splitting and purification processes in CMC are an intriguing but difficult area of CMC studies. Clearly, questions surrounding population growth and the quest for intimacy are foundational, and should provide the framework for analysis of this communicative process.

Thus, tools for the maintenance of intimacy, behavioral norms, and values have been developed by Phish.netters in a simultaneous attempt to contract and expand the community. Phish.net appears to be a community not just because its members share similar social goals, but also because those goals and the core values to be protected are developed through the same communicative process by which *all* communities establish their borders and values. Anthony Giddens (1984) has described this emergent construction of community values and norms as "structuration," and the construction of Phish.net norms mimics the process by which all communities build internal norms.

Structuration of Norms According to Group Uses and Gratifications

Structuration is the process by which the structure or rule set of a community is formed from the continual interaction of individual participants. Structuration takes the processes of repeated everyday interaction over time and develops them into the rules which form a community's structure. In this way, a community's rules are formed based upon the uses its participants have for those rules and based upon the gratifications that are derived from living under such rules. It suggests that rules are developed from within a community rather than being imposed externally as the rules of a large society are imposed upon the individual. Thus, to observe structuration in action is to observe the formation of social structure by those who choose to live within it. Because the grassroots formation of rules is not usually possible in a large society, structuration activity can be taken as a sign of group intimacy and therefore as a sign of community.

Analysis of structure and of social organization principles is often dominated by the suggestion that such structures are imposed from above by a bureaucratic rulership which limits the agentic freedoms of individuals affected by those structures. One prominent feature of computer-mediated communities which lends to the usefulness of the community metaphor and the distinction of intimacy between "community" and "society" is that the development of behavioral norms and other such structures stems from the needs and goals of the group and not from some centralized source of authority. "It is to meet the needs of the community, needs both given and emergent, that standards of behavior and methods of sanctioning inappropriate behavior develop" (Baym, 1995, p. 160).

Because population increases have threatened the intimacy of communication on Phish.net, structural norms in the form of "netiquette" have been developed and even recorded in the community's Frequently Asked Questions (FAQ) file:

> No question is stupid, but this file . . . [is] designed to answer literally *hundreds* of questions you might have; please check before posting a question to the net. Don't post a "subscribe" or "unsubscribe" message to the entire net. . . . Don't waste your time or other people's 'bandwidth' (mail space) fussing about someone's spelling. . . . When you respond to a post, make certain that personal responses go to a person (the poster), not the entire network group. . . . (Godard, 1994, pp. 4–5)

By directing a percentage of posts to either FAQ reading or personal e-mail communication these norms function both to encourage more personal interaction and shared knowledge among community members and to reduce the potential traffic of posts on the newsgroup. Other norms against full quoting of previously posted messages and against "me too" posts have also been established more strictly as the community's population has grown.

Among tapers, structural norms have been developed not only for the proper names of Phish songs, but also for the correct way to abbreviate these song titles when reporting information about set lists to each other. The song "Split Open and Melt" became known under the abbreviation "SOAM" until a new song was released with the same initials. "Scent Of A Mule" has forced the slow alteration of the two songs' abbreviations to

"Melt" and "Mule." The source for standardization of set list and song information is the *Helping Phriendly Book*—the ongoing fan-produced document of all known shows and set lists—and its key organizers, who even developed standards for the printed reporting of current and future set lists to the *Helping Phriendly Book* staff. Part of these standards involve a system of arrows adopted from previously existing structures developed by tapers of the Grateful Dead to communicate information on tape labels and through CMC about complex song transitions and interweavings. For example "Mike's Song-->I Am Hydrogen-->Weekapaug Groove" indicates the band's non-stop transition from the first song into the second and from there into the third. "Mike's Song-->Buffalo Bill-->Mike's Song" indicates a deviation from "Mike's Song" into a portion of "Buffalo Bill," which then returns to the remainder of "Mike's Song." These structures for standardizing communication between fans *and* the need to organize them arise from a combination of the unusual complexity and variety of the music played and the fannish desire of Phish.net tapers to accurately record all available information about the band and its activities. Group norms are thus structured out of communally felt needs.

The other need which arises for tape traders on Phish.net is for a shared understanding of how the tape trading process works. It is therefore outlined in the FAQ (Godard et al., 1994) for new tape traders and easily explained by any member of the trading community. It involves a minimum of a trade agreement and the exchange of snailmail addresses, but to ensure standards of trustworthiness and accountability, the practice of "outing" bad traders to the rest of the community has emerged as a simple way to express the seriousness of expectations upon a fan who wishes to trade tapes through Phish.net. The new trader easily observes that the tape lists of more experienced traders are organized in the same way, displaying shows chronologically by date followed by information about the venue, tape lengths, sound quality, and show highlights. Norms have also been established for the process of taping itself. Although the degree of imposed rules differs with the individual trader, many tape traders begin their tape lists with a paragraph of requests and expectations with which trading partners are expected to comply. Enough standards have been established that one can expect to be guided into a taping process with an experienced trader by a paragraph of qualifiers:

> No DAT. All my tapes are Analog. Please use Type II or higher tapes, preferably Maxell XLII's. No Dolby. No high-speed dubbing. If you are sending me blanks be sure to include return postage, a note of instructions, and how to contact you. If we are trading please try to be quick with tape turnaround as I usually am. (Watson, 1995a)

Again, these standards and the normative practice of stating them in such an upfront fashion have developed from the needs experienced by tape traders during their continued interactions on and off of Phish.net. As populations increased on the newsgroup, interaction among tapers also increased, leading to the structuration of extensive standards for fan practice in the community. Even in the venues, as populations increased, tapers felt their equipment being crowded. By contacting the band's management through Phish.net and by direct mail, these fans were able to establish the practice of "tapers' tickets." After the summer of 1993, the tapers' section of the venue floor was officially designated and limited by a specific number of tickets available only by mail from the band's management several weeks before general ticket sales. The designation of the tapers' section and its ticket procedure are structures which not only developed as the result of continued interaction on Phish.net, but are a visible and physical manifestation of the Phish.net community's ability to affect general audiences at the venues.

Structuration of normative behavior within the Phish.net community has also been the result of a repeated and continued need to affirm the foundational values of the community in the face of threats to those values. The united response to communally perceived threats further strengthens the metaphor of community as a descriptor for what occurs online. As with many other fan organizations, conventions, and groups, a primary purpose of fans coming together around a shared source product is to create a safe space for the expression of fan emotion. Because Phish.net was established by a fan, Matt Laurence, for fannish purposes, its most basic value is that the expression of fan emotion about Phish is to be accepted. Thus, posts whose content intentionally violates this value are seen as abnormal, disruptive, and a threat to the community. One such post which raised the ire of the community for a time by threatening the safe expression of fan emotion was the following:

> You all suck. Hippies suck. Your stupid brain gobbling band sucks. Why don't you all try getting out more? . . . Phish sucks. I hope that you all get beat up by some war mongering nazi morons that you pretend to hate, when really you are all just insecure about yourselves, and latch onto each other for support in your pitiful little lives that amount to nothing in the real world. (Newfeld, 1994)

Although its exaggerated tone suggests that this post was intended to raise ire rather than express the actual feelings of the poster, this post demonstrates several of the values which are upheld by the community by crossing them. In one paragraph, the poster homogeneously classifies and labels Phish.netters, who often claim to be heterogeneously individualistic and eclectic; she insults the band, which is the center of focus for the community; she suggests an insincerity of beliefs despite the community's claim to being educated and fed by "the tree of knowledge in your soul."[4] Finally, the poster negatively describes the benefit of mutual support which these Phish fans have found in each other and their online community. That this post was furiously flamed both publicly and privately is no surprise. Rather, it is the expected effect of structuration processes that standards of appropriateness for Phish.net posts be declared upon the basis of protecting the community's internal values.

Internal values thus show the marking points around which past, present, and future forms of structure are developed. Recognition that the structuration process also takes place inside computer-mediated spaces is embedded in the use of a community metaphor to recognize the development of new social norms. Thus, Giddens' theory of structuration is easily demonstrated by the organization of norms and values according to the emergent needs of the Phish.net community under conditions of population growth both online and in the venues. The structuration of behavioral norms is even seen to affect venue audiences due to the legislative efforts of actively engaged Phish.netters. That this process of structuration has accelerated with increasing population growth is further evidence that a community metaphor is appropriate for describing the ongoing interactive activities of the Phish.net community.

The Struggle for Possession of the Community Metaphor

Applying or Denying the Community Metaphor to Cyberspace

Perhaps one of the biggest difficulties in accepting the word "community" as a descriptor for CMC phenomena is the notion that communities first existed and currently exist in shared physical space. In CMC physical space has been replaced by a technology, a medium of communication. Rather than declaring that community must therefore be absent, I suggest that we stop thinking of "community" as shared communication in the same physical space. After all, the imaginary borders of nation-states prove that we humans do not always communicate towards shared norms with the people nearest us, but rather make determinations of *whom* we wish to build community with and whom we wish to exclude through the construction of borders. We should begin thinking of community as a product not of shared space, but of shared *relationships* among people.

Anthropology's origin in the roots of imperialist expansion and cross-cultural investigations of difference has perhaps been responsible for the field's focus on place-based phenomena and its emphasis on the importance of physical territory in determining group distinctions. This has been at the expense of recognizing "culture," that continuously productive and communicative activity in which all humans are inherently engaged and which I suggest is the source of the communion which makes community real to its participants. Benedict Anderson (1983) supportively suggests that "Communities are to be distinguished, not by their falsity/genuineness, but by the style in which they are imagined" (p. 15). By focusing on the human act of imagination, not only does it become appropriate to use the community metaphor for describing continuous group interaction, but the judgement of community is rightly returned to the minds of the participants involved rather than their detached observers.

For those of us seeking to apply cultural anthropology to an under-standing of the positive and negative potentials of the new CMC medium, Rheingold's (1993b) definition of "virtual communities" is well suited to this focus on human communicative and cultural practice: "social aggrega-tions that emerge from the Net when enough people carry on . . . public discussions long enough, with sufficient human feeling, to form webs of personal relationships in cyberspace" (p. 5). By focusing on social networks of relationship and interaction *quality* as the determinant of when "community" is present, CMC can better fit the illuminative assist-ance of cultural theory. We can now approach CMC users sensitized to look for the signs of high social interaction quality through their com-municative uses of the medium. Further, we have made a distinction between the *communication* that is made possible for users by a medium like urban subway graffiti, CB radios, or CMC, and the *community* that is formed only when that communicative ability is utilized to construct communion, and a structuration of norms and values via ongoing relationships of quality between participants.

By focusing on quality rather than a simple checklist of the ingredients which make community, we can openly engage the role of subjective evaluation. This means that agreement on what "community" means does not preclude disagreement on issues such as the degrees of sincerity, intimacy, and communion which are present in a CMC medium. Indeed, many scholars who have agreed with my thoughts on what "community" means continue to disagree with the basic idea that "real" community can be formed online.

The question must be raised as to whether there is a power motive behind this agenda. Is there something so powerful about the word "community" that some social groups would fight earnestly to keep the word from applying to other social groups? Does ownership of the term "community" have something to do with the ability of a social group to be well represented in a democratic society?

Refusal to apply "community" as a descriptor for online collectivities stems either from a desire to retain a purified notion of community in the hands of those who claim to know "true" community, or from an unwill-ingness to recognize CMC technologies as a medium with the potential to change traditional social arrangements. By combining both motives, we see that to apply "community" to online phenomena is to give those online denizens possession of the word. Its possession by online social groups may mean more than simply the right to apply it to others; it may also result in giving those online groups recognition of their own strengths, which are entailed by the use of the community metaphor to describe their activities and their existence as a new form of collective entity.

Anderson (1983) has stated that the rise of nation-states occurred because "a fundamental change was taking place in modes of appre-hending the world, which, more than anything else, made it possible to 'think' the nation" (p. 28). By theorizing community as based in the subjective experience and imagination of it's participants, the potential for changes in the nature of community is as present as the potential for new experience. Thus, the rise of CMC technologies can be seen as part of a fundamental change in modes of apprehending the world. New ideas can be seen as leading to both the development of the technologies and the development of new understandings of community. Certainly the proliferation of CMC technologies has altered the experiences of people in everyday life, and it can now be said that new modes of apprehending community have developed as a result of these changes to the realm of everyday experience. Hence, the rise and proliferation of CMC technologies is spurring debate about the nature and meaning of "community" among both scholars and CMC participants.

Uses of Denying the Metaphor

Cultural critics such as Neil Postman (1993) have maintained an argument against the use of the metaphor online based on a concern to retain the word's purity. Postman's main criticism of the term "virtual community" is that online collectivities do not contain the stake that exists in "real" communities. Critics like Postman point more deeply to the roots of the word "community," pointing out that the Latin root word *communis* or "common" is made up of two other roots, *cum*, meaning "together," and *munis*, meaning "obligation." Postman's work with the term "community" emphasizes this idea of common obligation as central to applications of the metaphor. He argues that although online collectivities like Phish.net may contain many other aspects of the community metaphor, they lack the essential feature of a common obligation. More accurately, online communities lack the consequences of not meeting or participating in the common obligation of most communities.

Postman fears that calling online collectivities "communities" alters the meaning of the term and discards one of its most vital elements. For him, application of the metaphor to cyberspace discussion groups pollutes the concept and changes it so that the notion of common obligation is forgotten. Postman wants us to remember that a community involves living amongst people with whom we may disagree strongly, but with whom we continue to communicate for the purposes of meeting our common obligations. He points out quite rightly that Internet discussion groups are formed out of common interest, not common obligation. In the Phish.net forum, one need not deal with persons who don't share a common interest in the band Phish. On Phish.net the upholding of common obligation across personal differences does not exist because it does not need to exist. The possibility has been precluded by the structuring of the medium into discussion groups based on common interest.

Postman is correct that the long-term result of applying the "community" metaphor to such groups may be to eliminate from human consciousness the understanding that living in a community means that we have obligations to each other even across a sea of personal differences. However, just as the emergence of nation-states transformed the meaning of "community" in our collective consciousness to fit a new world situation, so the rise of CMC technologies is operating to alter the meaning of this term again. Is that entirely bad news? I think not. Metaphors such as community change as humans adapt to new and emerging environments. In times of great change, the older form of such a metaphor slips away because it is no longer as useful as it once was. Hence we have seen our understanding of "community" shift from simple geographic proximity to communication and intimacy as social organization grew with the Industrial Revolution.

Postman's "community" is a noble form of the metaphor—recognition and expression of common obligation always is—but I fear that the usefulness of his metaphor is being lost. If we cling to Postman's version of the metaphor, we find that there are fewer and fewer places in the present day to which the word "community" correctly applies. Instead, Postman's community serves the purpose of establishing a nostalgia for the type of community which we used to have. His work often compares what we call community today to the "real" community which humans had during the nineteenth-century era of cottage industry and small village life. To be sure, I too am nostalgic for this older form of community, and were I to engage in a critique of how little common obligation exists in today's world I would certainly adopt Postman's form of the metaphor. However, it is precisely *because* so little common obligation exists today that I find Postman's "community" metaphor to be less than useful for describing the strength of present-day collectivities. When so little of the present-day world fits the metaphor which Postman champions, then the metaphor becomes nostalgic—something to be fondly remembered but not applied easily any more.

Uses of Applying the Metaphor

Postman's critique works by recognizing the absence of common obligation online and then using that basis to deny the entire metaphor of community to online collectivities. His motive in denying the metaphor is to keep the metaphor somehow pure in meaning. My application of the metaphor to online collectivities like Phish.net has motives too. Part of the motive is to alter the "community" metaphor so that it better applies to the types of social collectivity which exist today. In applying the metaphor to something new, I and other CMC theorists are not simply *expanding* the definition of "community," we are changing it, and we may be changing it for the better.

Even in the offline world our differences are not being bridged with talk, and with the advent of narrowcasting and personalized marketing we are finding less and less of a need to bridge the gaps of public opinion into a unified whole. Today there is enough fragmentation to prevent most actions of organized social good from being enacted on a large scale. Differences in public opinion are quite often too large to be bridged effectively. Any attempt at overhauling national social policies thus results in the maintenance of separate communities rather than a national whole.

Under-represented groups in the United States find that they cannot mobilize enough support nationally to create a change in their daily conditions of living. Political action designed to bridge the public gap has failed again and again. Those who champion Postman's noble metaphor of community as common obligation are most often faced with the task of dragging other community members kicking and screaming into their part of the obligation. Attempts to construct community usually result in the increased frustration of organizers and the increased cynicism of non-participants toward the entire idea of community. Structured communities such as those created by coincidences of geographic proximity or by other details which we seldom think about during daily life almost always have this experience of pulling together against the will and desire of many individual members.

Structured communities result in something like class reunions, a few really gung-ho organizers, moderate participants, and several clumps of people commiserating about how they wish they weren't a part of this particular group. This is not an effective method for being better represented in the larger social debates of our time. Yet, under-represented groups in US society have struggled along with this form of community grassroots organizing for many years. There was no choice for the most part, and so the question—of why grassroots struggles for greater representation were conducted in this odd way against the grain of the "apathy" that is apparently human nature—became moot. Practiced community organizing routines were simply the best known way to do such work. Today, Internet technologies may offer an improved set of tools for the formation of groups and for their struggles to be represented in the public sphere.

The communities which form naturally online do so with such apparent ease because they are based upon a trait which is also central to grassroots representation movements. Online communities are communities formed around a common interest. Thus, when participating in one of these communities, one can maintain the assumption that everyone involved is actually interested enough to initiate their own participation in the community. Communities online form willingly as volunteer communities as each individual chooses to join. Structured communities are dictated to the individual by an outside source; you are told that you are a member of the community and that you have obligations. When it comes to organizing a movement for greater representation in the democratic public sphere, online volunteer communities hold a considerable advantage at the level of both form and content over offline structured communities.

Applying the metaphor of community to online forums does not have to mean imposing a static definition over a clearly different situation. Instead we should be exploring the meaning of that metaphor and then changing it to update its applicability to today's world. The distinction which I have made between structured and volunteer communities is only one aspect of the online/offline difference. But I have chosen to focus on this difference because it assists the expansion of thinking about how to use new technologies for the achievement of greater representation in the public sphere. Careful application of the community metaphor in studies of online phenomena can assist the larger project of revitalizing the democratic process and finding pathways to social change by illustrating the uses of "community" as a metaphor and as a model for thinking about and organizing movements for social change. By drawing out the connections between being a community and gaining representation, Internet scholars can make an important contribution to the improvement of democratic representation.

"Community" and Being Represented

Using the community metaphor in CMC research helps one to recognize the formative and transformative processes which community structures undergo. The recognition of such processes is an important stepping stone to the development of the consciousness that change can occur and that it can be caused by the united work of online participants. The community metaphor applied to CMC groups allows those groups to recognize the pathways to change within a discourse (that of offline communities) which is already understood intuitively by CMC participants. In Marxian terms, recognition of themselves as a "community" is the first step to creating the common consciousness which enables attempts at improvement in the conditions of the participants' daily lives. When they understand their existence under a "community" metaphor, online participants become able to recognize and to address their common situations of under-representation in the larger social democracy.

Communities in the offline world serve as models of human behavior in large-group situations. They function as models of gradual and lasting social change. But communities are more than a valuable reference point for those wishing to organize for greater representation. In a pure democracy, individuals and their views would all be equally represented in public debates. The United States is a representative democracy in which individuals are somehow grouped together and then represented as a group by an individual delegate in debates among other such delegates. The method by which individuals are grouped together to be represented by a single delegate is one aspect of how the democratic process fails to function as well as it might. We need to examine that method of grouping to understand why some are apparently better represented than others.

The US Constitution and various legislative rules governing elections group American voters by their residence within a particular state. This is precisely the type of structured community dictated by arbitrary geographic distinctions which I suggested earlier may not be suitable for attempts to organize communal participation. Communities to be represented in public debate do not exist only by state, however. Politicians often appeal to communities of voters gathered around particular issues. Whether it is the community of tobacco growers across the South or the community of pro-choice voters across the nation, politicians learn to recognize such social aggregations around particular issues or circumstances and they learn how to address such communities with the promise of fair representation. The recognition of various aggregations by politicians means that individuals not attached to other individuals in a recognized community will most likely remain unrepresented. Representative democracy means that individuals *need* to form groups if they hope to be represented at all.

"Community" has thus become an organizing term by which we make distinctions among the multitude of individuals in our nation. It is a term for organizing those individuals into a few distinct groups which we can recognize and deal with in the forum of public sphere debates. The logic of organizing a mass public into a few distinct groupings is shared by both the political process and the cultural process of the United States. In the cultural process, producers of mass media materials determine the content of the nation's culture through their efforts to meet consumer interests. Capitalism and democracy share an interesting trait: the party which fails to serve the interests of a large public will fall victim to competing parties. Thus, both politicians and mass media companies have an incentive to assess and satiate public demand better than their competitors. Both politicians and production companies can be "voted out" should they fail to correctly assess and satiate public demand. Thus, both politicians and mass media companies need to organize the complex public into distinct communities which can be appeased.

Because "community" is an organizing term for those at the top of our society, the rest of us must join existing communities or form new ones should the old communities not suit our needs adequately. Thus, being a part of a community is necessary to gaining representation. A group must be recognized from above as carrying enough importance to have its demands assessed and sated. If the participating individuals online hold their interests in enough esteem to warrant spending the time and effort to be there, then it is no wonder that they would fight hard to be recognized as a "community." Being recognized by others as a "community" is a most necessary step to having the views of the group heard and represented by others in a democracy such as ours.

How Phish Fans Got Their Say

Phish.net has become a voice for the multitudes of Phish fans which it represents. That is not to say that 50,000 people are representing an even larger distribution of fans. Rather, the singular community called

"Phish.net" has become a representational device for the many Phish fans within and without the Internet forum. Phish.net has managed to win concessions from both the band and the larger record industry. Although the concessions may appear small and meaningless, what is most important is the model by which these Phish fans won better representation for themselves in the public sphere of American music culture. That model is based upon the intuitive and unspoken recognition of Phish fans as a community by those in positions of power throughout the record industry. For Phish fans to win their requested concessions from those in power, the industry had to somehow sense that Phish.net is a community or a group of people powerful enough to be worth the effort of appeasement.

Phish.net's successes fall within the cultural sphere, and the community's strategy relies upon the logic of capitalist production and competition to recognize Phish.net as a profitable market. This logic is quite similar to the logic of gaining democratic representation in the political sphere. To be heard by the record industry powers-that-be, and to "get their say," Phish fans could not remain separate individuals. They had to first prove to record industry executives that as a group they were worth listening to because of the collectivity's large size and tight coherence.

These are the features of an important market. To warrant attention in the media industries, a group of people must be both large and coherent in their tastes or views. Such a group constitutes a market worthy of producer attention. Such a group also constitutes a community. Without fulfilling these requirements, demands for representation fall on deaf ears, and perhaps logically so. Such is the nature of a capitalist democracy. Thus: to those in power, whether in the cultural or political spheres, showing proof of a group's community status is akin to *being* either a valuable market or a population subset worthy of representation. Phish.net clearly "got their say" by utilizing the strategy of this capitalist-democratic model.

A successful example of Phish.net's technological ability to connote large size, tight coherence, and therefore high importance behind posted fan requests can be found at the end of the band's 1994 album *Hoist*. During the time when the band was recording this album, Phish.net was receiving and displaying many individually posted requests for a professionally released live version of the song "Split Open and Melt" which had become a fan favorite during the previous year of live concert touring. Whereas individual fan letters to the band and Elektra requesting this might be lost among a flurry of other requests lacking importance in the scheme of media systems logic, the ability of the Phish.net community to display both the size and apparent consensus of this request signalled producers as to the comparatively high importance of the community/market. Qualities of the CMC medium made the request *appear* (from the industry's perspective) to originate from a community measured at roughly 50,000, even though the number of fans posting the request may not have been significantly larger than the number of individuals who wrote traditional letters of fan request.

When the album was eventually released it contained as its last song "Demand," a clear reference to the communal consumer-fan voice of the Phish.net community. This track contains a two-minute piece of original music followed by the sounds of a live Phish concert tape being inserted into the tape deck of a moving car. These two sounds of a live Phish tape and a moving car are of such familiarity to tour-dedicated Phish fans that this was immediately understood by Phish.netters as a response to their actively organized, persistent, and powerful voice. The volume of the live tape being played is then turned up to reveal the instrumental jam portion of "Split Open and Melt," which then carries on for another seven and a half minutes. This instance, in which Phish fans gained quick and certain results from their active communication with the record industry, is seen by the community as one of the clearest examples of Phish.net's designation as a representative for the larger community of Phish fans. Further, it is strong evidence that consumers can be served when they make their demands from the unified voice-piece of a community. By being recognized as a community, Phish.net was able to win for Phish fans a greater role in the determination of cultural production processes.

CMC's facilitation of immediate fan feedback which can be easily accessed by the band's members means that fan opinion on new songs can be assessed and acted upon between shows in a tour. Fans now make a practice of debating the pros and cons of new songs as soon as they are played somewhere. As the tapes disseminate over the next few days, more and more Phish.netters post their opinions of the new material to the community. The band has been known to alter the tempo, length, and frequency of songs according to the expressed opinions of their fans on Phish.net. However, the band's response to fans' criticisms is not an example of direct democracy. Rather, it is the result of the record industry's belief that Phish.net *represents* a larger fan community/market.

Because observance of an online community does not permit one to truly assess the balance of agreement or disagreement within the community regarding an issue, observers may instead take what is printed in the online forum as being the thoughts and feelings of many more people than it may actually represent. The fact that Phish.net is known to have 50,000 subscribers is mistakenly taken to mean that some verbalized requests are actually coming from 50,000 organized individuals. Online technologies thus assist groups bound by common interest to become communities and to be recognized as important within the public sphere. When the folks at Phish.net managed to fulfill the standards of large size and tight coherence, either truly *or* through the illusion of computer-mediated presentation, *then* they achieved the benefit of democratic representation in the determination of cultural content.

Having now won that gift of representation, the Phish.net community has affected the very direction of American music culture through its recognized presence. For example, when the Dave Matthews Band noted that their music shared certain (though vague) similarities with the music sought by

Phish fans, the band's management disseminated demo tapes of that band through the Phish.net community. This was accomplished through what is known as a "tape tree,"[5] a process now assisted by the speed of e-mail technology. The band's popularity skyrocketed when their demo tapes were disseminated by the Phish.net community. Within a single year, the Dave Matthews Band went from charging $5 at small clubs to playing their current venues of over 15,000 at more than $20 per ticket. They now also have several videos on MTV. Although it is difficult to claim a truly causal effect, Phish.netters did play a significant part in bringing that band into the public realm, and in doing so they helped to designate a new wing of music. The music industry now recognizes "Jam Bands" as a new category of American music and is giving heavy promotion and success to several such bands, including Blues Traveller, Aquarium Rescue Unit, and the Black Crowes. American music culture has lurched in a new direction, and the recognition of Phish.net as a "community" lies at the heart of the change.

Democratic Representation and the Question of Virtual Communities

The model for achieving democratic change as demonstrated by Phish.net in the cultural sphere could easily apply to other groups desiring greater representation in the political sphere. It also may explain why the debate over virtual community is so heated. "Community" permits representation. Thus to deny a group the status of community is to deny them their due representation in the public sphere. With this in mind, let us return briefly to the debate about online community and expose the political motives behind some of its terminology.

The most glaring offender in the terminology of the old debate is the most popular term of all: "virtual community." Using the word "virtual" implies that what we are trying to call community is not *actually* community. By naming it so, such communication phenomena can never be "true" community. This arrangement appears to best serve those who argue against the existence of community online. We must question why the terminology should hold such a judgement.

The distinction between "virtual" community and "real" community is unwarranted. The term "virtual" means something akin to "unreal" and so the entailments of calling online communities "virtual" include spreading and reinforcing a belief that what happens online is *like* a community, but isn't *really* a community. My experience has been that people in the offline world tend to see online communities as virtual, but that participants in the online communities see them as quite real. The fact that the term "virtual" has stuck so hard is due in part to the title of Rheingold's (1993b) pioneering book on the matter, but it is also a result of the fact that users of online technologies are not self-represented. Rather, they are represented to us by offline scholars wishing to compare these online communities to "the real thing" in their offline world. Such an argument smacks of the same culture-centric viewpoint which has permeated anthropology for decades. It reflects the usual refusal of scholars to accept the views of those they study *as stated* by those subjects. As such I reject the distinction as it has been handed to me.

I am not refuting that there are differences between communities formed offline and online. Indeed I have elaborated upon some of those differences and discussed the ways in which those differences might be helpful for certain purposes such as movements for grassroots representation. But the distinction of real communities from virtual communities is not the same as the distinction between online and offline. The distinction as handed down to us tells us immediately that online phenomena are not real communities. The danger of accepting this distinction as given is that voluntary online aggregations of people around issues of common interest will not be recognized as worthy of representation within the public sphere. By accepting the distinction between real and virtual communities, we will blind ourselves to recognizing that these online collectivities may be the new form which representative democracy is taking. Acceptance of the distinction as given precludes those in power from recognizing the importance of group demands and precludes those out of power from recognizing the pathways to greater representation which are bound up in the metaphor of "community."

Thus, thinking about the term "community" and rethinking the distinction between what humans do online and offline may be a key process to the revitalization of democracy. Changes in the power structure of our nation and our culture may rely upon this rethinking and alteration of the term "community." Barry Barnes (1988) suggests that:

> [People] may . . . change the distribution of power by reflecting upon it, learning about it, seeking to better understand and represent it; for a distribution of power is an aspect of a distribution of knowledge and what is known to be cannot be separated from what is. . . . Thus the capacity of people to grasp and represent a distribution of power sets limits on the possible form that such a distribution can take. (p. 92)

This complex process of re-thinking "community" may thus be the key to representation in the public sphere. Rethinking "community" permits people to recognize the pathways to social change and to discover the standards such as large size and tight coherence which must be fulfilled to gain public representation in our present democracy. Further, to rethink the meaning of, and the power attached to, a word like "community" may be the key to uncovering why it is that such a debate over online communication should occur at all.

Notes

1. The band's 7/16/93 Mann Music Center, Philadelphia, PA, rendition of "You Enjoy Myself" features the lyrics "Water your team, in a bee hive, I'm a sent you." These alternate

lyrics are quoted from the bass player's first joking response to the debate in the "Phish Update" Newsletter (1993a).

2. Based upon the mythic *Helping Friendly Book*, which is treasured by the Lizards of Gamehenge as containing the secrets to "eternal joy and never-ending splendor."

3. According to Gamehenge mythology, in the song "Colonel Forbin's Ascent" the mighty prophet-god Icculus agrees to assist the Lizards in stealing back the *Helping Friendly Book* from the evil King Wilson who has enslaved them. But Icculus advises Colonel Forbin that "all knowledge seeming innocent and pure becomes a deadly weapon in the hands of avarice and greed."

4. This again comes from Gamehenge mythology as a positive effect of possessing the *Helping Friendly Book* in the song "Colonel Forbin's Ascent."

5. A tape tree is when someone makes five copies of a tape for five people, each of whom then copies the tape for five more people, etc., etc. The result is massive dissemination of a tape with minimal damage to the tape's sound quality through recording generations.

References

Anderson, B. (1983). *Imagined communities: Reflections on the origin and spread of nationalism*. London: Verso.

Bacon-Smith, C. (1992). *Enterprising women: Television fandom and the creation of popular myth*. Philadelphia: University of Pennsylvania Press.

Barnes, B. (1988). *The nature of power*. Urbana and Chicago: University of Illinois Press.

Bassin, I. (1994, November 6). Problem w/ Scene. Posted to Phish.net.

Baym, N.K. (1995). The emergence of community in computer-mediated communication. In S.G. Jones (Ed.), *CyberSociety: Computer-mediated communication and community* (pp. 138–163). Thousand Oaks, CA: Sage.

Brendan. (1994, April 16). Re: Beacon (I was at all three). Posted to Phish.net.

Carey, J. (1989). Mass communication and cultural studies. In J. Carey, *Communication as culture: Essays on media and society* (pp. 37–68). Boston: Unwin Hyman.

Cooke, K., & Lehrer, D. (1993, July 12). The whole world is talking. *The Nation*, p. 61.

Giddens, A. (1984). *The constitution of society*. Berkeley: University of California Press.

Gladfelter, S. (1994, April 16). 4/15/94—brief highlights & lowlights. Posted to Phish.net.

Godard, E. (1994, September 17). The New Phish.net FAQ File.

Goodman, J. (1995, March 2). Personal communication. E-mail.

Heling, J. (1994a, October 11). Re: splitting the net a bad idea. Posted to Phish.net.

Heling, J. (1994b, December 1). Personal communication. E-mail.

Introne, Lucas, aka "Lucas the Lurker". (1994, October 10). Splitting the net. Posted to Phish.net.

Jackson, J.O. (Spring 1995) It's a Wired, Wired World. *Time*, Special Issue: Welcome to Cyberspace. *145*(12), 80–82.

James. (1994, April 17). Re: Beacon (I was at all three). Posted to Phish.net.

Jenkins, H. (1992). *Textual poachers: Television fans and participating culture*. New York: Routledge.

Jones, S.G. (1995). Understanding community in the information age. In S.G. Jones (Ed.), *CyberSociety: Computer-mediated communication and community* (pp. 10–35). Thousand Oaks, CA: Sage.

Karpenstein, N. (1994, April 18). Apology. Posted to Phish.net.

MacDonald, A. (1994a) *The polemics of pleasure: Women's community and computer-mediated communication*. Unpublished MA thesis, Annenberg School for Communication, PA.

MacDonald, A. (1994b) *Uncertain utopia: Science fiction media fandom & computer-mediated communication*. Unpublished paper, Annenberg School for Communication, PA.

MacKinnon, R.C. (1992). *Searching for the Leviathan in Usenet*. Unpublished master's thesis, San José State University.

McKechnie, D. (1994, December 2). Personal communication. E-mail.

McLaughlin, M.L., Osborne, K.K., & Smith, C.B. (1995). Standards of conduct on Usenet. In S.G. Jones (Ed.), *CyberSociety: Computer-mediated communication and community* (pp. 90–111). Thousand Oaks, CA: Sage.

Morgan, J. (1995, January 17). Personal communication. E-mail.

Newfeld, G. (1994, April 12). Hippies suck. Posted to Phish.net.

Phish Update. (1993a, February). Waltham, MA.

Phish Update. (1993b, Summer). Lexington, MA.

Postman, N. (1993) *Technopoly: The surrender of culture to technology.* New York: Vintage Books.

The Random House Dictionary of the English Language. (1987). (S.B. Flexner, Ed.) (2nd ed., unabridged). New York: Random House.

Rheingold, H. (1993a). A slice of life in my virtual community. In L.M. Harasim (Ed.), *Global networks: Computers and international communication* (pp. 57–80). Cambridge, MA: MIT Press.

Rheingold, H. (1993b). *The virtual community: Homesteading on the electronic frontier.* Reading, MA: Addison Wesley.

Rioux, J. (1994, October 10). Splitting the net. Posted to Phish.net.

Robson, K. (1994, December 5). Personal communication. E-mail.

Rogovin, S.R. (1994, April 16). An observation. Posted to Phish.net.

Silverman, L. (1994, October 20). Top 50 posters to rec.music.phish. Posted to Phish.net.

Snyder, C. (1994, April 15). Phish IRC Bot. Posted to Phish.net.

Sondericker, J. (1994, October 20). Personal communication. E-mail.

Stew, "The Dude of Nice." (1994, November 5). Anti Wilson Revolution, IDEAS. Posted to Phish.net.

STMT. (1994, April 16). Re: an observation. Posted to Phish.net.

Trimpe, J.J. (1994, December 3). Personal communication. E-mail.

Watson, N. (1995a, March 10). Dr. Swatso's Phish List. Posted to Phish.net.

Watson, N. (1995b). *The Phish.net fan community: What CMC means for theories of power and the practice of culture.* Unpublished MA thesis, Annenberg School for Communication, PA.

Welsh, J.M. (1994, April 13). Not to be bitter, but. . . Posted to Phish.net.

Welsh, J.M. (1995, February 6). Personal communication. E-mail.

Williams, R. (1976). *Keywords: A vocabulary of culture and society.* New York: Oxford University Press.

6

Gay Men and Computer Communication: A Discourse of Sex and Identity in Cyberspace

David F. Shaw

> *Language is a skin: I rub my language against the other. It is as if I had words instead of fingers, or fingers at the tip of my words. My language trembles with desire. The emotion derives from a double contact: on the one hand, a whole activity of discourse discreetly, indirectly focuses upon a single signified, which is "I desire you," and releases, nourishes, ramifies it to the point of explosion (language experiences orgasm upon touching itself); on the other hand, I enwrap the other in my words, I caress, brush against, talk up this contact, I extend myself to make the commentary to which I submit the relation endure.*
>
> —Roland Barthes, *A Lover's Discourse* (1978), p. 73

Roland Barthes's study of the discourse of love presents an ideal starting point for an analysis of human communication via the computer. First, *A Lover's Discourse* (1978) takes as its object the text of words and thoughts of individuals in the physical absence of the other—in this case, the lover. For Barthes, the other is *inscribed* within this text—moreover, "he inscribes himself within the text" (p. 79). Likewise, inherent in computer-mediated communication (CMC) is the physical absence of the other—be he lover, friend, family, or stranger. CMC also produces a text; one in which by his mere participation the other is inscribed. This text, like Barthes's, can be read as a discourse of absence. According to Barthes, "The discourse of Absence is a text with two ideograms: there are *the raised arms of Desire*, and there are *the wide-open arms of Need*" (p. 16). Second, and more specific to the object of this study, given Barthes's homosexuality, his discursive analysis of love and absence must necessarily be read as one of homosexual love and homosexual absence operating under the ideograms of *homosexual desire* and *homosexual need*.

I wish to analyze and deconstruct the CMC of gay men. If, as Barthes illustrates, love is most readily understood in the physical absence of the lover, then perhaps the best way to understand communication lies in the uncharted territories of cyberspace where men sit alone at their keyboards producing and inscribing themselves within interactive texts of homosexual desire and need. For my research I conducted interviews with twelve gay men who use Internet Relay Chat (IRC). Some of the interviews were conducted on IRC, some via e-mail, and others over the phone—whichever the respondent preferred. While my sample does not purport to be statistically significant, my research role of particpant-observer afforded me the opportunity to establish a bond of trust with the users I identified as frequent CMC participants. Further, the in-depth and open-ended interviews offered some keen insights into the uses and gratifications motivating gay men's computer-mediated communication.

IRC and the Social Bond

Real-time CMC is best exemplified by the IRC. It, like similar services available from private subscription services such as America Online (AOL) and Prodigy, offers real-time chat with an unlimited number of users. The format of IRC looks very much like a playwright's script. Each line of text begins with the sender's computer nickname ("nick" or "handle") and is followed by the text the user wishes to broadcast to the other users. As the conversation progresses, each line of text rolls off the top of the computer screen to make room for the new lines of text being transmitted through the bottom of the screen. CMC takes place in channels, and channels are created by users who join based on topic and interest. There are generally between 10,000 and 15,000 users on the IRC at any one time, operating as many as 5,000 different chat channels from around the globe.

Of all forms of CMC, real-time chat (as exemplified by IRC) best illustrates Rheingold's definition of the virtual community. IRC is made-up of "social aggregations that emerge from the Net" and it "forms webs of personal relationships in cyberspace" (Rheingold, 1993, p. 5). Of all forms of CMC, IRC is most intriguing because of its dualistic personality—that is, it is both interpersonal and mass-mediated communication. At once, users can carry on one-to-one discussions with each other and broadcast messages to the entire channel of users.

Rheingold (1993) characterizes the IRC as follows:

> IRC is what you get when you strip away everything that normally allows people to understand the unspoken shared assumptions that surround and support their communications, and thus render invisible most of the web of socially mediated definitions that tell us what words and behaviors are supposed to mean in our societies. (p. 178)

As inferred above, IRC communication is void of all physical contexts; there is no physical body language, physical appearance, change in tone of voice, or facial expression to enable the intended decoding of a typed message. Lacking these mostly visual cues, many argue that CMC has a much narrower bandwidth (i.e. fewer cues to determine the correct reception of message meaning) than real face-to-face interpersonal communication and other forms of mass-mediated communication (see Baym, 1995; Kiesler, Siegel, & McGuire, 1984; Walther, 1992). In short, there are only letters, words, and symbols. But IRCers are bricoleurs of physical context, actively employing all of the letters, numbers, and symbols the computer keyboard offers in order to create and convey these physical contexts.

Bodily movement, for example, can be rendered in physical action commands. If Bob types "/me rubs Jim's back," upon entering this command a line of text reading "Bob rubs Jim's back" appears amidst the texts of other users (flagged by a "*" to distinguish it from the dialogue on the channel). Tone of voice is indicated by using emoticons (Baym, 1995, p. 152), capital letters, bold face type, exclamation marks, and asterisk/parenthetical descriptors—for example "I AM SO ANGRY!!!" or "do you really mean that? *gasp*."

Most users provide other users with brief physical descriptions of themselves. Regular channel users can register these brief descriptions with the "bot" (the robot channel administrator created by one or more of the channel users). Physical descriptions are typically typed in the form "Bob is 24, 5'11", 170#, Bl/Bl, athletic build." Thus, if Bob is a registered regular on the channel, when he logs on the bot identifies his e-mail address and nickname, announces that he has joined the channel, and automatically provides other channel users with his brief biography. Perhaps the best way appearance is communicated is via the exchange of GIFs and JPEGs (graphic information files: photographs that have been electronically scanned and coded to be sent over the Internet). Once they have been sent to another user's computer, s/he can use image converter programs to translate the electronic data back into a picture and view it on his or her computer screen.

Rheingold (1993, p. 180) argues that in the physical absence of the other, IRCers are likely to try on different personalities. Elizabeth Reid characterizes IRC as a "playground" where:

> people are free to experiment with different forms of communication and self-representation. From that playground, IRC habituees have evolved rules, rituals, and communication styles that qualify them as a real culture. (cited in Rheingold, 1993, p. 180)

This self-regulated self-representation has been the cause of much negative press surrounding CMC. Countless popular press articles chronicle horror stories of online scams, charlatanism, and gross misrepresentation of the self. For example, a *Time* magazine feature describes the online revenge victims concocted against a computer Casanova (Cole, 1993, p. 58) while *People* magazine tells the story of a woman who conned more than 100 men by asking for travel money to visit them (Sanz, 1994, p. 40).

But for every online scam, there is a success story. Cyberspace is a world divided by interest rather than geography. Like Lyotard's performativity, the computer extends users' grasps, enabling them to meet more people, and, theoretically, the ideal person. In light of this, it should seem only natural that onliners are forming real friendships, relationships, and marriages (see, e.g., Chidley, 1994). Relationships formed in cyberspace and actualized in the flesh are increasingly catching the eye of the media as the newest "computer-dating" phenomenon fuels the public's fascination with the electronic superhighway (see *MacLean's*, January 17, 1994; *People*, February 21, 1994; *Time*, July 19, 1993). Daytime television is filled with fascination over the subject; *Jenny Jones*, *Carnie*, *Geraldo*, and *Maury Povich* have all focused on "Computer Sex and Dating," as "Unusual Ways Couples Met." The Fox television hit *Beverly Hills 90210* used CMC as a scripting device to introduce an unlikely affair between two of its protagonists. Even the lesbian magazine *Deneuve* (renamed *Curve*) ran a cover story on two women who met through the computer.

However, the press surrounding online relationships and communities tends to ignore one of the largest online communities—gay men. A 1994 "*Wired* Top 10" list cited the ten most populated chat rooms created by members of America Online, the nation's largest private subscriber service. Among the top ten were three gay channels: men4men (#3), Men Who Want 2 Meet Men (#6), and Young Men4Men (#8). Of the seven other channels on the list, one was lesbian, one was "Swingers or Group," and the remaining five were heterosexual—most appeared to be sexual topics. Similarly, IRC's "gaysex" and "jack-off" (also gay) channels are usually among the most populated IRC channels—sometimes surpassing the population of "sex," the complementary heterosexual chat room. The fact that gay men, a minority population, constitute such a significant proportion of CMC users deems further investigation. This chapter queries how, why, and to what end a group of gay men uses the IRC. In doing so, it attempts to uncover the uses and gratifications of gay men's computer communication—an approach which Rafaeli (1986, 1996) regards as essential to the study of the Internet. This chapter will further demonstrate that the social architecture of IRC and CMC deems it an "undernet" of self-discovery and shrouded experimentation which both resonates with and parallels the lived experiences of many gay men.

Gay Men and IRC

> *My theory of popularity, which I define as an easy interrelationship between the reader's experience of the text and his or her social experience, is one that is best arrived at by a study of the text itself.*
>
> —John Fiske, *Television Criticism* (1991), p. 447

Ask a gay man for simple directions to the local gay bar. Under the viaduct, over the railroad tracks, down a dirt road, across an alley, in the back door of a non-descript building, or shrouded from the street by smoked glass windows—it is quite difficult to find. Word of mouth will tell you it's there; a patron will show you the way. Once inside it's a cavernous room filled to the rim with other gay men. Some are there to meet with friends. Some are there to drink, make new friends and conversation. Others are there for sex. Some passively observe the environment while others actively participate in it. Whatever the reason one goes to a gay bar, there is common solace and excitement in the fact that it is one of the few places in society where by their mere presence all patrons can be assumed gay.

Similarly, IRC exists as a word-of-mouth community. Logged on to a local server, there are no signs saying "This way to IRC." Once arrived at, given that as many as 5,000 channels exist at a given time, finding the online gay community proves equally difficult. Entering this community via the "gaysex" channel, users find themselves in a large "room" with as many as seventy other gay men. Not all of the men logged onto the channel are contributing the dialogue: some "lurk" (observing and waiting for the right moment to join in), and some "whisper" (sending private messages to one another). For those participating in the dialogue(s) there is (are) political talk, gossip about other #gaysex-ers, tales of sexual bravado, GIF exchanging, advice seeking, and just about anything else imaginable. As texts scroll up their screens, users can eavesdrop on many conversations at once. While heterosexuals wander into the channel from time to time (most to "gaybash," further paralleling the lived social experiences of gay men), there is comfort in the fact that the regulars are gay men. Additionally, interlocutors can be "kicked" out by channel ops (those rooted firmly enough within the community to earn the status of channel operator) or banned by administrative bots and channel ops.

In making such a comparison between these two meeting places, it is not my intention to reduce the term "gay bar" to those bars characterized by large crowds, loud music, flashing lights, and pulsating bodies. This type of bar, however, draws the widest range of gay men. Admittedly, the umbrella term "gay bar" encompasses the range of corner bars, piano bars, leather bars, and discos to under-age gay dances and drag shows. Similarly, the IRC's #gaysex is the most (gay) mainstreamed channel created by its gay male users. Other frequently populated gay channels include:

- #jack-off
- #gaysm (sadism and masochism)
- #gaymuscle
- #gaygifs (for the exchange of GIFs)
- #gayboygifs
- #gayboysex
- #gayteensex
- #gayraunch
- #gblf (gays, bisexuals, lesbians, and friends)
- #gay40+
- #gayNYC (LA, DC, UK, etc.—any city, state, or country abbreviation).

Depending on their communications software and service provider, most users can be logged on to several of these channels at once, carrying on multiple conversations in multiple software windows.

The gay bar analogy, however, came up in most of the interviews I conducted. While not overtly posited as an equivalent experience, IRC was mentioned as an alternative way of meeting other gay men. Additionally, when asked what the appeal of IRC was for them, the bar was the only real social experience the interviewees cited.

"Meateatr,"[1] a 27-year-old computer engineering student from Colorado, responded:

> In the gay world, a gay itch is satisfied by going out to a club or a party which requires a certain time commitment, while IRC is literally at my fingertips (at work and home). There is always some group of gays online to talk 24 hours a day.

"Thor," a 26-year-old attorney from Texas said:

> It's a very different way of meeting people than any other way I've ever found . . . you meet people through non-visual means unlike in a bar where you see someone and say "Oooh—they look nice, I want to meet them." Here you just have to get to like people from what they say.

"Musician," a 29-year-old music education student from Illinois, describes himself as "very shy" and finds IRC appealing because:

> I get to meet other gay men. I'm pretty shy so it's hard for me to meet people face to face in a bar. On the computer I can flirt and talk to people and get a sense of their reaction by the things they type: the grins, descriptions they say. . . . the computer makes it easier.

"Dolphin," a 32-year-old graphic artist from Nebraska, and "Netboy," a 26-year-old accounting clerk from Colorado, stated the relationship most clearly:

> I appreciate it because it's a way of perhaps meeting somebody other than the normal routes of . . . hmm . . . bars. (Dolphin)

> The best thing is meeting people outside of the bar scene. (Netboy)

For others, the sense of community—specifically gay community—is the primary appeal:

> I just like talking to other gay people about gay issues, but my primary purpose is for entertainment. ("Exec," a 25-year-old Urban Studies student from San Francisco)

> Every time you get on you feel like you know these people pretty much. A lot of people where I went to school would be on and we'd be sitting there talking and it'd be like "hey let's all go do something." You feel like you know them all; you see the same people and they're on all the time. ("Queen," a 20-year-old Business student from Texas)

All but two of the men I interviewed used more than one form of interactive CMC. All have access to the Internet and IRC, a few subscribe to America Online, and all but two have accounts on local BBSs (Bulletin Board Services). The primary appeal of local BBSs was that users could meet other local subscribers.

How Do Gay Men Find the Online Community?

All of the people I interviewed use computers for work or school. Finding IRC and its gay users followed a fairly typical pattern. First, users were introduced to e-mail and N-talk (interactive discussions with up to three people). Soon they found their way to the bulletin boards and newsgroups where people would place posts for meeting one another. Like the personals, users could respond to postings along with sending and receiving GIFs of one another. It was usually through these postings that the gay men I interviewed were directed to the IRC. All but one of the men I interviewed found the IRC through another gay man he either already knew or someone he met through a BBS. The last man found the IRC through a heterosexual female friend, and "stumbled" onto the gaysex channel on his own.

The men have been using the IRC anywhere from three months to two years. All of them collect GIFs of other users and random gay pornography that has been sent to them in GIF form. Their collections range from a dozen to 300 images. All cite the IRC as the primary use of their server accounts and they log on in varying amounts.

Dolphin had access to the Internet through a private subscriber service and only recently gave up his account because his high use and the hourly charge for service were becoming too much of a financial burden. Others log on so sporadically that they guessed their weekly use was only three to four hours. Meateatr's use, for example,

> varies widely due to work, school, and/or horniness. Sometimes I will go for several weeks between logons. Other times I will log on just to see if any locals are on. Sometimes I get on with the intent of not staying on long, but then I get hooked into a dirty conversation with a guy. I guess I'm saying my IRC activity is pretty random.

Most of the men said that they average ten to fifteen hours per week. "Scorsese," a 24-year-old film student from New York, responded anecdotally:

> Maybe an hour, an hour and a half a day? And that would be on the short side! You've heard of "IRC inches?" . . . somebody says eight and you know it's probably five. I guess this works the same way—but backwards.

At the other end of the scale is Thor, who logs on for roughly twenty-five hours per week. Early in my interview with him, Thor said he initially spent so much time on IRC because he had fallen in love with a man from Europe whom he had met online. He flew from California (where he had just finished law school) to Europe to meet the man. He stayed for a month before moving to Texas for work. He says most of his time is spent on IRC because it is a free way to communicate with the European man, his first lover.

#gaysex and "Real" Social Relationships

After communicating via the computer, all of the men had met at least one other IRC #gaysex-er in person. The results are a mixed bag of excitement and disgust, promise and letdown, nonchalance and embarrassment.

The disappointment of his first face-to-face (F2F) has left Meateatr reluctant to try it again:

> I met one guy and it wasn't very cool. I had an opportunity to do it again via a local BBS, and I declined in fear of a repeat of my first bad experience.

Others, like Exec, approach the face-to-face more cautiously:

> It depends . . . if I have had a long going relationship talking with someone for an extensive period of time . . . then maybe a face-to-face would be appropriate.

Netboy says he's "somewhat interested" in meeting people face-to-face, but:

> I have to get to know them first before actually meeting them face-to-face. I have not had a relationship with anyone from the computer, but have had sex with guys after meeting them.

When asked if they had ever had a computer-turned-physical affair with another gay man, all but three indicated that they had. Of the three who said they had not, one was suspiciously evasive:

> You mean like did I go visit someone and have sex with them? . . . I would say no. No. I mean . . . no. Let's just say no. We'll say no.

Thor, however, is very interested in meeting other users and has met twenty-eight IRC #gaysex-ers:

> I've met people the same day I've talked to them for the first time. And I've met people who I've talked to for months in the same town as me. I've also spent months trying to get someone to meet me. Some people get on when they're horny and want to meet you right away. My first meet—I talked to the guy for three and a half months and flew 5000 miles to meet him. He was the first guy I've ever been with. I came out in February and wasn't with a guy until last November. That was my first. Since then, I've only been with one person who wasn't on IRC.

Part of the fear in the face-to-face stems from Rheingold's discussion of IRCers trying on different personalities, and Reid's characterization of the IRC as a "playground." Several of the men I interviewed discussed the disappointment when people's online personalities don't match their real personality. Michael Reison, a Boston psychotherapist, characterizes online relationships as "instantaneous and less threatening," they are in his words "all your fantasies" (There's something electric, 1994, p. 24). First impressions are, however, often wrong. As quoted earlier, many of the men are reluctant to meet other IRCers right away—they want to get a sense of knowing them first, before the face-to-face. Many regular IRCers will argue that real personalities emerge over time. Scorsese, for example:

If I notice that there's a guy always logged on and I never see him talk to the rest of the channel, no matter how much he messages me and how much he wants to talk to me, I know the guy's gotta be really quiet and nervous. That's not my type.

Others, like Meateatr, are more cognizant of the playground effect:

[I have] a strange feeling of distrust of those I am conversing with. You can be anything your abilities will allow you to be on IRC, and this often is someone/thing completely different than the truth. However, sometimes the fantasy is worth ignoring the possible lies involved.

Musician, however, believes that while some IRCers are there to play, others are there in sincerity:

I think some of the people are there to play, as far as mind-playing with you. But I think there are also some other people on the channel who are interested in trying to find maybe a partner.

But What Does He Look Like?

Anyone who has ever spent one night in a gay bathhouse knows that it is (or was) one of the most ruthlessly ranked, heirarchized, and competitive environments imaginable. Your looks, muscles, hair distribution, size of cock, and shape of ass determined exactly how happy you were going to be during those few hours.

—Leo Bersani, "Is the Rectum a Grave?" (1988), p. 206

Being a *body* constitutes the principle behind our separateness from one another and behind our personal presence. Our bodily existence stands at the forefront of personal identity and individuality. Both the law and morality recognize the physical body as something of a fence, an absolute boundary, establishing and protecting our privacy. Now, the computer network simply brackets the physical presence of the participants, either by omitting or by simulating corporeal immediacy.

—Michael Heim, "The Erotic Ontology of Cyberspace" (1991), p. 74

As mentioned earlier, the chief way in which appearance is communicated is via typed physical descriptions within the #gaysex text. Additionally, most users have GIFs of themselves and exchange them upon request. Generally GIFs are traded and it is not uncommon to see users asking "does anyone have a GIF to trade." None of the men I interviewed thought that anyone had ever misrepresented himself in a GIF—that is, pretending that a photograph of another better-looking man was him. Many regulars make their GIFs available at the "Gaysex Gallery," a user created Web site featuring user GIFS and links to user homepages. There is also a seldom broken rule that a user will not distribute a GIF that another user has sent him. GIFs of users come in all states of undress, relatively few are what most would consider pornographic or distasteful (GIFs made from erotic imagery from open market pornography fill this void). GIFs, however, can be difficult to view. Monochrome and low-resolution monitors make some GIFs look worse than black and white photocopies of glossy magazine covers. An inexpensive scanner can turn the wink of an eye into a photographic black hole.

While it may be easy to communicate to a bodiless communicator, once a mutual curiosity has been established there is the desire for more. To fill in these bodily gaps, the men send photographs to one another and begin communicating by phone. Parks and Floyd (1996, p. 92) found that CMC users used an average of 2.68 channels of communication (e.g. direct e-mail, phone, postal service, and face-to-face communication) in maintaining and developing social relationships with other users. Most of the men I spoke to said looks were very important to them and they eagerly exchanged GIFs with other users. Looks, and not necessarily personality, were the primary causes that led to Meateatr and Dolphin's disappointments in their first and only face-to-faces.

Several of the men I interviewed remarked that gay culture has an extraordinary visual bias and that they found the IRC to be a refreshing non-visual break. Ironically, all of the men collected GIFs and had had at least one face-to-face meeting. Further, as noted above, they indicate that looks are, indeed, important to them. The antilogy reveals itself: while bodiless communication was the initial appeal, all had made overt efforts to attach bodies to other communicators. In short, not only do the users create the missing contexts from which to communicate, they also create a context for an idealized concept of gay culture which is necessarily rooted in and leads to their lived homosexual experiences.

For Bersani (above epigraph), an impersonal and solipsistic version of desire is the only way around the insidious forms of power he sees as suffusing sexuality. Heim, however, renders the solipsism inherent in bodilessness self-annihilating. It follows that the CMC texts produced by the men are variations of Barthes's presence/absence duality. Inasmuch as users try to attach real bodies to other communicators, they try to tap into that "forefront of personal identities" Heim writes about. Thus, there exists a genuine desire to meet other users on a personal and present level. On the other hand, as noted above, some users are reluctant to meet others because they fear they will not live up to their projected images and fantasies. These fantasy texts thrive in the absence of the other user. The other is imagined and his text becomes a mere prop for the desires of the user. Thus, while the two quotes that lead this section appear to be antithetical approaches to the role of the body in gay men's communication, they are in constant negotiation on #gaysex—rendering them inseparable.

As noted earlier, in his shyness, Musician finds CMC to be an ideal forum for communicating with other gay men. Yet, there is a concomitant desire to physically meet other #gaysex-ers:

> It's hard for me to meet people in real social situations because physicality is how people decide who they want to meet. . . . I'm not so hung-up on looks, but it does play a role in how I choose somebody. If the personality wins out, then I would go with that. It's hard to say because you get a really limited perspective

of somebody from the computer. . . . I try to talk to people who live nearby—for convenience sake.

For others, like Dolphin, a disappointing face-to-face can reinforce the original appeal of the medium:

What's neat about it is you actually—even though people lie and cheat and all that kind of stuff over it—you get the sense that you're actually talking to someone right off the bat instead of just eyeing each other.

Meateatr, on the other hand, spoke earlier of a distrust that stemmed from his face-to-face and says he's becoming increasingly antagonistic to other users:

[IRC] has reinforced my observation that gay males are very visually-oriented. . . . I was on one day and didn't know anyone who was on and nobody would talk to me. So I finally said "anyone want my GIF?" A bunch of guys responded and I sent it to three or four of them—all of the sudden all these guys were messaging me "ooh you're cute," "I want to talk to you." I told them to "fuck off" and left.

Thor, however, represents this ongoing negotiation best. Consider his earlier words on the appeal of IRC in light of the fact that he has met twenty-eight #gaysex-ers:

you meet people through non-visual means unlike in a bar where you see someone and say "Oooh—they look nice, I want to meet them."

Conclusion

The gay men I interviewed ranged in age from 20 to 32. All had received, or were in the process of receiving, university degrees. Some characterized their IRC use as "addictive," others "sporadic." Some log on until the early morning hours and sleep all afternoon, while others fill in the gaps between classes. For some, the IRC is mere entertainment. For others it has been an integral part of their coming-out process and the formulation of a gay identity. Some know only how to use IRC and word-processing software, while others work with and study computers all day. However, despite the differences in uses and users, several common themes became evident.

Most of the men in the online gay community found IRC through another member and all had introduced at least one other friend to the community. They all want to meet other gay men, and most posit CMC as the only alternative to a gay bar. Thus, for the gay men participating in CMC, the virtual experiences of IRC and real-life experience share a symbiotic relationship; that is, relationships formed within the exterior gay community lead the users to the interior CMC gay community, where they, in turn, develop new relationships which are nurtured and developed outside the bounds of CMC.

While the format's physical absence of the other is appealing, all of the men actively transgress the bounds of bodilessness through the exchange of GIFs, photographs, phone calls, and ultimately in the face-to-face. For many gay users the face-to-face meeting remains the ultimate goal; it offers them a way to meet other gay men and increase their circles of friends and significant others. The face-to-face, however, yields varying results. For some it is a disappointment, for others it is a way to have sex, make friends, or begin a relationship—cyberspace, like real life, is full of promises but makes none.

The texts users produce online are, like Barthes's love, discourses of absence. They are replete with *homosexual desire* and *homosexual need*. The desire is manifest in the fantasies projected onto other #gaysex-ers as well as the desire to meet other gay men and fight the constraints of the medium. The need is manifest in the text's unspoken sense of community that drives members to return to one of the few places in society where gay men convene. Most importantly, while the playground potential of the IRC inarguably exists and people will (and do—even on #gaysex) try on different personalities, the uniqueness of #gaysex lies in the fact that it presents an opportunity for gay men, who often go through life hiding this most vital aspect of their identity, to try on this real identity.

Note

1. In respect of their privacy, I have changed the respondents' computer nicknames. I have tried to create alternative names which embody the essence of their chosen nicks.

References

Barthes, R. (1978). *A lover's discourse* (R. Howard, Trans.). New York: Hill & Wang.

Baym, N.K. (1995). The emergence of community in computer-mediated communication. In S.G. Jones (Ed.), *CyberSociety: Computer-mediated communication and commmunity* (pp. 138–163). Thousand Oaks, CA: Sage.

Bersani, L. (1988). Is the rectum a grave? In D. Crimp (Ed.), *AIDS: Cultural analysis, cultural activism* (pp. 197–222). Cambridge, MA: MIT Press.

Chidley, J. (1994). Love connection: Trading cologne and makeup for a computer and a modem. *MacLean's, 107*(3), 46–47.

Cole, W. (1993, July 19). Heartbreak in cyberspace. *Time*, p. 58.

Fiske, J. (1991). *Television criticism: Approaches and applications.* White Plains, NY: Longman.

Heim, M. (1991). The erotic ontology of cyberspace. In M. Benedikt (Ed.), *Cyberspace: First steps* (pp. 59–80). Cambridge, MA: MIT Press.

Kiesler, S., Siegel, J., & McGuire, T.W. (1984). Social psychological aspects of computer mediated communication. *American Psychologist, 39*(10), 1123–1134.

Parks, M., & Floyd, K. (1996). Making friends in cyberspace. *Journal of Communication, 46*(1), 80–97.

Rafaeli, S. (1986). The electronic bulletin board: A computer-driven mass medium. *Computers and the Social Sciences,* (2), 123–136.

Rafaeli, S. (1996). Why communication researchers should study the Internet: A dialogue. *Journal of Communication, 46*(1), 4–13.

Rheingold, H. (1993). *The virtual community: Homesteading on the electronic frontier.* Reading, MA: Addison-Wesley.

Sanz, C. (1994, February 21). Where love has gone. *People*, p. 40.

There's something electric between us (1994, February 14). *Newsday*, p. 34.

Walther, J. (1992). Interpersonal effects in computer-mediated interaction: A relational perspective. *Communication Research*, *19*(1), 52–90.

Wired Top 10. (1994). *Wired*, 2(2), p. 32.

7

Virtual Community in a Telepresence Environment

Margaret L. McLaughlin, Kerry K. Osborne, and Nicole B. Ellison

The revolution in global networked communications has given rise to a new generation of social technologies, including mechanisms for the formation and cultivation of interpersonal relationships (Baym, 1995; Reid, 1991; Rheingold, 1993; Smith, McLaughlin, & Osborne, in press; Walther & Burgoon, 1992; Wilkins, 1991). Individuals united by common goals and interests encounter and engage one another in online bulletin boards, mailing lists, chat rooms, and Web spaces. Unlike face-to-face interaction, in which relationships are initiated and then topics of mutual interest sought, Internet users can go directly to the topics that interest them and pursue interaction with like-minded others (Rheingold, 1993).

There is evidence to indicate that for some of these venues conversational dialog is consumed by many but produced by relatively few (McLaughlin et al., 1995), and that virtual collectives are more properly characterized as "pseudocommunities" (Beniger, 1987, p. 369), networks not of primary interpersonal relationships but rather of impersonal associations integrated via a mass medium. Further, issues of personal identity can be compromised and confounded in the virtual commons, as the current limitations of bandwidth are exploited to create new opportunities for self-presentation and social experimentation through predominantly text-based messaging:

> The physical world . . . is a place where the identity and position of the people you communicate with are well known, fixed, and highly visual. In cyberspace, everybody is in the dark. . . . On top of the technology-imposed constraints, we who populate cyberspace deliberately experiment with fracturing traditional notions of identity by living as multiple simultaneous personae in different virtual neighborhoods. (Rheingold, 1993, p. 61)

Shirky (1995), however, points out that identity is flexible in physical communities as well, as we switch among multiple personae in accordance with situational constraints.

Participation and identity issues notwithstanding, the temptation to label online aggregates "communities" has proven virtually irresistible to most observers of cyberspace (see, e.g., Baym, 1995; Curtis, 1992; Fernback & Thompson, 1995; Frederick, 1993; Jones, 1995a; Kollock & Smith, 1994), in large part due to the early emergence of analogs in computer-mediated communication (CMC) to social structures and discourse processes found in face-to-face communication. Kollock and Smith (1994), for example, illustrate the creation of community in Usenet by analyzing newsgroup postings according to Ostrom's (1990) design principles of communities which produce and maintain collective goods. These principles include: clearly defined group boundaries; rules for use of collective goods that are consistent with needs; access to participation in rule modification; independence from external authorities; a system for member behavior monitoring; graduated sanctions; and access to conflict resolution mechanisms. Each of these principles, say Kollock and Smith, obtain in newsgroup communities. The issue of non-participation is classified by the authors as free-riding, no less problematic in non-electronic communities.

Face-to-face analogies are not, however, the sole basis for conceptualizing certain online aggregates as communities. As Jones (1995b, p. 26) notes, there seems to be a prevailing sentiment that new technologies require us to invent novel strategies for organizing social relations. Baym (1995) has identified a number of phenomena which reflect how the underlying technology of CMC systems is being adapted to create new ways of relating. These include new forms of expressive communication (emoticons, graphic accents, and other uses of ASCII text to convey affect), new electronic variations on the management of personal identity (gender-bending, anonymous remailing), and new sources of acculturation, such as online primers, guides to "netiquette," and FAQs (Frequently Asked Questions). "Reply-to" and threading conventions built into most online messaging systems impose a degree of interactivity and order on the unpunctuated stream of discourse that matches and often exceeds the level of co-orientation found in face-to-face conversation.

McLaughlin et al. (1995) locate community in the emergence of standards of conduct, many of which are peculiarly applicable to the electronic commons and aimed toward the goal of preserving the group. The concern for community well-being is shown by reproaches made to participants whose behavior in some way threatens that well-being, such as "bandwidth piggery," which makes participation costly and jeopardizes future interaction. Strategies for the management of virtual spaces with respect to issues of power and control, authority, dominance, and submission have evolved as well, as human and non-human agents (moderators and Webmasters, listservers and cancelbots) serve as gatekeepers, adjudicators, and imposers of sanctions for misconduct.

In virtual spaces, as elsewhere, the primary challenge of community formation is an organizational one: to convert the vision of the founders to a structure that can sustain itself and nourish the members (Fernback & Thompson, 1995). As Ostrom (1990) notes, the question is how a group of individuals can "organize and govern themselves to obtain collective benefits where the temptations to free-ride and to break commitments are substantial" (p. 10). Mechanisms for forming groups around common interests have long existed on the Internet, and are most highly evolved on the older, text-based network, Usenet. In terms of virtual space, Usenet newsgroups are literary spaces, created with language alone, hosting topically arranged discussions that a participant can read and reply to whenever the mood strikes. Shirky (1995) classifies chats as more spatially complex than newsgroups, and argues that synchronicity (users interacting together in real time) promotes a greater sense of community than asychronicity can: "When people use real time chat, they are usually less interested in what's being discussed than in who is doing the discussing, less interested in text than in community" (p. 92).

The logical conclusion to Shirky's complexity algorithm implies that the increased complexity of the multimedia-capable World Wide Web (WWW), with its inclusion of graphics, audio, and motion video resources, should give even greater stimulus to the formation of electronic communities. On the WWW, it is a relatively simple matter to provide the foundation of a rudimentary community by developing a page of resources and posting announcements to potential members in appropriate locations. Whether or not anyone will come, or more to the point come back again and contribute resources, is hard to predict and sometimes difficult to monitor. Newsgroups and chats require questions and answers to exchange information, and community resources are emergent and inherently collaborative. WWW pages, on the other hand, offer pre-packaged resources which consumers can access without contributing so much as a question. Hyperlinking technology facilitates the search for resources such that consumers may prefer to hop from site to site rather than incur interpersonal expense. Where benefits can be obtained without expenditure, there may be little or no incentive to reciprocate communication, and even those who do take a moment to sign a "guestbook" (an electronic form soliciting information from the visitor) or answer a questionnaire may be engaging in an act more closely akin to tossing a quarter in a box marked "donations" next to a stack of free newspapers than to contributing to the store of community resources.

Equally difficult to predict is whether or not the virtual space can serve as a locus for the formation of personal relationships. With rare exceptions, Web "surfers" retrieve biographies and pictures, fill out forms and questionnaires without ever experiencing a sense of the presence of another. While the increasingly popular access counters can inform surfers that they are among large numbers of visitors to a Web site, these machine-generated numbers are merely a tabulation, like the index on a turnstile, and consumers downloading files and filling out forms are invisible to each other. Typical Web sites invite contributions through private e-mail or questionnaire response. Unless a Web site includes in its design a feature which automatically displays form submissions, these contributions are made in virtual privacy, and only the recipient, that is, the Web site owner, benefits. If a Web site is to accommodate relationship formation, the owner must provide and maintain some virtual venue in which visitors can commune. It is not enough for surfers to know that there are other surfers "out there somewhere," they must be able to identify and message each other somehow. For this, surfers are at the mercy of the Web site designer or owner. The popularity of Usenet gives evidence that even the asynchronous technology of newsgroup messaging is satisfying to electronic communicators. Thus, the Web site owner who promises to update pages to include messages from the visitors provides a minimal opportunity for relationship formation. However, the realization that the owner must make constant efforts to update the page, or footnotes indicating great passages of time since the last update, may prompt visitors to pass on what seems likely to be a futile attempt at ongoing interaction.

Finally, virtual communities whose existence is primarily online, as opposed to physical world communities who conduct some but not all of their activities offline, are at a disadvantage in that there is little in the network or in network technology as currently constituted that encourages commitment. There are few "no-exit" relationships in cyberspace, and the term "surfing the Net" is an apt descriptor of the depth of much online activity.

Paradoxically, then, while the architecture of the WWW includes both the rich complexity and the capacity for synchronicity which, following Shirky's (1995) logic, should facilitate the formation of electronic communities, that same architecture renders the WWW even more susceptible to the free-riding that Ostrom (1990) identified as a threat to community formation and well-being. The organizational challenge of community formation in this virtual space may, ironically, be even greater than that of its text-based ancestors, and the question to be answered is: "Can the WWW ever live up to its already popular conception as a global community, or will the technologically advanced network revert to little more than a global-access data base, as was the original Internet?"

The Tele-Garden

To explore some of these issues we undertook an experiment in creating a planned virtual community, one in which the virtual space invites participation and encourages return visits. The Tele-Garden is a telerobotic art installation accessible via the World Wide Web in which remote visitors can participate, manipulating an industrial robotic arm to control a color CCD camera, plant phlox, eggplant and other flora, and water their own and others' seedlings. The Tele-Garden was created to provide a testbed for a new generation of low-cost "point-and-click" devices for control of a robotic apparatus over wide-area networks, to explore the ability of networked telerobotics to create a sense of telepresence (extending the body through space), and to provide a laboratory for the study of emerging online community.

Visitors to the site on the WWW can manipulate the robotic arm with an attached color video camera, enabling them to navigate the garden and view it from multiple perspectives, as well as view the activities of current robot operators, and exchange messages with others at the site via a messaging system called Village Square Chat. Members can make "fly-by" or time-lapse movies of the garden and post them for viewing and critique by fellow gardeners (Goldberg et al., 1995).

A sense of community membership is encouraged through a registration procedure, a searchable membership list, and pointers to the homepages of members, as well as logs in which planting and watering activity can be recorded. In theory, members have to return to the Web site frequently to water and monitor the progress of seeds they have planted. A resource allocation scheme was put in place such that in order to plant his or her first seed, a member must demonstrate commitment by accumulating a minimum of 100 "hits" or accesses of the system. Additional opportunities to plant could be earned by accumulating 500 and then 1,000 hits.

As of May 6, 1996, the Garden had a total of 7,102 registered members with active accounts. Between July 1, 1995 and May 8, 1996, these members accrued 141,442 hits. The number of people who visited the Garden as Guests tallied 67,694 as of May 6. These guests were active as well, accruing a total 260,482 hits. Most visitors were directed to the Garden by friends, came across it through Yahoo! or similar search/cataloguing engines, or read about it in the popular press and narrow-interest publications. Additional publicity for the site was garnered when it was awarded the Kobe Award at the Interactive Media Festival in June 1995.

The logs from the Tele-Garden's Village Square Chat are yielding a rich vein of data on communication patterns and practices in the new interactive medium, in particular those factors known to indicate community formation: the emergence of primary interpersonal relationships; the development of group identity and distinctiveness; the evolution of norms, standards, and sanctions; and the creation of mechanisms for control of the community space. Our study of the Tele-Garden user interface provided feedback on how the system could be adapted to accommodate the needs and limitations of its audience. In the studies reported below, archives of message logs were examined for evidence of community-conscious discourse, part of a continuing effort to understand the underpinnings of the virtual collective. Study 1 reports on a quantitative analysis of coded message log data during the initial stages of the Tele-Garden project, focusing on gross indicators of community. Study 2 reports on a qualitative analysis of messages posted to Village Square Chat during a period of developing community, four to six months after the project was initially opened to the public. Particular attention is given to a small group of heavy users of the Tele-Garden system, and to their constitution as a dynamic, working community within the larger community of registered members. Of special interest are the efforts by members of this community to work out standards of appropriate conduct and develop methods of dealing with putative violations of standards.

User Interface Study

In a pilot assessment, the telepresence system used in the Tele-Garden was tested with a focus group who evaluated the interface using an online questionnaire measuring user satisfaction with screen factors such as the display of graphics, the underlying logic of the hypertext structure, system feedback, steepness of the learning curve with respect to techniques for driving the robotic arm, richness of the telepresence experience, and quality of the messaging system. After the first interface study, refinements to the Tele-Garden in the form of expanded help menus and a tutorial were added to the system. The questionnaire used in the study and a detailed report of the results of the focus group study is available at http://www.usc.edu/dept/annenberg/museum/members/study.html.

Study 1

Coding of Village Square Chat Messages   Archives of messages posted to Village Square Chat between July 26, 1995 and October 15, 1995 served as the database for the present investigation. Messages were posted from 841 unique userids; total message volume was 7,942. A coding sample of 800 messages was drawn from the archive at four intervals approximately seventeen days apart. The first sample of 200 contiguous messages began on August 18, after planting had been implemented in the garden. Subsequent 200-message samples were drawn on September 4, September 21, and October 9.

Archived messages were of the following form:

IQ(FORUM)(userid) (Sun,Oct 15 05:16:52)$Well, it's time for me to hit the shower and get ready to go to church. Don't anybody step on my seeds while I'm gone. <g>

IQ(FORUM)(userid) (Sun,Oct 15 05:16:53)$[Username] . . . you of course know I was only teasing . . . [Username] did tell me 40 hits are needed . . . I believe it is why so many people decry there [sic] seed is not sprouting . . . that and these dang eggplants are super slow germinators that need tons of water. . . .

Messages actually seen on-screen in the Village Square Chat window feature the individual user names, which for most members include at a minimum their real first name and last initial. We have stripped off the names from the examples and refer to individual posters as userid1, userid2, etc., to distinguish different speakers within a contiguous series of messages. The id numbers do not identify any particular speaker across episodes. Identical reloads of previous messages and posts from "AIs" (scripts) were not included in the 200-message samples. Thus we postponed consideration of such interesting exchanges as the following for another day.

Data recorded during coding for the present investigation were date, time, message category, use of language other than English, intended message recipient (developer or member/guest), message length, Tele-Garden role of the message poster (developer, member, guest), total number of messages the poster had contributed to Village Square Chat, the poster's location (USA/other), the poster's total number of "hits" or accesses of the Tele-Garden pages, and whether or not the poster listed a WWW homepage.

Messages were coded into one of three categories: conventional, interpersonal, and communal. Messages coded into the conventional category included greetings and farewells, announcing one's availability to communicate, chatting about the weather, and other staples with which everyday social intercourse is managed among strangers. Conventional messages rely on cultural-level understandings about how discourse is opened and closed, and what strangers may properly say to one another. Conventional messages assume little or no interpersonal-level knowledge of other interlocutors, nor do they disclose personal information about the speaker to which others would not have ready access.

Messages coded into the interpersonal category were those in which the personal identities of the message poster and/or others online or among the membership were invoked, but the messages did not specifically address issues related to the Tele-Garden as a community. Messages coded into the interpersonal category were those which: (1) served to establish the individual's identity or persona; (2) acknowledged the persona of one or more other members; (3) sought a personal relationship with another member; and/or (4) evidenced an existing relationship with another member.

Members established their unique individual identities by such techniques as naming and then announcing the names of their plants, providing pointers to or inviting other members to their homepages, and announcing their planting and watering activities. Acknowledgement of others included demonstrating pre-existing awareness of another member's homepage, number of hits, or planting and watering activities, complimenting others on their plants or movies, or reporting on a visit to their Web pages. Pursuit of interpersonal relationships was evidenced by such messages as invitations to migrate to another chat forum or to send e-mail, disclosing personal information to which other parties would not ordinarily have access, or pointing out commonalities with another.

Finally, messages were categorized as interpersonal if they evidenced an existing dyadic exchange with another named member. References to sending or receipt of e-mail were included. References to planned meetings in Village Square Chat, mutual friends or real-world encounters were coded into this category, as was engaging in online play (e.g. chess in Village Square Chat, or, as one member announced, $Party in Q [sector]9! :))

Messages were categorized as communal if the primary focus of the message was on the Tele-Garden, its members, and their joint activities as members of a virtual community. Messages were coded as communal if they: (1) were oriented to the establishment of norms, standards of conduct, or the socialization of newcomers; (2) addressed the scheme for allocation of resources in the Tele-Garden's virtual economy; (3) bespoke a sense of group identity or group self-consciousness; (4) contributed to the collective knowledge store or wisdom of the virtual commons; or (5) evidenced collaborative activity in the pursuit of common goals.

With respect to the establishment of norms and standards, the ability to extend the reach of the body through space via teleoperation of the robotic arm increases the range of action beyond what can be accomplished through text-based messaging. In the absence of an imposed code of behavior, an increased range of possible action should lead to the development of new rules and norms to govern conduct and foster cooperative interaction. For example, during the period in question there was no mechanism inherent in the Tele-Garden apparatus to prevent members from sabotaging each other's plants by crushing them with the robotic arm, planting on top of another's plant, posting pornographic pictures in the chat window, or writing a script to flood the garden with repeated clicks of the "water" icon, and in fact some of these events did occur, although most members were unaware of them.

The scheme for allocating resources in the garden, in which the ability to plant is provided in exchange for a fixed number of accesses of the system, requires members to weigh their own self-interest versus that of the members at large. Sometimes the self-interest wins, as members waste bandwidth hitting "reload" and posting messages to themselves in order to accumulate hits.

Messages addressed to the appropriateness of these and other anti-social or negligent actions (e.g. planting on top of another's seedling) were coded into the communal category. Posts which reflected a sense of group self-consciousness or group identity (references to Gardeners or Fellow Tele-Gardeners), use of garden/water-related metaphors (e.g. Hurricane Felix), explicit references to the Tele-Garden as a virtual community, metacommunication about messages posted in Village Square Chat, participation in rituals such as paging other members to watch while a first seed is planted, or fantasizing about the garden and its members were coded as communal messages. Also included were philosophical discourses about the meaning of the garden.

Much activity in the Tele-Garden revolves around building the collective knowledge store of the group through questions and answers about how the system works, particularly with respect to the machinations of the robotic arm. Other items in this category of communal-level messaging included seeking or providing information about Web browsers, providing (software) bug reports, and sharing links to other resources on the Web about gardening and telerobotics.

Posted messages which evidenced collaborative action to achieve communal goals include reports of taking action for the common good, such as watering dry areas, volunteering to water others' plants during their vacation, making proposals for improvements or additions to the system, and discussing ways to influence the developers.

Analysis of Study 1 Data   Intercoder agreement between two coders was assessed on a reliability sample of 100 messages. Obtained percentages of agreement were: date, 1.00; time, .99; message, .80; use of language other than English, 1.00; intended recipient of message, .96; message length, .95; Tele-Garden role, .98; number of messages posted, .98; location of the message poster, .99; number of hits, .99; and listing of a home page, .95. Disagreements with respect to machine-coded variables were due to keystroking errors and were corrected; other discrepancies were reconciled and recoded. Because there is no record of number of hits, homepages, or place of residence for unregistered members, missing data for "Guests" (n = 47) posting messages to Village Square Chat reduced the number of observations . available for certain of the analyses to 753. Obtained frequencies from coding of the messages were: conventional messages, n = 160; interpersonal messages, n = 268; and communal messages, n = 372. Thus slightly less than half (46.5 percent) of the messages posted during the sampled periods were oriented to the Tele-Garden as a virtual community.

Predictors of Conventional, Interpersonal, and Communal Messaging   A series of contingency-table analyses were carried out to determine if the type of message posted was associated with any of the categorial variables: whether the message was in English or in another language; whether or not the message was explicitly addressed to Tele-Garden developers; whether the person posting was a developer, member, or guest; whether or not the message was posted from someone living outside the United States; and whether or not the message poster provided a pointer to his/her own homepage. Significant associations were found for all but one of the variables. Posts in languages other than English were found only in the conventional message category (chi-square = 17.05, p < .01). Guests were more likely to post conventional messages than other types, whereas developer and member messages were more likely to be interpersonal or communal than conventional (chi-square = 20.92, p < .001). Proportionately fewer interpersonal and communal messages were posted from members outside the United States (chi-square = 21.36, p < .001). Proportionately fewer conventional messages were posted by members providing links to their own homepages (chi-square = 18.62, p < .0001). No significant associations were obtained between message type and the intended message recipient.

A stepwise discriminant analysis was conducted on the coded messages to assess which of the continuous variables—message length, poster's number of messages, and poster's number of hits—distinguished among conventional, interpersonal, and communal messages. A preliminary analysis indicated that there were significant univariate differences for message type for all three of the variables. Mean lengths for messages by type were: conventional, 6.92, interpersonal, 16.09, and communal, 16.73, $F = 40.5$, $p < .0000$. Mean number of messages posted to Village Square Chat by authors of conventional messages was 163.07; by authors of interpersonal messages, 273.80; and by authors of communal messages, 307.57, $F = 9.27$, $p < .0001$. Mean number of hits by authors of conventional messages was 1441.20; by authors of interpersonal messages, 2526.40, and by authors of communal messages, 2721.44, $F = 11.23$, $p < .0000$. A discriminant analysis designed to test the multivariate-analysis-of-variance hypothesis that message type differed on one or more linear combinations of the three variables produced one discriminant function which maximally discriminated between the three message types (Function 1, lambda = .87, chi-square = 105.33, $p < .0001$). The second discriminant function did not account for a sufficiently large amount of the between-group variability to warrant further attention. Group means on the discriminant function were conventional, −.80, interpersonal, .12, and communal, .22. The obtained value of Box's M (105.31, $p > .0001$) indicated that the group covariance matrices were not homogeneous, however. Further, a test of the predictive ability of the discriminant function indicated although the linear combination of the three variables was able to reclassify 74 percent of the conventional messages correctly, there was much confusion between the interpersonal and communal messages and the overall success of reclassification was only 43 percent. Hence, any obtained differences must be interpreted with caution.

Discussion of Study 1   One of the Tele-Garden developers characterized the role of the founders in maintaining the garden as a sort of purposeful neglect:

> Strangers will rub shoulders with strangers, raising questions of cooperation versus competition in the use of limited resources. The garden could evolve as a green and blooming oasis, or it could become a barren plot. The garden's future has been left up to its "gardeners." (Goldberg, cited in Mankin, 1995)

Our preliminary analysis of the messages sampled from the initial three months of Village Square Chat logs suggests that a significant number of the messages, although less than half of them, could be classified as communal, orienting to the Tele-Garden as a collective of individuals united by common interests. Clearly the data indicate that most communal talk during the data collection period was produced by a core group of registered members who access the system frequently, post messages frequently, tend to be homogeneous with respect to language and national origin, and tend to be more rather than less embedded in the Web as a social network, as evidenced by their having a higher proportion of homepages listed.

However, our observations also indicated that although the Tele-Gardeners were a virtual collective united by demography and common patterns of participation, the road to true community still lay ahead of them.

A visit to the Tele-Garden on a typical day during the first data collection period would likely have revealed that the garden tended to be dry. The image returned by the robotically mounted CCD camera often showed large areas of parched-looking soil. The aerial view indicated that the pattern of planting was uneven; some spots were bare, and others were overcrowded. While analysis of messages posted to Village Square Chat indicated that approximately half of the messages reflected a community-consciousness on the part of the members, that awareness did not seem to have manifested itself in a top-down, concerted collaborative effort to take care of the whole garden. Although the group had members who were extremely verbose, it did not appear at this point to have had leaders. Such collaborative activity as there was consisted mainly in one individual helping another to reach his or her individual goals. Little of the talk was directed to organizing for collective action to benefit the garden, nor was there much discussion of how resources ought to be allocated. The allocation scheme was taken as an externally imposed given, to be either acquiesced to or worked around through various stratagems.

Reading through the message corpus, coders were struck by two things: (1) the repetitive and largely unproductive nature of most of the discussion, centering on whether the robot was working, when the robot would be working, how the robot worked, and how resources were allocated; and (2) the apparent absence of a core of primary interpersonal relationships formed through the Village Square. Such personal discourse as was present and available through the public messaging windows tended to be devoted to fairly superficial topics. Members' personal knowledge of each other appeared to be limited largely to their respective numbers of hits, their country of origin, and so on. Although there were occasional indicators of relationships being conducted offline, in comparison to the lively and sometimes intimate discourse which characterizes many other conferencing and chat venues, in particular Usenet news and chat forums on commercial online services, Village Square Chat messaging seemed peculiarly flat, largely overwhelmed by members' continuing wonder at the technical accomplishments of the project. It would not be too much of a stretch to say that, early on, the community itself did not attract because the charms of its members were eclipsed by the technology.

A write-up of Study 1 was posted on the Web and a pointer to it provided by the Tele-Garden developers. Available evidence from an access counter and logs of posts to Village Square Chat indicated that only a handful of members consulted the report, although all of the individuals whose messages were quoted in the report were aware of the existence of the study, having been asked for permission to incorporate their posts as examples in the write-up.

Study 2

The Tele-Garden continued to develop and attract new members as well as visits from old ones for many months after the first study concluded. Subsequent analysis of the messages logs began to suggest our initial conclusion that what little evidence of true community was present could stand to be re-examined. There are several grounds on which the methods used in Study 1 are susceptible to criticism. First, it is probably the case that even virtual communities take time to form, the instantaneous nature of their communications notwithstanding. Perhaps relationships that were in a nascent state during the initial analysis crystallized after the data collection period concluded. Perhaps as time passed the members became inured to the technological brilliance of the project and the "gee whiz" quality of the discourse was replaced by a meatier vein of discussion.

Also, in the initial study the methodology was to examine and catalogue every message sent to Village Square Chat during a prescribed coding interval. Indeed, many of the posted messages continued to consist of banal, stultifyingly trivial prattle. But among a small group of participants, primarily the "big hitters" (members who had accumulated a lot of hits), a tightly knit, protective community began noticeably to emerge. To analyze messages sent by every passer-by who happened to serendipitously click on a hot link while surfing is perhaps not as useful as examining only the dialogue of those few individuals who visited the Garden on a daily basis, communicated with each other outside of the Garden, and actively cared for the Garden, as well as contributed to the Village Square Chat. Indeed, given the transient nature of much of the interaction on the Internet and the architecture of the World Wide Web, it would be surprising if each and every user of the Garden became a part of the community, especially given the large number of registered members.

A third issue lies in the coding of greetings and farewells, announcing one's availability and chatting about the weather, and other staples with which everyday social intercourse is managed among strangers, as conventional messages, meaning that they neither assume interpersonal-level knowledge of other interlocutors, nor convey personal information about the speaker. It may be the case that such messages are common among strangers, but they are also common among people with intimate knowledge of each other: parents, spouses, friends. Almost all of the heavy contributors to the Garden greet each other, and in fact appear to be slightly miffed when their presence on the system is not acknowledged in this way. In the interaction captured below, for example, one participant recognizes another and says hello. Realizing that there are others logged on, and that she has committed a *faux pas*, she then acknowledges all the other people present at the time. This example illustrates a general tendency for greetings to be exchanged between friends as well as strangers; therefore to code all greetings as conventional might be problematic.

IQ(FORUM)userid1 (Tue,Jan 16 08:51:45)$Hi Hans!
IQ(FORUM)userid2 (Tue,Jan 16 08:52:40)$Where are my manners?
$Hi to everyone else here, too!

One might also question the validity of the coding scheme, in that it fails
to take into account the unique aspects of long-distance, asynchronous
communication. For example, two strangers at a bus stop who discuss the
rain are probably engaging in conventional communication. One could
argue that the unique variable that makes the bus stop conversation about
the weather impersonal and banal is that fact that the two strangers are
located in the same immediate physical environment: they both see that it
is raining. However, the same conversation when exchanged by two
strangers conversing via the Internet might serve an entirely different
purpose. Communicating about this type of information may be a way for
participants to transcend the communication barriers imposed by the lack
of a shared physical environment.

For the second study, we took a closer look at the message logs from the
Village Square Chat from November 6, 1995 to January 27, 1996. As in
the earlier study, many of the postings fell into the category of mundane,
trivial banter. Most of the members had a fleeting or superficial relationship with the Garden and other members. But during this stage in the
life of the Tele-Garden message logs began to evidence the existence of a
close-knit, intimate community among a small group of participants,
perhaps twelve or so members, who logged in frequently, spent considerable time chatting in the Village Square, recognized each other and
commented on absences, exchanged private e-mail, and on occasion paged
each other with "PowWow" (a conferencing software) so that they could
surf the Net or visit other chat locales together. Below we examine in
detail some of the canonical indicators of community as they are played
out among the emerging group of regulars. Of particular note is the
increasing complexity and richness of the messages in comparison to the
examples provided for Study 1.

Fixed Identity of Members   One hallmark of community in the "real
world" is that members are likely to be known to one another and to have
a fixed identity; that is, they can be counted on to be Joe and not Jim (or
Joe and not Joan) from one day to the next. The architecture of the Tele-
Garden discourages anonymity, because members must have a valid e-mail
address in order to register, and members are encouraged to provide
pointers to their homepages. A member's materializing in the Village
Square generates acknowledgements, and prolonged absence invites
comment:

IQ(FORUM)userid1 (Fri,Nov 10 13:50:11)$great . . . I gonna have my secretary
call eve . . . she hasn't been here all day . . .

Member identities are assumed to be genuine; in fact, they are used by members to hold one another accountable for conduct. For example, one person popped into the Garden, sent the following message, and then left:

IQ(FORUM)userid1 (Sat,Dec 30 10:10:30)$You are all losers! Get a life and plant outside!

The remark elicited the following response:

IQ(FORUM)userid2 (Sat,Dec 30 10:38:43)$I wonder if hypocrytical [sic] (because he too is a member) Mr. userid1 usually plants his bean crop on December 30th? If so, his outdoor heating bill must be enormous. Very foolish of you userid1.

Another member sent the person in question a scalding e-mail and then reported it to the Tele-Garden group.

IQ(FORUM)userid3 (Sat,Dec 30 13:56:44)$just a copy of my E to userid1 . . . $Just a note to let you know how much the garden gang appreciated your fertilizer. . . . $with the s**t you post the plants should do well . . . btw . . . nice homepage. . . . $ $
Userid3 $
"The Garden Mayor" $
http://www.*******.***/~****/

Members will frequently draw upon available resources to learn more about each other. Since the Tele-Garden provides links to members' homepages, many explore members' Web sites to gain information about their appearance, hobbies, interests, and families. These homepages, which can be easily accessed by clicking on the hyperlinked Uniform Resource Locator (URL) next to the member's e-mail address and location, serve as constructed identities to replace the usual person perception process that results from face-to-face interaction.

Distinctions between real and "play" or "pretend" identities in the garden are clear. Members may re-register and adopt a new persona for fun, but rarely was a persona assumed to make fools of others or to show off programming mastery, as occurs not infrequently on Internet Relay Chat (IRC) (Marvin, 1995).

Pursuit of Interpersonal Relationships   Often, members who want to "speak" privately will leave the Garden to engage in more intimate discourse. Frequently they will make plans to call each other on the telephone, send private e-mail, or use conferencing software like PowWow. In the following episode, a member who wants to talk privately includes a link to software that will enable another member to converse with him outside of the Tele-Garden environs.

IQ(FORUM)userid1 (Tue,Jan 16 00:16:24)$userid2 Honey . . . have you fallen and can't get up? $
IQ(FORUM)userid2 (Tue,Jan 16 00:17:03)$can you put on pcAnywhere?
IQ(FORUM)userid1 (Tue,Jan 16 00:17:33)$If I knew how I would. $
IQ(FORUM)userid2 (Tue,Jan 16 00:19:02)$I think my page makes a reference to the latest version I use . . . <A HREF="http://www.********.***/~ld******/*****.htm">hint</A>
IQ(FORUM)userid1 (Tue,Jan 16 00:19:34)$Wow that was sly, userid2!!!
IQ(FORUM)userid2 (Tue,Jan 16 00:21:03)$d-click the icon, dial-up can't be active. Hit the [be a host button]. $and wait for call . . .
IQ(FORUM)userid1 (Tue,Jan 16 00:22:29)$Bye all!

Rites and Rituals   As in other virtual communities, members of the Tele-Garden engage in many rituals associated with community, such as greeting each other and exchanging mail. The Garden members also engage in virtual rituals that are indications of community formation in the real world but have little meaning in cyberspace: for example, "going out to drinks after a hard day at the office." The Tele-Garden Happy Hour includes virtual drinks, toasts, and a friendly bartender. It is especially interesting that elements of this ritual that have no real meaning as virtual simulacra are fastidiously observed. For example, one participant will usually "pick up the tab," although obviously one has not been created. Also, participants will sometimes "decline drinks" if it is too early in the morning or if they have to drive, a curious condition in which real and imaginary worlds are seemingly enmeshed.

The Tele-Garden community also engages in rituals unique to the Tele-Garden, its architecture, and mythology. For example, when one member earns enough hits to plant a seed, the moment is usually publicly acknowledged and the proud parent congratulated. In one incident two members who had formed a close relationship decided to plant a seed together. The online event was fraught with marital and sexual innuendo: a location was carefully chosen, witnesses summoned, and festive cocktails dispensed.

IQ(FORUM)userid1 (Sat,Nov 11 17:46:31)$yes userid2 . . . cant you tell the garden has been a bit quiet . . . we are here for a special occasion tonight . . .
IQ(FORUM)userid1 (Sat,Nov 11 17:56:12)$dont do that userid3 . . . I didnt get 8000 hits by not knowing my $way around this garden . . . go to d4 . . . my old spot . . . all those seeds planted around me are Eggplants . . . and they aint going nowhere . . . $we will consumate [*sic*] this relationship on the 8000 hit . . . lol
IQ(FORUM)userid2 (Sat,Nov 11 17:59:24)$userid3 ,You know the old saying. Them that plants together,------together.
IQ(FORUM)userid1 (Sat,Nov 11 17:59:55)$7994 . . . a couple more squirts my love and we will be ready . . . lol $
IQ(FORUM)userid3 (Sat,Nov 11 18:00:26)$userid2 . . . lol . . . would you like one of my famous Strawberry Margarita's? Anyone else?
IQ(FORUM)userid1 (Sat,Nov 11 18:00:58)$hey userid2 we need a witness . . . and bring userid4 . . . well party . . .
IQ(FORUM)userid3 (Sat,Nov 11 18:01:01)$I watered a bit for us, so the ground would be ready . . .

IQ(FORUM)userid2 (Sat,Nov 11 18:01:42)$userid3, I'd love one. Could userid4 have one too. I'll pay allround [*sic*].
IQ(FORUM)userid2 (Sat,Nov 11 18:08:07)$userid2 bows head in reverence waiting for the moment.
IQ(FORUM)userid2 (Sat,Nov 11 18:10:38)$userid2 holds userid4's hand to add tenterness [*sic*] to the occasion . . .

Hierarchy and Social Status   Social status in the real world is constituted by many things: age, wealth, power. The Tele-Garden community uses hit counts as a sort of ready-made hierarchy in which top hitters are granted respect and admiration. This hierarchy is observed by those with very few hits and little social capital as well as by those comfortably ensconced in its higher regions. In this incident, a "Top Hitter" proposes to discount the comment made by a newbie with very few hits and therefore little social capital:

IQ(FORUM)userid1 (Mon,Nov 6 15:36:12)$He only has 223 points. He doesn't count yet. Unless he is nice. He already proved he nothing to say.

The members of the Garden seem to have slightly ambivalent attitudes toward the issue of getting hits. On one hand, accruing hits implies a long-term relationship with and commitment to the Garden, and therefore translates into respect and power in the Garden. On the other hand many members seem to consider it tasteless to try to accrue hits just for the sake of getting a higher hit count. These contradictory and sometimes confusing thoughts about hits are illustrated by the following discussion:

IQ(FORUM)userid1 (Sun,Nov 19 05:40:53)$My daughter thinks that userid3 is overwatering his plants $just to get points. She thinks that maybe the garden will become so boggy $that the robot will fall through.
IQ(FORUM)userid2 (Sun,Nov 19 05:42:06)$I reckon that it is not a garden at all but some computer $program!
IQ(FORUM)userid1 (Sun,Nov 19 05:45:03)$Some people will post messages just to get hits. Shame isn't it !
IQ(FORUM)userid2 (Sun,Nov 19 05:46:55)$Does it actually count though? $
IQ(FORUM)userid1 (Sun,Nov 19 05:47:51)$userid1 it is not true that some people post to get hits. $Some other people are well known for talking to themselves $Are you sure, userid1 ? $Yes I'm certain.
IQ(FORUM)userid4 (Sun,Nov 19 06:00:12)$userid1. It's a real problem in the Garden. Some people are overclicking, just to make hits. $I got 8400 hits but really work hard for it trying to respect the community and have the Garden grown correctly.
IQ(FORUM)userid3 (Sun,Nov 19 06:01:59)$userid4 do you think I have been some of those people?
IQ(FORUM)userid1 (Sun,Nov 19 06:02:05)$OK userid3—We accept your excuses for the watering. $Considering we're amateurs building up hits $for our first seed, we have no right to criticize. I am also middle aged (a horrible expression) $Hope your seed grows up soon !! $
IQ(FORUM)userid1 (Sun,Nov 19 06:03:41)$userid4. We have great respect for anyone with so many hits. $Bonne chance, mon ami

A Distinctive Culture   The Tele-Garden community's creation of an alternative universe, unique to the Garden, also speaks to the strong culture of play created by the WWW site. For example, two participants appropriate the online personae of Adam and Eve (as befitting a Garden) and engage passionately in dramas featuring these characters, at times to the discomfort of others who happen to be in the Garden. Sometimes the scenes created by the participants are quite vivid and detailed:

> IQ(FORUM) userid1 (Fri,Nov 10 14:02:53)$Ignored by [system admin], the Barbarian is virtually alone in the garden. Apple cores are on the ground. The snake is still in the tree. The piano is silent. No bar tender, but it's still early. The Barbarian waits a bit longer.
> IQ(FORUM)userid2 (Fri,Nov 10 14:03:21)$hey [system admin] . . .
> IQ(FORUM)userid1 (Fri,Nov 10 14:04:37)$Adam appears, looking spiffy in his newly pressed fig leaf.
> IQ(FORUM)userid1 (Fri,Nov 10 14:06:16)$The barbarian decides to go off and compute the language of graph isomorphism, intending to return later.
> IQ(FORUM)userid2 (Fri,Nov 10 14:06:21)$A soft errie [sic] blues waifts [sic] from the willows . . . satanic beauty slides on bark so rough, eve can here it approaching. . . .

At other times the members evoke a medieval virtual world, complete with its own lexicon and carefully ordered court consisting of a Queen, a Prince and Princess, and various knaves, ladies, barons, and knights. Here, one participant explains the world to a newbie:

> IQ(FORUM) userid1 (Thu,Dec 28 15:59:42)$Alan—I have met some of the nicest people on the Net here—it really is a good place.—we meet often—chat and drink together and a lady called userid2 believes it is like King Arthur's Court and some of them have been given Royal Titles and have to CHAT accordingly. $She is Princess Eve—userid3 is Queen—userid4 is a Baron etc.

This incident, in which "Queen" userid3 asks "Prince" Adam about HTML, is a good example of the pseudo-Olde English dialect they use:

> IQ(FORUM) userid3 (Wed,Nov 29 05:31:48)$I hope to have it finished by March. $Well so much for being creative. All that and you missed it $Well the jest was: $Pray tell sweet Prince but if our memory is not flawed we remember that thou had at one time bespok of semding us a how to on making our very own home page. Has thou forgotten or is it ins some way that our mind has mis-remembered?

Commitment   Another indication of the strong community formed in the Tele-Garden can be seen in the way the members speak about the Garden, and in the fact that many of the regulars have pointers to it on their homepages. They often articulate their devotion to the Garden and the extent to which they value the relationships they have formed there:

> IQ(FORUM)userid1 (Thu,Dec 21 14:22:15)$The power of the garden! $Yesterday userid3 had an awful day at work—came home tired and fed up—she entered

the garden—had a long chat on her own with userid2—came down afterwards feeling 100% better. $Long live the Garden. $It can even solve your problems.

The oft-rumored closure of the Tele-Garden, due to expiration of its funding, is a steady topic of conversation among the participants. Many express grief at the thought and several times members actively searched for another virtual forum in which to meet.

"Sinning" in the Garden　In addition to the characteristics of the Garden detailed above, which seem to be indicative of nascent community, there were numerous incidents of remedial sequences in the Garden, episodes in which a guest member acted or spoke in a manner that others felt was untoward, and was publicly chastised for his or her behavior. These episodes are considered to be one of the hallmarks of community, according to the accounts and explanations literature (McLaughlin et al., 1995). Most such episodes, unlike a protracted sequence we will describe later, appeared to have been fully worked out within a single, encapsulated series of messages. Polite reminders that the Garden resources needed to be shared by all were not uncommon. Such episodes were important to the development of a set of shared understandings about how the system could be used to maximize outcomes for everyone:

> IQ(FORUM)userid1 (Tue,Jan 9 23:02:49)$I agree, I was just wondering how much you were going to water there . . . $otherwise I was going to water my plant.
> IQ(FORUM)userid2 (Tue,Jan 9 23:04:39)$Sorry userid1, I have my camera turned off to speed up pages. I'll move.
> IQ(FORUM)userid3 (Tue,Jan 9 23:04:52)$I understand userid1 just a little parental responsibility showing I guess. Userid2 10 squirts a day no wonder my 1st didn't survive. Now thats something they should mention when they revamp.

As hierarchy and status within the garden have much to do with the degree of commitment a member has demonstrated to the project, failure to recognize a regular as such could generate a reproach:

> IQ(FORUM)userid1 (Sat,Dec 30 21:06:25)$Thanks userid2 but i'm not new!!! . . .
> IQ(FORUM)userid2 (Sat,Dec 30 21:07:39)$userid3, click on the center of the robot arm. It'll take you to the Village Square. You can chat easier here and there's an Update button to update the chat for you.
> IQ(FORUM)userid2 (Sat,Dec 30 21:08:27)$Yes, now I see you're not new, userid1. I had you confused with userid3. Sorry.

One form of untoward conduct which was recurrent and which was particularly galling to the members was when less frequent visitors seemed to imply, or in some cases baldly proclaim, that the members' intense involvement in the Tele-Garden community was *prima facie* evidence that they "had no life."

IQ(FORUM)userid1 (Mon,Nov 6 15:23:13)$Now this is living. What more could anyone want.
IQ(FORUM)userid1 (Mon,Nov 6 15:24:00)$Ta da. 6000+
IQ(FORUM)userid2 (Mon,Nov 6 15:24:36)$brb guys . . . My dog is going crazy . . . The someone I hate bark . . . $brb. . . .
IQ(FORUM)userid3 (Mon,Nov 6 15:25:00)$A life? (A guess)

Much negative reaction and a subsequent reproach to the purveyor of this "guess" led to an apology, an account, gracious forgiveness, but with no obvious concession by the perpetrator with respect to the positive values of the online life:

IQ(FORUM)userid2 (Mon,Nov 6 16:08:06)$Let me help you with that question. . . . first "click" on the $center of the robots arm . . . Here you will find members in the $garden and the amount of hits they have . . . Next to USERID1 (who $you told to get a life) is over 6000 hits . . . hits spent $helping us all enjoy life with her wit and wisdom . . . something $you have little of . . . [signature] . . .
IQ(FORUM)userid3 (Mon,Nov 6 17:51:50)$Hi ya'll, I come and go, You hardly know i've been here. $btw userid2, IT WAS JUST A JOKE! Tongue in cheek so to speak.
IQ(FORUM)userid2 (Mon,Nov 6 17:55:51)$well tell userid1 that the next time you see her . . . and in here $you come you go we always know . . .
IQ(FORUM)userid2 (Tue,Nov 7 17:00:03)$userid3 . . . not necessary . . . if i had a nickle [sic] for everything $my fingers said and my mind didnt know why . . . well actually $i do . . . thus this giant house . . . smiling . . . dont worry about it . . . $Eve make my friend userid3 here a Houston slammer . . . enjoy $the garden userid3

The sort of content that could appropriately be posted in the Village Square Chat window was rarely a source for overt discussion by the members, most of whom, like the developers, relied on everyday understandings and assumptions about what sorts of conversational events might occur there. Remedial sequences like those which follow served not only to clarify the values of the members with respect to appropriate limitations on the medium, but also to place the values of loyalty and friendship squarely at the heart of the Garden community.

In a precursor episode, the member who often assumed the online persona of Adam posted a questionable picture ("tiffany.jpg") to the site and was rebuked by another member who worried children might enter the Garden. This incident was followed by a lengthy and uncharacteristically serious discussion about CompuServe's decision to prevent subscribers in Germany from viewing certain newsgroups, The prevailing sentiment was anti-censorship, and the perpetrator appeared less than responsive to the concern expressed by the only woman member online. However, a subsequent posting by "Adam" of a similar picture a few days later invoked the ire of the system administrator, with the result that, after hastily removing the picture from view by uploading a lengthy text document, Adam expelled himself from the garden, apparently not from a concern that he had done something inconsistent with group values, but rather that his action would induce the developers to disable the much-liked feature by which HTML-proficient members and friends could include inline images in their posts:

> IQ(FORUM)system admin (Tue,Jan 2 18:32:23)$Ok, guys. Looks like I gotta disable the img in the village square. $Thanks for screwing it up for the rest of us!!!!
> IQ(FORUM)userid1 (Tue,Jan 2 18:32:28)$smiling . . . okay mich . . . sweet dreams . . .
> IQ(FORUM) userid1 (Tue,Jan 2 18:33:11)$sorry [system admin] . . . there was no one here . . . just playing . . . dont do that . . . $ never happen again. made w [sic] sure we were alone . . .
> IQ(FORUM)userid1 (Tue,Jan 2 18:33:41)$sorry man . . . we were just playing . . .
> IQ(FORUM)userid1 (Tue,Jan 2 18:34:18)$how about if your #1 fan just leaves the garden . . . wont come back if you want . . .
> IQ(FORUM)system admin (Tue,Jan 2 18:34:39)$Ok, but that's strike one.
> IQ(FORUM)userid1 (Tue,Jan 2 18:34:46)$okay? $
> IQ(FORUM)userid1 (Tue,Jan 2 18:35:12)$never again. the boys were just restless . . . $
> IQ(FORUM)system admin (Tue,Jan 2 18:35:27)$Yup.
> IQ(FORUM)userid1 (Tue,Jan 2 18:36:52)$olkay . . . well . . . sorry again . . . userid2 . . . your #1 now . . . tell my friends . . . goodbye . . . see ya all.
> IQ(FORUM)userid2 (Tue,Jan 2 18:38:56)$See you userid1, have a goodnight.
> IQ(FORUM)userid3 (Tue,Jan 2 18:41:54)$Hi [system admin]—Glad to see you're online! What's up with the robot?
> IQ(FORUM)userid2 (Tue,Jan 2 18:43:33)$[system admin]. Don't be shocked and don't disable anything. They have fun and I guess, I have fun as well.
> IQ(FORUM)userid4 (Tue,Jan 2 18:50:43)$Hello folks. I see the robot is still down . . . bummer. Does anyone know what the problem is?
> IQ(FORUM)userid5 (Tue,Jan 2 18:59:20)$Is userid1 serious about leaving?
> IQ(FORUM)userid6 (Tue,Jan 2 19:00:44)$Hi! userid5. That sounded serious

During the following week much discussion about the episode took place among the regulars, both in the Village Square and via private exchanges of e-mail among themselves and with the self-exiled member. No fewer than fourteen of the members made a comment or inquired about the episode. A recurring theme of the discussion was the desire that the departed member reinstate himself, as his lively presence was sorely missed. None of the members posted critical comments. Much talk was directed to the fine qualities of the member, in particular to his many positive contributions to the Garden community. There was also considerable retelling of the episode, reports from "eyewitnesses," and rumor-mongering:

> IQ(FORUM)userid1 (Tue,Jan 9 22:36:50)$userid2, a friend of mine told me that somebody is going around "reporting" to the garden authorities instances of "unsuitable" images posted in the Square. The fingered posters are subsequently e-mail threatened with termination. There also seems to be an effort to track down and delete members with "unnatural" user names. You know anything about this?

After some cajoling the member (the second speaker here) returned to the garden, without ceremony, a week later, marking (and closing) the episode with a little humor:

IQ(FORUM)userid1 (Tue,Jan 9 17:53:52)$userid2, been warm there in ol' So.Cal lately, enjoying the wonderful weather? Still on your [USC] Trojan high . . . smiling . . .
IQ(FORUM)userid2 (Tue,Jan 9 17:55:03)$userid1!!! Dont Say trojan . . . you remember what happened last time . . . $

Conclusion

The technological wonders of the Garden and its robot provided the initial impetus for WWW surfers to explore it. For a small group of them, however, it was the people and community they found there that made them stay, long after the novelty of the robot's magic had worn off. Ample evidence was obtained of the formation of primary interpersonal relationships, a group identity, the evolution of standards of conduct, and methods for repairing the social fabric when it was in need of a mend. The episode in which Adam expelled himself from the Garden is not exactly faithful in its re-creation of the biblical expulsion from the Garden of Eden. The new Adam's sin was hardly original; in fact it was among the most commonplace and pedestrian of Internet events. And in this electronic Paradise, God (system administrators are often said to have "God" powers) decided to give Adam a second chance. Moreover, although Adam elected to exile himself, all were happy to have him return. This episode, and others in which members of electronic communities create and reify group standards through individual and conjoint solutions, is in marked contrast to the kinds of unilateral and top-down governance practiced by larger online communities, who operate in an uncertain legal environment and must answer to multiple competing publics, making mistakes and alienating their subscribers in the process.

David Johnson (1996) has deftly summarized the delicate balance which exists between providers and their agents, on the one hand, and the user community, on the other:

there remain important questions raised by the potential of system operators, or majorities of communities of users, to oppress individuals and minorities.While those who disagree with local rules are free to migrate, many users will have invested very substantial amounts of time and effort in establishing a particular online identity (building a reputation based on a particular e-mail address or Web page location, for example). And many seek to participate actively in particular online cybercommunities, over long periods of time. For them, separation from their cybercommunities would impose a very substantial personal loss. Thus, the check on sysop power provided by the user's right to abandon an online area is importantly mitigated by the costs imposed on the user who walks away.

In all of the foregoing there is an important message to Web developers or to any who provides opportunities for individuals to post or to chat via their systems: even if the chat system is in their own estimation peripheral to the larger project, as it was in the case of the Tele-Garden, in making it available they are also creating an opportunity for interpersonal relationships and user communities to form, an awesome power indeed. Let us hope that all will use their God powers with care.

References

Baym, N.K. (1995). The emergence of community in computer-mediated communication. In S.G. Jones (Ed.), *Cybersociety: Computer-mediated communication and community* (pp. 138–163). Thousand Oaks, CA: Sage.

Beniger, J. (1987). Personalization of mass media and the growth of pseudo-community. *Communication Research, 14*, 352–371.

Curtis, P. (1992). Mudding: Social phenomena in text-based social realities. *Intertek, 3*(3), 26–34.

Fernback, J., & Thompson, B. (1995, May). *Computer-mediated communication and the American collectivity: The dimensions of community within cyberspace.* Paper presented at the annual meeting of the International Communication Association, Albuquerque, NM.

Frederick, H.H. (1993). Computer networks and the emergence of global civil society: The case of the Association for Progressive Communication (APC). In L.M. Harasim (Ed.), *Global networks: Computers and international communication* (pp. 283–295). Cambridge, MA: MIT Press.

Goldberg, K., Santarramano, J., Bekey, G., Gentner, S., Morris, R., Sutter, C., & Wiegley, J. (1995) The Tele-Garden. Available http://www.usc.edu/dept/garden.

Johnson, D.R. (1996). Due process and cyberjurisdiction. *Journal of Computer-Mediated Communication, 2*(1).

Jones, S.G., (1995a) *CyberSociety: Computer-mediated communication and community.* Thousand Oaks, CA: Sage.

Jones, S.G. (1995b). Understanding community in the information age. In S.G. Jones (Ed.), *Cybersociety: Computer-mediated communication and community* (pp. 10–35). Thousand Oaks, CA: Sage.

Kollock, P., & Smith, M. (1994). *The sociology of cyberspace: Social interaction and order in computer communities.* Unpublished manuscript, Department of Sociology, UCLA.

Mankin, E. (1995, June). Press release, University of Southern California.

Marvin, L.E. (1995) Spoof, spam, lurk and log: The aesthetics of text-based virtual realities. *Journal of Computer-Mediated Communication, 1*(2).

McLaughlin, M.L., Osborne, K.K., & Smith, C.B. (1995). Standards of conduct on Usenet. In S.G. Jones (Ed.), *Cybersociety: Computer-mediated communication and community* (pp. 90–111). Thousand Oaks, CA: Sage.

Ostrom, E. (1990). *Governing the commons: The evolution of institutions for collective action.* New York: Cambridge University Press.

Reid, E.M. (1991). Electropolis: Communication and community on Internet Relay Chat. Unpublished manuscript. Available http://www.ee.mu.oz.du/papers/emt/electropolis.html.

Rheingold, H. (1993). *The virtual community: Homesteading on the electronic frontier.* Reading, MA: Addison-Wesley.

Shirky, C. (1995). *Voices from the net.* Emeryville, CA: Ziff-Davis Press.

Smith, C.B., McLaughlin, M.L., & Osborne, K.K. (in press). From terminal ineptitude to virtual sociopathy: How conduct is regulated on Usenet. In F. Sudweeks, M.L.

McLaughlin, & S. Rafaeli (Eds.), *Network and net-play: Virtual groups on the Internet.* Menio Park, CA: AAAI/MIT Press.

Walther, J. (1995, May). *Computer-mediated communication: Impersonal, interpersonal, and hyperpersonal interaction.* Paper presented at the annual meeting of the International Communication Association, Albuquerque, NM.

Walther, J., & Burgoon, J.K. (1992). Relational communication in computer-mediated interaction. *Human Communication Research, 19*(1), 50.

Wilkins, H. (1991). Computer talk: Long-distance conversations by computer. *Written Communication, 8,* 56–78.

8

(Re)-Fashioning the Techno-Erotic Woman: Gender and Textuality in the Cybercultural Matrix

Dawn Dietrich

Rhetorics of Cyberculture

> MAN: *I acknowledge that the use of the term "man" for the concept of humanity is sexist. I use it here as a matter of convenience.*
>
> —R.U. Sirius [Ken Goffman] in Rucker, Sirius, & Mu,
> *Mondo 2000: A User's Guide to the New Edge* (1992), p. 100

As post-industrial culture is increasingly mediated through information technologies, a chief concern for postmodern theorists and feminists alike is how gender intersects with the construction of social matrices and networks. While the print media are still manufacturing verbal and visual representations of "New Edge" culture, increasingly these representations are assuming electronic form in cyberspace, constituting what Baudrillard (1983) terms a "telematic culture." The implications for gender, textuality, and identity within such a culture are great, especially as "technology" and "nature" become increasingly intertwined.

Currently, techno-journals and futuristic zines such as *Mondo 2000*, *Wired*, and *bOing-bOing* inscribe a kind of textual prologue for cyber-culture. They are valuable in themselves because they forge a much needed connection between late print culture and the new cyberspatial network, formatting the matrix of this social space in ways that begin to define it. *Wired* magazine, for instance, participates in a cultural dialogue concerning issues of network privacy, governmental regulation, and censorship. *Wired* also sponsors *HotWired*, its online counterpart, where participants can exchange information, chat with live guests, and buy, sell, or trade computers and software products. *bOing bOing* and *Mondo 2000*, while differing from *Wired* in their hyperbolic presentation, share the techno-journal's fascination with "New Edge" culture, which includes, in addition to a hacker-like obsession with computers, technological phenomena such as raves, body alteration, smart drugs, and techno-spiritual movements. Because the communications revolution has brought about a phenomenological change in our perceptions of lived experience (Sobchack, 1990), these publications could be said to provide a type of public service by offering interfacing media that connect the user-friendly world of print with the phenomenon of cyberspatial networking.

Yet, for all of their cutting-edge potential as links to the democratizing venues of cyberspace or as media for constructing alternative cybertextual practices, many of these techno-journals remain disturbingly vested in the politics of late capitalist culture (Sobchack, 1993). This includes heralding the new technologies in what amounts to an almost nostalgic longing for the ultimate "metanarrative"—the world sewn together through the electronic fibers of the Net—pronouncing technological libertarianism, and combining social consciousness with rampant consumerism.

A feminist analysis seems required, at the very least, to call into question these cultural assumptions, if not to (re)name the politics. To begin it is necessary to situate gender, on the level of representation, within the matrix of computer networking systems; for as Mary Ann Doane (1990) attests, "when technology intersects with the body in the realm of representation, the question of sexual difference is inevitably involved" (p. 163).

Though early representations of cyberspace denied sexual difference by positing the Net as a "gender-neutral zone," recent scholarship has focused on issues specific to gender difference(s) *within* various postmodern technologies. Allucquère Rosanne Stone (1991) offers a feminist interpretation of gendered technologies by deconstructing the act of *penetrating the screen*, an act which she attributes to the heterosexual male user who empowers himself by incorporating the surfaces of cyberspace *into* himself. Here, Stone, argues, "to become the cyborg, to put on the seductive and dangerous cybernetic space like a garment, is to put on the *female*" (p. 109).

Claudia Springer (1993) similarly discusses the "feminization" of virtual technologies, which she distinguishes from the "masculinization" of industrial machines and technologies. Specifically, Springer relates the invisible networking of cyberspatial systems to "conventional ways of thinking about female anatomy and feminine subjectivity" (p. 92). Drawing on Thomas Laqueur's two-sex model of human sexuality, Springer deconstructs women's "inferior" sexual status by arguing that women's bodies are read as the opposite of men's, due to their lack of male genitalia, as well as the association of women with interior, fluctuating spaces of the body (pp. 91–92). Springer sees the feminization of virtual technologies as central to understanding issues of identity and embodiment within cyberspace itself.

From this perspective, then, it seems plausible that male fears regarding *feminine spaces* may become collapsed with naturalized, or invisible, interfacing relations to create a threatening social matrix. As print representatives of the cyberspatial industry, the techno-journals bear out the implications of such a theory through a rhetoric which tends to be sexualized, and sometimes aggressive. It is ironic that even as these publications herald new forms of "egalitarian" networking, they replicate the sexist discourse(s) that mark late capitalist culture, particularly in respect to the representation of women and women's issues.

In large part this is due to the fact that most cybernauts are white males between the ages of 15 and 45. Not surprisingly, then, the rhetoric of these print texts tends to reflect white, heterosexual male perspectives, desire(s) and idealizations. Further, at the cyberspatial sites where many of these techno-journals are inscribed textually and graphically, the narratives tend to be gendered in a binary fashion, yet often lack markers for racial, ethnic, and class difference. Difference in other words, is both exaggerated for heightened visibility and erased for (potentially) exploitative purposes. And because these publications rely strategically upon various modes of ironic discourse, they are able to "neutralize" their own political stance, in effect, defending against criticism through the displacement of their (real) subject(s).

For example, consider *Mondo* editor Ken Goffman's (1992) entry on "Evolutionary Mutations," in *Mondo 2000: A User's Guide to the New Edge*. After drawing attention to the word "man" in the text by placing an outlined box around it, he writes the following textual note: "MAN: I acknowledge that the use of the term 'man' for the concept of humanity is sexist. I use it here as a matter of convenience" (p. 100).[1] On one level, one could imagine that this is a blatant sexist maneuver, or that the writer isn't addressing a mixed audience at all, given the implications of his intended (and informed) sexism (for surely he would recognize that his female readers would prefer their sex be acknowledged before the writer's convenience attained). Such a case might even be compared to the kind of androcentric thinking that governed science textbooks two decades ago, in which women never saw their own sex illustrated in the evolutionary process—only that of men (Morgan, 1972).

On another level, however, it seems possible to locate more specious resonances in this discursive strategy. By drawing attention to what is still, perhaps, a widespread convention of using the term "man" to represent humanity in general, Goffman focuses the reader on the importance of semantics in relation to gender, only then to contradict his gesture by using the term in a way that negates the logic of his statement. While it might be tempting to classify this move as an ironic one (in the classical sense that the writer can't be taken seriously or doesn't mean what he says, especially given Goffman's pen name, R.U. Sirius), the act itself appears more problematic. In this instance, the writer disarms potential critics by assuming a posture of liberal tolerance, only then to "compromise" himself by revealing his complicity in a discourse he appears to oppose. Given the embedded nature of power relations within discourse, this act appears disingenuous and, therefore, serves to reinforce patriarchal values, rather than undermine them.

Postmodern theorists, from Fredric Jameson (1981) to Linda Hutcheon (1994), have focused on irony as a particular rhetorical strategy which carries with it disturbing political implications, depending upon the expression used and the understanding necessary to interpret it. Linda Hutcheon writes,

> Unlike metaphor or allegory, which demand similar supplementing of meaning, irony has an evaluative edge and manages to provoke emotional responses in those who "get" it and those who don't, as well as in its targets and in what some people call its "victims.". . . The "scene" of irony involves relations of power based in relations of communication. (p. 2)

Given such a description, it seems necessary to question the evasive nature of such ironic rhetoric within the context of patriarchal techno-journals, for, in Goffman's instance, *Mondo 2000* is the same publication that prints its subscription cards over images of topless, fetishized women. Might one political outcome be that within certain contexts such rhetorical structures actually work to unsettle any grounds from which they might be criticized? If this is true, what privileges are granted this "ironic" stance? What "liberties" routinely left unchecked?

Another stylistic feature that warrants investigation is the liberatory rhetoric of the techno-journals. Couched within various masculine tropes ranging from the democratic imperative of the "founding fathers" to the *jouissance* of cyberhacking cowboys, this rhetoric has developed alongside an identity of cyberspace itself. "Technopaganism," the latest trope among such trends, raises questions about our very conception(s) of cyberspace. Described by Erik Davis (1995) in *Wired* as an "anarchic, earthy, celebratory spiritual movement that attempts to reboot the magic, myths, and gods of Europe's pre-Christian people" (p. 128), the new technopagans differ from their older counterparts in their claim to achieve divinity through the algorithms of computer interfacing design.

Part New-Age hype, part science-fiction fantasy, these multi-media gurus promise users everything from divine inspiration to physical disembodiment and gender equality—all through the "magic" of cyberspatial networking. And while it is true that most of the 100,000 to 300,000 participants practice their "religion" self-consciously, any levity regarding the matter is usually intermixed with an attitude of utter seriousness. Davis (1995) comments that "technopagans are driven by . . . [a] basic desire: to honor technology as part of the circle of human life, a life that for Pagans is already divine" (p. 128). In a subsidiary article in the same issue of *Wired* Paulina Borsook (1995) claims that this divinity can be symbolized by *female* personae. "Here," she writes, "there are brainiacs and artists and powermongers, in addition to the more traditional archetypes of sexpot and baby-maker and provider of harvests" (p. 133). And she continues, "in goddess-based spiritual practice, women can express their latent sense of potency without feeling they have to be crypto-male" (p. 133). Borsook goes on to state that "technopaganism is the grand exception to the 85-percent-male, 15-percent female demographics of the on-line world. It is one virtual community where rough parity—both in number and power—exists between the sexes" (p. 133).

But a closer look at the fundamental constituency of technopagans suggests a different picture. In Davis's (1995) article, which physically subsumes Borsook's, technopagans are defined as "white folks drawn from bohemian and middle-class enclaves," folks who happen to "work and play in technical fields, as sysops [systems operators], computer programmers, and network engineers" (p. 128). Coupled with the capitalistic enterprise that nearly always accompanies the pagan "rituals," this description comes dangerously close to resembling the mostly male community that generally inhabits cyberspatial networks. For reasons like this, the liberatory rhetoric of the techno-journals casts itself in a dim light.

And while one might hope to find some kind of radical decentering with the *online* counterparts to these techno-journals, there appears to be little difference. Though the technological factors themselves destabilize conventional print structure, it appears that electronic versions of print texts often remain *contextualized within print paradigms* (Aycock & Buchignani, 1995, p. 216).[2] Thus, despite *HotWired*'s claim on its "Welcome Page" (1995) that "the Net and the Web do not just constitute a refinement of old models of publishing and broadcast media, but a vital new medium", *HotWired* is remarkably similar to *Wired* magazine. This means that even with increased access (*HotWired* is free, provided the user has a means to connect with the site) and greater interactivity, the site functions much in the same way the magazine does. The content and the rhetoric are similar to *Wired* magazine, many of the same products are mentioned (or advertised), and most of the editors are male (Ned Brainard, David Kline, and Brock Meeks, for example).

Though *HotWired* prides itself on its financial and editorial independence from *Wired* magazine, it is partially owned by Wired Ventures LLC, the parent company of *Wired* magazine (*HotWired*'s Welcome Page, 1995); and despite claims that the two entities are separate, *HotWired* publishes an index to the articles in *Wired* and admits to being the magazine's home on the Internet. Similarly, there is little evidence to suggest that *HotWired* is the "model of cross-cultural discourse" (*HotWired*'s Welcome Page, 1995) it announces itself to be, though it would be interesting to look for alternatives in electronic journals that do not have print counterparts and which are not supported by corporate funds. For instance, some academic institutions back electronic forums that are designed to encourage critical discussion, and they often publish a wide variety of materials from a diverse group of writers. *C-Theory* is one such example. Sponsored by the *Canadian Journal of Political and Social Theory*, *C-Theory* is an international Web site for book reviews and articles that relate to critical theory and postmodern culture. The range of topics covered, the nature of the critiques received, and the diversity of the contributors themselves distinguish this electronic site from corporate sites such as *HotWired*, *FringeWare*, and *Net*.

Yet one cannot underestimate the power of corporate control on the Internet (see Mutch, 1995). Oftentimes, the rhetoric of the new communication technologies only serves to mystify and obscure the relations of production and labor which structure its very material enterprise. The euphoric praise nearly always associated with virtual systems can act as a kind of smokescreen, in which an emphasis on the end obscures any clear understanding of the means used to get there. This disparity between rhetoric and reality has the most devastating consequences for women, who are usually structured at the bases of operations; so that one has to ask not only to what extent women are disempowered socially through their representation in sexist media, but to what extent they are disenfranchised from a communications market that is tied to the fastest growing technologies in the world.

Virtually Feminine

> *Sometimes feminists attack us, but I don't think a*
> *true feminist should attack another woman.*
> *We should all work together. Why do we have to*
> *choose between being either a bimbo or a militant*
> *bitch? There are all different types of women.*
>
> —Sia Barbi, "Living Dolls," *bOing bOing*, p. 48

Savvy to marketing demands, nearly all of the techno-journals feature some female staff writers, so it appears on the surface of the texts that women's voices comprise a part of the discourse that is shaping the new technologies. Similarly, the occasional article that features a woman involved with the industry is usually written by a female staff person. Yet, many of these staff writers share a remarkably homogeneous voice, and it becomes clear after reading across several issues that it is a particular kind of female voice that is missing—one that would radically question or challenge the tacit assumptions governing the rhetoric of the techno-journals. In a strategic way, much like the use of ironic rhetoric, this practice not only spares the publications outright criticism, but creates an untenable position for feminists who wish to challenge the rhetoric without criticizing the few women who are working in the industry. Interestingly, recent studies have shown that women's conversations on mixed-gender networks often assume a *homogeneity that does not reflect the reality of the network of users.* Researchers attribute this phenomenon to the general lack of consideration or interest given women's topics and concerns (Kramarae & Taylor, 1993, p. 55). Might the same be true of the minority of women who are working within the male-dominant field of communication technologies? How much force is exerted upon the female voice in the context of the cyberspatial industry?

As an example of the unsettling rhetoric that typifies this particular circumstance, consider the lengthy article that Paulina Borsook (1993) wrote on Esther Dyson in *Wired* magazine. Though Dyson is one of the most powerful software consultants in the Silicon Valley, she is presented as a "Hollywood agent"—a personality. Throughout the article, Dyson is referred to by her first name, Esther, a stylistic technique one would be surprised to see in an article covering a top male executive or corporate head. Similarly, bracketed off in its own lavender box, Borsook has created a section entitled "Street Myths About Esther," which includes—in addition to the categories of "Really smart" and "Swimming junkie"— "Likes older powerful men" and "Almost married Bill Ziff" (p. 97).

The collapse of the "social" with the "professional" marks a distinct techno-journalistic style, which nearly always demarcates the feminine subject. While in other contexts this merging of the public with the private might be read as a creative feminist transgression, in this particular context it constructs a representation of woman through difference or "otherness." As a result, it is not enough for readers to know that this partner of Mayfield, Software, Inc. is "the most important woman in computing" (p. 95), they must also be familiar with her sexual preference and recognize the names of the powerful men with whom she is involved.

In another article in *Wired* magazine, Jan Davidson, the owner of a $40 million educational software empire, is introduced with the title, "She just wanted to be a *good teacher*" (Guglielmo, 1994, p. 44; emphasis added); and Sueann Ambron, one of the world's experts in multimedia and interactive communication, is announced by the title "The *Mother* of Multimedia" (Garner, 1994, p. 52; emphasis added), while posing in a kitchen apron, mixing bowl in hand.[3] Such fundamentally sexist representation was the subject of feminist criticism during the 1970s, but that it should garner critical attention today, nearly three decades later, suggests that network culture is not the liberal institution it promotes itself as being. Why are the few women in the industry presented in ways that are traditional and non-threatening? Why are the articles about women written mostly by female staff writers? Why are there no voices which admonish readers that these women are, in fact, exceptional, and not representative of women's status in the larger culture? Finally, what requirements must a female journalist meet in order to join the ranks of *Wired*'s staff writers? What kinds of pressures are exerted on her voice?

One can easily imagine the difficulty of asserting a feminist voice of change within a cyberspatial industry noted for its liberatory and sensa-tionalist rhetoric. Add to that its exploitation of high profile women, featured prominently as representatives of cyberspatial identities, and it seems unlikely that anyone is going to challenge the industry's represen-tation of women, at least from within that industry. For example, it can be easier to find photographs of techno-cultural novelist and art critic Kathy Acker than to read about her ideas.[4] The "visual format," a postmodern staple, seems to have set a kind of precedent in techno-futuristic publi-cations, for silent images of women abound in place of their voices and ideas. This is readily discernible from flipping through pages of the journals randomly, both in terms of article inlays and advertisements. Seductive young women appear modeling the latest technological gear; Asian women fuse the excitement of the exotic "Other" with the "out there" reality of VR equipment and fashion; and women's sexualized and objectified bodies merge graphically with the new technologies. (See the scantily clad Madonna-like figure hoisting a satellite dish above her head in the *Mondo 2000 User's Guide*, p. 95.) Within this context it is not surprising to find that the feminine voices allowed into the ranks are not necessarily those who oppose the conditions granting privilege and agency to the techno-journals.

Additionally, the sexism of the relations between women's bodies and the production of the new technologies is often belied by the slick presentation of aestheticized images. Though I oppose Net censorship, I don't think it is unfair to suggest that this type of print exploitation leaves women vulnerable to the propagation of "virtual sex" and other sex-peddling services offered on the Internet.[5] While it is easy to see what is objectionable about a "Virtual Sex Arcade," where you can negotiate "modifications" in the "Girl of Your Dreams," some of the arguments put forth for "virtual sex" are more insidious (Lebkowsky, 1993). Consider the argument that "virtual sex" may help to decrease violence against women, since computer-generated "whips, clamps, brooms, toasters, etc." won't leave marks (p. 18). Despite the rhetoric that claims such games are "harmless," they reify a cultural way of looking at women, which is destructive and demeaning.

Consider a second virtual myth: sexism against women may be reduced through CD-ROM and virtual reality programs because men can now log-in as the female gender and "take" the woman's point of view. This speculation sounds encouraging, but it essentially ignores the fact that identities of sexuality are constructed socially in ways that cultures powerfully inscribe onto bodies. Women are socialized in a manner that can't be replicated by assuming a "different point of view." Nor can the sexual hierarchy be overturned so simplistically, for Western culture continues to privilege the male within the confines of the phallocentric tradition.

Patriarchal representations of femininity, whether through Internet communications or CD-ROM games, are notoriously sexist; and yet these text- and graphic-based images are occupying the virtual space(s) where women could be defining their own relationship(s) to the new information technologies. Such lack of representation carries with it significant consequences, not the least of which involves the shift of political power from an industrial basis to one in which knowledge or the communication of information operates as the new "capital." The exclusion of women from the technologies which produce and regulate this knowledge dis-empowers them in fundamental ways, especially given that virtual technologies are controlled and managed on several powerful fronts: the government (especially defense contracting), corporate America, and the media and communication channels.

No wonder, then, that the rhetoric of the "techno-journals" and zines sounds absurd and conservative to feminist readers—harking back to the days of the "founding fathers" and the democratic ideals of such men as Thomas Jefferson (Barlow, 1994), for the reality of this "new egalitarian society" is decidedly less utopian for women. As an example, the Silicon Valley, one of the earliest centers of the new communications industry, continues to exploit thousands of Asian and Latina women and other immigrants in entry-level manufacturing jobs, where they endure sexual harassment, poor working conditions, and threats of deportation (Hossfield, 1994). Many of these women are exposed to toxic chemicals because there is so little adequate testing of these materials, and yet few are in any position to challenge corporate power. Recently, in an effort to put to rest rumors relating ethylene glycol to miscarriages in young female employees, IBM initiated a private study to examine the ill-effects of the chemical on its workers (Hossfield, 1994). Contrary to the company's expectations, the chemical was found to be linked with serious health problems, including a higher than normal risk of miscarriage in young women. IBM agreed to delete the chemical from its operating processes before the end of 1994, but not before it had brought unwanted grief to the women whose bodies and children bought the price of the new technologies.

Thus, even while acknowledging the admirable accomplishments of female corporate managers, software developers, media artists, and scholars, it is important to recognize that women in the larger culture are still marginalized at the periphery of the communications industry, usually at its base in the lowest paying jobs. The social biases established early in education, which separate women from the disciplines of math and science, represent deeply embedded cultural prejudices against women in the technical sciences. Consequently, fewer women are qualified in the areas of research that are shaping the communications industry, and those who are are often held back in positions of less pay and authority (Balsamo, 1993).

It is no surprise, then, that on a representational level many of these same injustices are present. Yet to begin to resist at the textual level is not to bypass the revolution, for our rhetorics have the power to shape the very potential of the new technologies. And here the politics *are* clear-cut: any general advancement for women within this "techno-culture" will have to begin by transforming the sexist images and the rhetoric that attends them. In place of these texts, women need to introduce their own voices, reappropriating the very "languages which have" been used against them. This is, of course, easier said than done, for it means making inroads in a discipline and industry traditionally foreclosed to women. It means doing battle against powerful ideological prejudices, and, most difficult of all, reshaping one's own conception of the female.

(Re)-Fashioning the Cybercultural Matrix

I prefer a network . . . image, suggesting
the profusion of spaces and identities and the
permeability of boundaries in the personal body
and in the body politic.

—Donna J. Haraway, *Simians, Cyborgs, and Women:*
The Reinvention of Nature (1991), p. 170

In the face of these challenges I would like to propose a textual strategy by which women may appropriate a cultural space and begin to define their own relationship(s) to the new information technologies. Though I have cited the cybermatrix, including its print representatives, as the locus of conservative gender politics, I also believe it has the potential to constitute a subversive, feminist space, literally a site where women can "re-member" their own gendered self—identities. Cyberspace offers the potential for virtual communities, or "consensual loci," where women can join voices/texts to articulate (and activate) issues pertinent to them (Stone, 1991). In an effort to reconstitute a feminist "subject" in the context of postmodern decenteredness, this task becomes an effort both to inscribe textual space and follow through with active (political) choice.[6] In this instance, cyberspace becomes a narrative space, a potential authoring site in an economy where textual circulation can recover political agency. In referring to feminist science-fiction writers Joanna Russ and Pamela Zoline, Scott Bukatman (1993) describes this rhetorical act as "turn[ing] text into tactic—a *technology*—that . . . challenges the masculinist formations of science fiction and culture" (p. 314).

Not surprisingly, the notion of cyberspace as a radical domain for women necessarily raises several issues of concern. As Anne Balsamo (1993) and other feminists have argued, female bodies are inscribed culturally into specific paradigms that determine the nature of identity and subjectivity. For women in Western cultures, this has been a paradigm fraught with difficulties, for the physical body has been the site of fervent battles regarding female sexuality, reproduction, and identity, so much so that it becomes impossible to separate feminine subjectivity from a particular system of embedded power relations. Because of these patriarchal tensions, it is necessary to situate female subjectivity within a gendered and politicized context in the cybercultural matrix. Put differently, women stand to gain little as quasi-disembodied subjects within a network environment *without reference to the material conditions of their subjectivity.*

Yet, as will be demonstrated in this chapter, projecting a gendered self into cyberspace can be a very painful experience for women. Issues involving gender politics and representation cut to the core, and many women are simply tired of buttressing the same fronts time and time again. In short, there do not seem to be easy answers to these difficult social issues. Nonetheless, I would like to suggest a strategy for constructing an electronic space that might be more negotiable than the cyberspace we know at present. Drawing on Donna Haraway's (1991) mythos of the cyborg, I imagine an electronic space that is about "transgressed boundaries, potent fusions, and dangerous possibilities," called for in order to resist dominant (rational) power structures embedded within patriarchal culture (p. 154). In this instance the fusion of machine and organism becomes a progressive, and transgressive, hybrid—an artificial site for ongoing political activity, which necessarily involves deconstructing "incompatible" frames of reference.

In other words, situated between a gendered, material body and an ethereal, cyberspatial identity; between patriarchal culture and feminist community; between "inside" and "outside," the female participant must embrace ambiguity and conflict in order to appropriate a cultural space for feminist discourse. Because this space is electronic, such a tactic necessarily involves issues of subjectivity and embodiment. In her book, *The War of Desire and Technology at the Close of the Mechanical Age*, Allucquère Rosanne Stone (1995) acknowledges the relationship of physical bodies to the epistemic structures by which they become encoded in culture; and she is particularly careful to ascribe gender, discourse, and meaning *to the physical body itself*, as an embedded cultural phenomenon. She identifies this concept as "a body unit grounded in a self" and suggests that telling any personal narrative seems to depend upon this material identity (pp. 84–85).

If we think of a cyberspatial identity as mediated through this physical "self," the *discursive feminine body* can be read/narrated in such a way as to preserve a sense of presence, politics, and history in a medium increasingly characterized by shifting fields of meaning. In this sense, an electronic community of women becomes a symbolic space, an engaged social space, that defines itself through a particular textualized culture. Overriding geographical limitations, women can gather together in ways that challenge the constraints of time and space, allowing them to explore the potent relations among agency, authority, and discursive community (Stone, 1995, p. 97).

Despite recent feminist theory regarding the totalizing effect communities can have when they attempt to reach "wholeness," the idea of a textualized, feminist cyberspace may posit an alternative concept of "community" (Young, 1990, pp. 300-323). Referring back to Haraway's politics of the cyborg, it is possible to embrace the idea of community without assuming the totalizing structures that delineate patriarchal hierarchies. In the first instance, Haraway (1991) points to the political necessity of seeing from "both sides" (machine and animal), "because each [side] reveals both dominations and possibilities unimaginable from the other viewpoint" (p. 154). She then goes on to differentiate between "communal unity," and "affinity" and "coalition" as organizing communal factors. Haraway powerfully identifies the corpus of the cyborg as a self-conscious coalition—a political kinship forged from radical feminist initiative and action—and necessarily involving difference and contradiction. For Haraway, building effective unity does not eradicate the revolutionary subject, for the permeability of boundaries in both the body and the body politic assures transgressive leakages as well as radical fusions. New couplings must, of necessity, bring about new coalitions.

The question then becomes how to ally the new technologies with progressive political movements. And here Haraway (1991) points to the empowerment of feminist textuality, of having access to the signifying practices that "mark the world" (p. 175). Haraway writes, "Feminist cyborg stories have the task of recoding communication and intelligence to subvert command and control" (p. 175). What is particularly interesting about Haraway's conception is that such political empowerment is *constituted from textuality*—in other words from women's collected voices, stories, and myths. And it is here that I believe a community emerges within the cyberspatial matrix: women join the circuitry of the electronic network, responding to one another's dialogue through digitized conversation.

Steven Jones (1995) likewise, defines the nature of electronic exchange as involving aspects of community, if only because of the *ritual sharing of information*. His observation is interesting, for it underscores the role that technology plays in establishing new relations among users. Judy Smith and Ellen Balka (1988) similarly report that using "talk terminology" may affect the way we conceptualize words on the network. Using the term "chatting" to describe the mode of writing that takes place on the electronic network, Smith and Balka speculate that this type of informality (where the writer doesn't reread or rewrite her message to correct spelling or grammar errors) may invite more people of differing educational levels and interests to enter into electronic discussions. Research like this demonstrates the powerful sociological impact that electronic communications can bring to bear on human behavior and social relations.

At the same time, the Internet is a powerfully conservative venue, mirroring gender-based ideologies that circulate in the larger culture. Challenging women to identify the issues of their gendered realities means confronting behavior that has developed in response to patriarchal pressures. This situation creates a double bind for women that potentially marks cyberspace as a difficult, even uncomfortable, social space. Consider Stacy Horn's development of a *mixed-gender* electronic bulletin board called EchoNYC (Glenn, 1996). This online service constitutes a virtual community comprised of artists, writers, and filmmakers. Because the bulletin board is art-based, rather than technical or business-oriented, Horn has attracted a diverse clientele, including 40 percent female membership. She attributes this high percentage of women to her aggressive recruiting practices and confrontational politics. Yet, even Horn was surprised to find that once the women were online, they seldom interacted, engaging in the kind of electronic behavior known as "lurking" (listening in to conversations, but not speaking). Horn addressed the issue by initiating a discussion of the possible reasons for this behavior, and she found, as Stone had earlier speculated, that the women were *projecting embodied identities into cyberspace*. In other words, as the female users wrote themselves into this virtual community, they did so in an imagined social space very much defined by their experiences in a patriarchal culture. As a result their discourse patterns were "gendered," meaning, in this case, that the female users were less participatory than their male counterparts, and often silent.

This is not too surprising given the studies which demonstrate that women participate more readily on all-women networks (Ebben & Kramarae, 1993; Thorne, Kramarae, & Henley, 1983). Yet left unchecked, this type of networking behavior can underscore, rather than undermine, conservative gender relations. For Stacy Horn, it was a topic worth taking up with the EchoNYC participants, and she was quick to remind the women of the importance of their voices to the overall success of the network. Eventually, Horn did succeed in recruiting as many female forum leaders as male, suggesting, perhaps, that confrontational politics may be one way to afford real political change within virtual communities. Had Horn remained uninterested in the demographics of her online service, it seems certain that business would have prevailed as usual.

Similarly, there are women who are shaping communication technologies to meet their own political ends. One of the most successful projects is the Women's Opportunity and Resource Development (WORD), which is run out of Missoula, Montana, and develops electronic projects geared specifically toward women and lower-income people (Smith, 1992, p. 70). All of the state's women programs are online, and the agency offers thirteen displaced home-maker programs, including one which teaches women with small businesses how to do cash flow accounts electronically. With state and federal support, the agency is also able to provide loans to women to start their own businesses and enter into a profitable market economy. WORD represents an online community project that has resulted in real social changes in the culture at large. It doesn't seem too great a leap, then, to imagine that these same communication technologies can further other feminist initiatives. Already, in fact, women are stepping forward in an effort to shape social perceptions regarding electronic networks. At the 1995 SIGGRAPH Computer Graphics Conference in Los Angeles, Jill Scott presented "Frontiers of Utopia," an interactive cyber-spatial community, where participants hypertextually engage eight different women, whose histories and lives differ in time and geographical location. Designed to present alternative views on women's relationships to history and technology, this interfacing design melds feminist issues with high-tech capabilities.

In a similar fashion, GRANITE (Gender Relations and New Technology) organizes an international network of scholars and policy-makers online, and WON (Women's Online Network) coordinates political efforts to promote women's issues within mainstream culture. Furthermore, the University of Illinois at Urbana sponsors the Women, Information

Technology, and Scholarship Colloquium at the Center for Advanced Study, an interdisciplinary group that works to ensure equity across new communications networks. And though none of these organizations can ensure that women will appropriate a feminist cyberspace or begin to define their own relationships to the new information technologies, they represent structural attempts to intervene in the patriarchal domination of electronic technologies. They are reminders to us that we can join voices to articulate issues pertinent to ourselves—that cyberspace offers the potential to *reconstitute* a feminist "subject"—literally turning text into tactic.

Given the need for continued development of feminist communities amidst dwindling state and federal resources, cyborg politics demand that we reimagine social and political possibilities for communicating through electronic media—that we *utilize* and *mobilize* the powerful venue that cyberspace offers. This means working within existing structures, such as the cyberspatial print industry represented by *Wired*, *Mondo 2000*, and *bOing bOing*; its electronic counterparts; and educational, governmental, and corporate institutions. It also means continuing to cultivate the margins of electronic culture, where greater experimentation is taking place; for in this post-industrial present we are left with radical information technologies, possibilities for new social matrices, and issues of textuality and gender to explore further. Though we stand little to gain by idealizing these new technologies, we can embrace their difference(s) with the hope that they might introduce new ways to textualize both our (social) space(s) and our bodies, allowing us to reimagine a feminist politics of the future.

Notes

1. See also Gareth Branwyn's (1993) defense of his sexism against "the gnarly grain of short-sighted feminism" (p. 24).

2. The authors demonstrate that "the urge to contextualize in conventional terms as a means to comprehend and situate discourse seems to be quite powerful in . . . [the] electronic environment despite its ideology of resistance to contextualization" (Aycock & Buchignani, 1995, p. 216).

3. It is true that Ambron's business is called the "Paramount Technology Group's Media Kitchen," so the photograph and title cleverly comment on the company's name, but in a more problematic way the maternal metaphor also governs the rhetoric of the article. This includes everything from author Rochelle Garner's (1994) noting Ambron's "overwhelming Momness" to seeing her as the "nurturer of [Silicon Valley's] visionaries" (p. 52). In this instance, where is the line drawn between playful commentary and sexist depiction?

4. Vivian Sobchack (1993) cites the example of Avital Ronell, whose publication, *Telephone Book*, "was followed up in the glossy fourth issue [of *Mondo 2000*] with Professor Avital Ronell herself . . . posed glamorously in a head shot to die for (what was to become part of M2's signature style of male homage to smart women: part *Cosmopolitan*, part *Playboy*)" (p. 581).

5. Researchers are just beginning to document the impact of sex-related behavior to women's online participation. Their research concludes, generally, that the climate of the Net *can exclude women and minorities* from participating in the conversation. See Cheris

Kramarae and H. Jeanie Taylor (1993) for information on everything from sexual harassment to electronically transferred digitized pornographic pictures.

6. See Susan Bordo's (1993, pp. 283–284) discussion of the negative reactions to postmodern "decenteredness".

References

Aycock, A., & Buchignani, N. (1995). The e-mail murders: Reflections on "dead" letters. In S.G. Jones (Ed.), *CyberSociety: Computer-mediated communication and community* (pp. 184–231). Thousand Oaks, CA: Sage.

Balsamo, A. (1993). Feminism for the incurably informed. *South Atlantic Quarterly, 94,* 681–712.

Barbi, Sia (1996). Living Dolls. *bOing bOing, 14,* 44–48.

Barlow, J. (1994, March). The economy of ideas: A framework for rethinking patents and copyrights in the digital age. *Wired,* pp. 84–90, 126–29.

Baudrillard, J. (1983). *Simulations.* (P. Foss, P. Patton, & P. Beitchman, Trans.). New York: Semiotext(e).

Benedikt, M. (Ed.). (1991). *Introduction to cyberspace: First steps.* Cambridge, MA: MIT Press.

Bordo, S. (1993). *Unbearable weight: Feminism, Western culture, and the body.* Berkeley: University of California Press.

Borsook, P. (1993, November). Release. *Wired,* pp. 94–97, 124–126.

Borsook, P. (1995, July). The goddess in every woman's machine. *Wired,* pp. 133, 181.

Branwyn, G. (1993). The painfully personal confession of a politically-correct salivating porn fanatic. *bOing bOing, 10,* 24–28.

Bukatman, S. (1993). *Terminal identity: The virtual subject in postmodern science fiction.* Durham, NC: Duke University Press.

Davis, E. (1995, July). Technopagans: May the astral plane be reborn in cyberspace. *Wired,* pp. 126–133, 174–181.

Doane, M.A. (1990). Technophilia: Technology, representation, and the feminine. In M. Jacobus, E.F. Keller, & S. Shuttleworth (Eds.), *Body/Politics: Women and the discourses of science* (pp. 163–176). New York: Routledge.

Ebben, M., & Kramarae, C. (1993). Women and information technologies: Creating a cyberspace of our own. In H.J. Taylor, C. Kramarae, & M. Ebben (Eds.), *Women, information technology, and scholarship* (pp. 15–27). Urbana: University of Illinois Center for Advanced Study.

Garner, R. (1994, April). The mother of multimedia. *Wired,* pp. 52, 54–56.

Glenn, J. (1996, January/February). Media diet: Stacy horn. *Utne Reader,* p. 110.

Goffman, K. (1992). Evolutionary mutations. In R. Rucker, R.U. Sirius, & Q. Mu, *Mondo 2000: A user's guide to the new edge.* New York: HarperCollins.

Guglielmo, C. (1994, February). Class leader. *Wired,* pp. 44, 46.

Haraway, D.J. (1991). *Simians, cyborgs, and women: The reinvention of nature.* New York: Routledge.

Hossfield, K. (1994). *Small, foreign, and female.* Berkeley: University of California Press.

HotWired's Welcome Page. (1995). http//www.hotwired.com/.

Hutcheon, L. (1994). *Irony's edge.* New York: Routledge.

Jameson, F. (1981). *The political unconscious: Narrative as socially symbolic act.* Ithaca, NY: Cornell University Press.

Jones, S.G. (1995). Understanding community in the information age. In S.G. Jones (Ed.), *CyberSociety: Computer-mediated communication and community* (pp. 10–35). Thousand Oaks, CA: Sage.

Kramarae, C., & Taylor, H.J. (1993). Women and men on electronic networks: A conversation or a monologue? In H.J. Taylor, C. Kramarae, & M. Ebben (Eds.), *Women, information technology, and scholarship* (pp. 52–61). Urbana: University of Illinois Center for Advanced Study.

Lebkowsky, J. (1993). Virtual sex: Fucking around with machines. *bOing bOing, 10,* 17–18.

Morgan, E. (1972). *The descent of woman.* New York: Stein & Day.

Mutch, D. (1995, November 3). Business is booming on the Net, and business has control. *Christian Science Monitor,* p. 8.

Rucker, R., Sirius, R.U., & Mu, Q. (1992). *Mondo 2000: A user's guide to the new edge.* New York: HarperCollins.

Smith, J. (1992). *Linking women: Computer networks as a feminist resource.* Presentation to Women, Information Technology, and Scholarship Colloquium. Center for Advanced Study, University of Illinois.

Smith, J., & Balka, E. (1988). Chatting on a feminist computer network. In C. Kramarae (Ed.), *Technology and women's voices* (pp. 82–97). New York: Routledge & Kegan Paul/ Methuen.

Sobchack, V. (1990). Toward a phenomenology of cinematic and electronic presence: The scene of the screen. *Post Script, 10,* 50–59.

Sobchack, V. (1993). New age mutant ninja hackers: Reading *Mondo 2000. South Atlantic Quarterly, 92,* 569–584.

Springer, C. (1993, Winter). Muscular circuitry: The invincible armored cyborg in cinema. *Genders, 18,* 87–101.

Stone, A.R. (1991). Will the real body please stand up? Boundary stories about virtual cultures. In M. Benedikt (Ed.), *Introduction to cyberspace: First steps* (pp. 81–118). Cambridge, MA: MIT Press.

Stone, A.R. (1995). *The war between desire and technology at the close of the mechanical age.* Cambridge, MA: MIT Press.

Thorne, B., Kramarae, C., & Henley, N. (Eds.). (1983). *Language, gender, and society.* Rowley, MA: Newbury.

Young, I.M. (1990). The ideal of community and the politics of difference. In L.J. Nicholson (Ed.), *Feminism/Postmodernism* (pp. 300–323). New York: Routledge.

9

Approaching the Radical Other: The Discursive Culture of Cyberhate

Susan Zickmund

The Internet has transformed the nature of community and identity within the United States. Along with other groups, this new medium has affected the cohesiveness of subversive organizations. Individuals propagating Nazi ideologies have traditionally operated in isolation, with limited ties to organizational structures. Yet with the emergence of electronic mail and the World Wide Web, subversives are now discovering the means of propagating their message beyond the narrow confines of pre-established alliances.

Subversive literature functions as the discursive articulation of a community, and expresses its historical consciousness and cultural identification. Based on this historical and cultural background, an argumentative *Weltanschauung* has developed which fosters a rhetoric of antipathy, one baring the unique markings of American radicalism. Individuals who propagate this discourse are unified in complex structures of a shared subversive ideology. They are "interpellated," a phenomenon Althusser defines as the discursive process of evoking a collection of individuals into a group through an ideological screen (Charland, 1987, p. 148).

This ideological "interpellating" becomes especially important when examining subversive culture in cyberspace. Here a person loses the spatial markers that determine group membership. Benedict Anderson (1983) argues in his work *Imagined Communities* that communal structures, such as shared spatial, cultural, and linguistic domains, are necessary in order to bind members together. Yet within the Internet a defined spatial dimension does not exist. The virtual reality of cyberspace does not conform with our traditional notions of community, one which allows individuals to physically interact on a day to day basis (Rosello, 1994, pp. 131–132). These cybercultures lack what Heidegger (1962) defines as the "everydayness" of life, which is required in order to create *das Man*, or the larger structures of society which, in turn, shape the individual sense of Being-in-the-world.

Access to Radical Materials

The difficult access to radical materials has traditionally plagued subversive organizations. For example, Germany constitutionally banned the publication or distribution of Nazi documents after World War II (Charney, 1995). In the 1990s the German government also outlawed skinhead, heavy metal music with lyrics promoting hate, after neo-Nazi youths burned the residence of Turkish *Gastarbeiter*. Yet with global access to the Internet, the autonomy of one nation to restrict radical literature has been greatly reduced. Documents posted on the World Wide Web are now available to anyone with the technological capacity to gain access. This freedom to disseminate materials over the Internet has led to a thriving radical culture. This communication technology is also creating new legal issues as it bypasses national control mechanisms, thereby challenging traditional notions of national sovereignty. The implications of this change were recently illustrated when Germany attempted to assert control over literature available within its own borders by calling on CompuServe to restrict access to radical materials (Brenner, 1996). While the server at first attempted to abide by this restriction, the company has now decided, in a striking reversal, to restrict *Germany's* access to the Web, rather than hamper the availability of information for patrons. In the future such issues may be rendered moot as a US court recently decided in favor of maintaining free speech over the Internet. A judge supporting the decision argued that it is better to allow the cacophony of voices on the Internet to control itself without the use of governmental or judicial intervention (Lewis, 1996).

Historical Development

The radical right is a compendium of disparate groups with different, often conflicting, ideologies which nonetheless share certain elements in common: a vociferous sense of hatred extending toward one or more groups (typically involving racism and anti-Semitism), disdain toward the authority of the federal government, and a strong or loose familial tie to the Ku Klux Klan or other Nazi-based organizations which originated in the first half of this century in America. Elinor Langer (1990) in her work "The American Neo-Nazi Movement Today" estimates membership in these organizations as approximately 20,000 to 100,000 persons, a number that is substantial, but nonetheless equaling only a fraction of all Americans.

Historically, US radicalism can be traced back to anti-immigrant and anti-religious movements. While Gustavus Myers (1960), in his study the *History of Bigotry in the United States*, found seeds of prejudice in the very birth of the nation, serious political confrontation began only with the American anti-Catholic movement which blossomed during the 1830s. This movement led to the formation of a political party dubbed the "Know Nothings," which ultimately collapsed into the newly created Republican Party. The Klan itself began in the American South during the 1860s in reaction to the turmoil caused by the Civil War. Formed as a social club for bored Confederate soldiers, its members wore bed-sheets in order to frighten emancipated slaves. Within several years of its foundation, Klan orders had sprung up over the South and were responsible for terrorist activities and deaths, most via lynchings of African-Americans (Katz, 1987). In the 1920s the Klan reached the peak of its membership after D.W. Griffith's pro-Klan film, *Birth of a Nation*, was released. At its peak, about 20 percent of the white males were listed as members, including representatives of Congress (Lipset & Raab, 1970, p. 111). During this time the Klan targeted predominately blacks and Catholics. In fact, many of the robes and rituals of the Klan were meant as parodies of Catholicism. Members considered themselves to be the upholders of the law, structures of order, and Protestant Christian virtues. One study of early twentieth-century Klan membership found that the two most prominent professions in the organization were religious ministers and police officers (Katz, 1987).

The civil rights movement of the 1960s changed the relationship of the Klan to legal authority, an aspect that would continue to reverberate throughout contemporary radicalism. The prosperity of the post-World War II years had reduced the membership of the Klan, confining it to the deep and less prosperous Southern region. When the "Jim Crow" Southern states refused to abolish segregation, the national government, under the Kennedy and Johnson administrations, sent troops into the states to enforce these federal laws. The Klan strove to disrupt the activities of the Northern government agents, as Southerners brandished the Confederate flag as a sign of rebellion against the liberal, educated, and largely East Coast forces of the government. While today law suits and organizational infighting have largely diminished the Klan, splinter groups now flourish across the country, each maintaining a confrontational role with the US government (Bennett, 1988).

The contemporary American extremist right today generally descends from these earlier Klan organizations as well as the American Nazi movement. Together they share strident racial sentiments, often augmented by a religious or a semi-cosmological view of the creation of humanity. These groups include such divergent organizations as the religiously oriented Christian Identity sect to the secular, California-based organization White Aryan Resistance (WAR). Christian Identity members believe that Aryans are the real chosen people of the Bible, that Jews have actually descended from Satan, and that all non-whites are "mud-people," the offspring of a rejected creature made before Adam (Barkun, 1994). James Ridgeway's (1990) work on American extremism takes its title, *Blood in the Face*, from the Christian Identity belief that only true human beings, that is, whites, have the capacity to blush or have "blood in the face." Members of this organization view this phenomenon as the proof that persons of other races do not constitute human beings.

Another prominent group, the White Aryan Resistance (WAR), was founded by television repairman Tom Metzger. Metzger ran a talk show entitled *Race and Reason* on a cable-access channel in San Diego throughout much of the 1980s (Ridgeway, 1990). On his program, guests discussed the genetic inferiority of Jews and minorities and the imminent threat to the white race posed by affirmative action and inter-marriage. Metzger's group produced newsletters, magazines, radio programs, and videotapes promoting their racist message. In her work, Langer (1990) describes one such tape where

> a WAR video opens with a laugh track over a scene of bulldozers burying bodies at Auschwitz, the narrator stating: "When the people can no longer tolerate the Jews, those people who don't believe in the Holocaust will want one; and those who do believe in the Holocaust will want another one. . . . The next holocaust won't be a hoax." (p. 85)

Groups supporting such views have increasingly become active in the Northwestern part of America, such as northern California, Oregon, Washington, and Idaho, where agencies in 1989 reported a 400 percent increase in anti-Semitic activities (Langer, 1990).

Another important organization, one which did not directly descend from the Klan or Nazi movement, is that of the skinheads (Hamm, 1993). This loosely structured movement emerged during the 1980s from the economically depressed blue-collar urban centers in Britain. Their distinctive hair-styles and rebellious clothing were at first meant as signs of protest against dominant English society. Strident racial views developed amongst a portion of the skinhead following, often directed toward Pakistani immigrants who sought employment in London. From this group a subset of the culture emerged which embraced racial discrimination (Kovaleski, 1996). This racist segment of the movement spread throughout the Western world during the 1980s and 1990s, promoted in part by the distinctive version of heavy metal music its members produced.

Finally, an older radical group is known as the Posse Comitatus, a name that extends from one of the organization's central desires: local rule. While Posse members do not play a significant role on the Internet, their ideology has influenced the belief structures of other radical organizations. In this way they effectively crystallize a variety of radical views. The Posse Comitatus members believe that the national government is involved in a vast conspiracy to destroy farmers, white people, and the American family (Ridgeway, 1990). They adhere tenaciously to the belief in ZOG (the Zionist Occupational Government), which they see as a synonym for the US government. Posse members argue that ZOG is controlled by the International Jewish Conspiracy, a group of powerful Jewish financiers who together essentially rule the world. As a result of this belief, members refuse to pay taxes, carry social security or driver's license cards, and instead frequently stockpile weapons and await the day of the ultimate confrontation with the Jewish-controlled authorities (Ridgeway, 1990).

In addition to these dominant organizations, other groups, comprised of tax revolters and anti-environmentalist ranchers in the Northwestern

United States, have arisen over the years to add to this anti-government sentiment. Many of their members subscribe to the conspiratorial fear of ZOG, as do most radical hate groups. Indeed, a belief in ZOG has become one of the chief tenets of the radical right. It finds expression in the widely held conspiracy theory that the power of the US government and the Federal Reserve Board operate at the very center of ZOG. This sense of world-wide conspiracy has recently been further embellished for these groups by an unwilling supporter when President Bush, in a 1990 speech during the Gulf War, described the development of a "New World Order" of nations. Within American radicalism, this term has come to stand for the Jewish-backed UN powers that are to invade the United States with the goal of depriving Christians of their rights, liberties, and lives (After Oklahoma (2), 1995).

Subversives in Cyberspace: Web Sites and Belief Structures of the Radicals

While these groups have a long history in the United States, the technology of the Internet has been critical in terms of increasing visibility. Rabbi Abraham Cooper of the Los Angeles-based Wiesenthal Center argues: "along with all of the wonderful educational opportunities being born every day via the Internet and on-line resources, hate groups are aggressively utilizing the same avenues to promote their hate-filled agendas" (cited in Schwartz, 1995, p. 22). In order to understand this use of the Internet, I will first discuss the emerging radical cyber-sites, before explicating some of the dimensions which have transformed radical *individuals* into a subversive *community*.

Aryan and white power groups in cyberspace are represented on a variety of Web sites, the most prominent being Reverend Ronald Schoedel's "Christian Identity On-line," the "National Alliance," and the "Stormfront White Nationalist Resource Page." Listserves for white supremacists include "Stormfront-L" and the "Aryan News Agency." The two most popular Usenet newsgroups—which are the focus of this chapter—are alt.politics. nationalism.white and alt.politics.white-power. These newsgroups have been featured in journalistic analyses as well as praised by the radicals themselves as being central to the growing radical network. In addition to such traditional forms of access on the Internet, Tom Metzger has extended technology even further by advertising on the "White Aryan Resistance Web Page" a free provider for any racist homepage that may have been censored by commercial servers.

Another prominent radical group to be represented on the Internet is that of the skinheads. The Alta Vista search engine reveals a plethora of American organizations on the Web, both at national and regional locations. These include "Wolfpack Services" and "Skinheads U.S.A. Links Page." The listserve for skinheads has been appropriately named "Resist-

List," the title reflecting the hostile ethos cultivated by group members. The most prominent newsgroups for skinheads are alt.skinheads and alt.skinheads.moderated, although upon accessing the moderated newsgroup, I found few postings compared to the heavy traffic evident on the non-moderated net. Radical cyberculture in general has also cultivated ties to international sources, targeting lands with strict censorship laws, such as Germany. These organizations include: "Denmark (D.N.S.B.)," "Norway Resources," "Swedish Resources Page," "British National Party," "Stormfront: Spanish Language." The nation most prominently represented here is that of Germany, with Web sites listed for "Zündelsite: German Language" (n.d.), "Stormfront: German Language" (n.d.), "Nationale Volkspartij/ CP'86" (n.d.), and "Germanica Online" (n.d.).

The dominant trafficking of subversive discourse still travels through America. Here members can be easily routed to a variety of groups through a clearing station, such as the Aryan Re-Education Link. This station is a linking service for thirty-four separate radical Web pages. The groups represented tend toward the skinhead spectrum, but white supremacists are advertised as well. Twenty-two of these groups are iconically represented by their logo, and it is here that an examination of symbolic, cultural discourse can begin.

Subversive cultures operate within what Wittgenstein (1953) describes in his *Philosophical Investigations* as a "language game." Wittgenstein argues that language itself functions within a community and that discursive game rules formulate the notions of rationality that exist within that culture. As one moves from one society to another, the rules and norms of the language game change. Based on these assumptions, linguistic, tropological, and symbolic communication can reveal much about the unifying dimensions of a culture.

With the radical cybercommunities, the dominant metaphoric association used by group members is that of war. Symbolically, the radicals associate themselves with icons of political oppression, violence, and death. Organizations tending toward Aryan beliefs typically employ the swastika symbol of the Third Reich, such as that used by the "Independent White Racist Homepage." Skinhead groups are more likely to turn to images of violence, including the insignia of the "New Jersey Skinhead Page," where a threatening fist has the word "skin" tattooed across the fingers. Various dimensions of dress and body culture reinforce these symbols. White supremacists frequently wear military clothing, at times donning full camouflage attire. Skinheads in particular prefer a paramilitary style, the most prominent cultural artifact being their military boots which members wear (Hamm, 1993). So important are these boots that they have become an insignia of identification, with members using greetings such as "Heil Bootboy."

This cyberculture reflects, in general, an overall fixation on war. For example, the architects of the Third Reich function as heroic key figures for both white supremacists and skinheads (Talty, 1996). The importance of the Nazi era is made apparent in part through the commodification of fascist regalia. For example, on alt.politics.white-power, a man selling an "early edition of Hitler's *Mein Kampf*," received a response of interest from Christian Identity leader Reverend Ronald Schoedel (1996). The NSDAP mail order catalogue features hundreds of Nazi items and military paraphernalia, including a swastika stick pin (item #211), "War Songs of the Third Reich" (#201), and a photograph book entitled, "The Hitler We Loved and Why" (#189) (Mail Order Catalogue, 1996). The solicitation of Nazi goods reinforces cultural icons while encouraging a consumerist orientation towards radical materials. In this way, this virtual marketplace for Nazi goods offers for sale valued symbols and texts as it spreads and strengthens the ideas which these items signify.

This war-centric *Weltanschauung* colors the belief structure of many of these radical members. Historian Richard Hofstadter (1965) has labeled a preoccupation with war and conspiracy as the discursive characteristics of the "paranoid style." Grand conspiracies, Hofstadter argues, indicate a form of political psycho-pathology. This pathology causes individuals to interpret unrelated events as ones causally linked, revealing designs of tyranny and oppression. The acceptance of ZOG as the dominant mechanism of world control clearly demonstrates a "paranoid style." Yet it is also important to go beyond the stylistic aspects of political psycho-pathology in order to understand how this paranoid discourse leads to a sense of group cohesion.

One central, unifying bond of this movement lies in its mythic belief structures, ones which blur the traditional distinction between fabricated narratives and standard conceptions of history. Within these myths, demon figures, such as ZOG, function to discursively ground narrative structures which, in turn, keep the community together. The constructed demonic "conspirators" constitute essential elements within this process: they become the catalysts for the unfolding of a series of narratives which then give rise to an all-encompassing worldview. To understand the significance of these devil figures and the way in which they are depicted, one must turn to the radical subversive's approach to the Other.

Approaching the Other

With the development of existentialist philosophy and the rise of mass racial genocide, academic communities have come to address the issue of the Other. Theunissen (1984) argues that "few issues have exercised as powerful a hold over the thought of this century as that of 'the Other'" (p. 1). The academic conceptualization of the Other has been richly endowed by many traditions. Building upon the existentialist terminology of Heidegger and Sartre, contemporary critics are now addressing the Other from the perspective of feminism and post-colonial theory. A shared conception held by these schools of thought views the Other as a disempowered agent, one depicted as a serviceable being whose labor is appropriated by the dominant society. Sampson (1993) contends that

> the other is a figure constructed to be serviceable to the historically dominant white male group. In order to provide this service, the other cannot be permitted to have a voice, a position, a being of its own, but must remain mute or speak only in the ways permitted by the dominant discourse. (p. 13)

The Other can become colonized and become narratively depicted as the antithesis of the colonizer. Thus, while the colonizer is rational, the Other is irrational, while the colonizer is hard-working, the Other is "lazy," or "stupid." Boehmer (1995) writes that "images of the native, alien or Other, reflected *by contrast* Western conceptions of self-hood—of mastery and control, of rationality and cultural superiority, of energy, thrift, technological skillfulness" (p. 81). The act of naming becomes important in the process that defines the Other. Derogatory terms function not only to demoralize, but also to provide a label that mandates an essential identity. The supremacist discourse examined here harbors a two-fold portrait of the Other. These two prevailing constructions serve differing yet interdependent purposes within the movement, and can be best categorized as: the Other as social contaminant; and the Other as powerful conspirator.

The Other as Social Contaminant

The construction of the Other as social contaminant is evident throughout the literature of the radical subversives. Here the Other metaphorically becomes a cultural disease, one whose very presence within the nation is sufficient to destroy the social stability and the special values which made the nation strong at its founding. This depiction of the Other holds strong ties to the genre of racist discourse articulated earlier in American history, as well as in racist Nazi propaganda of the 1930s and the French anti-Semitic discourse of the nineteenth century (Dinnerstein, 1994; Ridgeway, 1990). The importance of constructing completely *new* myths—the radical's discursive *inventio*—remains less critical in this context than the question of how cybercultures appropriate antecedent genres in fostering current narrative structures.

African-Americans as the Other   In current radical discourse, the dominant manifestation of this social contamination is embodied within the image of the African-American. In developing this portrait, radical members draw upon racist images generated in American history and in the US mass media during the first half of the century. This Othering of African-Americans involved depicting them as a brute, primitive force, one biologically designed to corrupt American society. One man wrote on alt.politics.white-power:

> The problem with African Americans is that they are presently destroying our cities as they have been doing for 35–50 years. . . . The African American

menace has attacked our cities and suburbs with more force than all of the hostile Indian tribes and French/English forces combined and organized against us in colonial and post-revolutionary days. Yet, we continue to treat our enemy as citizens. (Bertleson, 1996)

This portrait of African-Americans isolates them as a nefarious and particularly foreign source of contamination. According to such logic, black Americans personify and trigger urban–suburban decay. In this respect they become the causal agent for the impersonal forces affecting the populated sectors of US society. The depiction fulfills what Boehmer argues above: the African-American serves as the antithesis to dominant society, thus negatively mirroring the cultural and social superiority of the colonizer. A contributor on alt.politics.nationalism.white articulated racist statements which depicted Africans as primitive: "Africa sucks, it is a stone age continent and Africans are bringing the stone age to Europe and America. Why are we allowing it?" ("Rad," 1996a). Here again African-Americans become the counter-image to the civilized, productive, side of society. This cultured, civilized portrait is used in turn to define the Aryan racists themselves as ideal.

Such strident racism often loosely hides larger fears about society. The façade concerning the "dangers" of African-Americans as a unique cultural group becomes more apparent when removed from the US context. The consistency of social fears, the *interchangeablity* of the Other, and the racist reaction to the Other surfaces as subversives from other nations post materials on the Internet. For example, the Canadian "Scarborough Skinhead Web Page" distributed a strikingly similar message:

Are you tired of seeing your community turning into gang hang outs? Are you tired of seeing drugs sold in your area? Tired of CANADA spending millions of your tax dollars on immigration not including the price of keeping landed immigrants and refugees in the country. Keeping these claimants could result in the loss of your job, your tax money and your CANADIAN heritage. . . . Third world immigration is killing our people and our way of life. GET INVOLVED AND STAND UP FOR YOUR WHITE RIGHTS. (Scarborough Skinheads, n.d.)

The list of concerns here, such as high taxes, personal safety, and job security, points to the importance of economic and social anxieties in generating racist discourse. Examples of international radicalism serve to make clearer the rough outlines of the supremacist genre which drives such tracts. Further characteristics of this genre emerge as we explore alternative constructions of the Other, including a devil figure created outside of the racial criterion.

Homosexuals as the Other Homosexuals function in this context as a socially constructed Other designed to show the degradation of society. The Web page entitled "Cyberhate" (n.d.), chose as its motto: "Keeping America White, Straight, and Proud!!" This slogan excludes by default the Other based upon the criteria of race and sexual orientation. Another Web entry, the "CNG," a self-described "cell-based White Nationalist organization," included a work entitled "The Homosexual Threat," by Jeff Vos (1996). In it Vos provided a quote, filled with ellipses, which was attributed to a periodical entitled the Gay Community News. Vos appropriated the voice of the Other in rendering a social manifesto, threatening:

> We shall sodomize your sons . . . we shall seduce them in your schools, in your dormitories. . . . [author's ellipses] All laws banning homosexuality will be revoked. . . . Be careful when you speak of homosexuals because we are always among you . . . the family unit . . . will be abolished. . . . All churches who condemn us will be closed. Our only Gods are handsome young men. (Vos, 1996)

This narrative of a homosexual "threat" was reminiscent of the anti-Communist genre of the 1950s. The physical danger to society's young males is further exacerbated by the conspiratorial presence of the atheistic gay men. From this alleged "data" against gays, Vos (1996) called out in his tract to condemn homosexuals: "for these sick individuals have caused too much pain and trouble in too many children's lives for society to continue to turn a blind eye to their excesses." Reflecting again the conspiratorial threat of the anti-Communist discourse, the author alerted his readers that "we are in a war. Make no mistake about it. There is an enemy, and the enemy has made significant gains."

Drawing upon Hofstadter's approach to political psycho-pathology, this portrait of the Other can function as a Rorschach test, revealing psychological tokens embedded within the discourse (Black, 1983). A close reading of the Web site literature reveals that as blacks, homosexuals, and the other generic minority groups "destroy" society—via violent behavior or sexual degradation—it becomes the responsibility of the subversives to serve as the preservers of society. Yet unlike the Christian fundamentalists who can look to their religious tenets and knowledge of the Bible, supremacists and skinheads must look to another criterion to support their superior status. They focus on a biological criterion which serves as the foundation for an elaborate cultural tapestry: skin pigmentation. Whiteness, then, functions as the talisman which makes the supremacists and the skinheads the mirror opposite of the Other.

The immense importance of securing "whiteness" as an unabridgeable category helps to clarify the biological foundation which frequently characterizes supremacist discourse. On one newsgroup an advocate argued that: "Actually, racism is good and necessary for the continued breaching off of new types of human beings from the existing stocks . . . at some point, homo sapiens sapiens refused to breed with the sub-men around him" (Strom, 1996). The biological foundation for distinguishing between the supremacists and the Other enhances the essentialist nature of these radical arguments. The distinction, of course, becomes problematized when extended to homosexuals, for here no inherently racial criterion exists upon which to base condemnation. Yet race again emerges when discussions focus on preserving Western civilization, for in this case homosexuals are indicted—whether from the grounds of biological determination or from their free choice of sexual preference—for failing to propagate the white race. Thus, ultimately, attributes of the enemy are traced back to deterministic, essentialist, biological impurities embedded within the body of the Other.

The Other as Conspirator

An examination of the Other as conspirator reveals a distinctly different power relation between the supremacists and the Other. While African-Americans are depicted as savages and subhumans and gays as sexual perverts, it is the Jew who is most ubiquitously condemned in the literature of the radical right. Yet here the prototypical image of the Jew differs from the previously described construction of the Other. Issues of power, wealth, and control predominate. There are two prominent constructions, one involving the Other as a conspiring impersonal agent, the other focusing upon essentialized traits of the individual Jew.

The image of the Jew as a dominant conspiring agent functions as a point of consistency amongst subversives. Langer (1990) emphasizes the importance of the powerful Jew as an image which subversives generally subscribe to. Rhetorically, the empowering of the Jew plays a key role in the radical genre. The Jew, imbued with power, personifies changes in mass society. As Neibuhr (1937, p. 149) has argued, radicalism is often a revolt against the forces of modernization. These forces, such as recessions and high interest rates, result in unemployment and economic disruptions. Members of groups with low status can do little to influence the fluctuations of domestic or world markets. Yet these impersonal threats of the modern world *can* be confronted once they are anthropomorphized in the form of a particular ethnic group. The radicals' discourse generates a mythical narrative that converts social problems into conflicts between distinct and identifiable entities. Such a strategy creates a framework for its proponents which allows them to counter detrimental forms of change. Jews, with their supposed access to "power," personify these forces more effectively than groups such as African-Americans who still hold little influence within society. Thus the Jew is constructed as the agent which lies hidden within institutions possessing hegemonic power, structures which they then use to manipulate society. The government, the media, and even the spread of academic knowledge or ideological doctrines may emanate ultimately from this source.

The Other within these narratives is suffused with an almost super-human power. Such an endowment is imperative if the Jew is to have sufficient capacity to control national or even world events. For example, Dr William L. Pierce (1996) of the National Alliance demonstrated this belief in the dominate power of the Jews. In his tract posted on the National Alliance Web Directory, he argued that the negative reaction to the skinhead movement was caused by a monolithic Jewish conspiracy.

Here the Jews were the cause behind "drug usage among skinheads. They encouraged rap music and racial mixing." Having failed at this attempt, "the Jews tried to brainwash the public against skinheads through their controlled media." Finally, Pierce maintains, Jews began to perpetuate a system of propaganda, whereby the "minions" of the Jew, the American Civil Liberties Union and the Anti-Defamation League of B'nai B'rith, began to turn the police against the skinheads: "All of these Jewish propaganda organizations are well-connected politically, and so they can approach police departments draped in the false cloak of authority."

The subversive literature also indicts the Jew for wreaking havoc upon American society by orchestrating the slave trade in the New World. The entrepreneurial spirit of the Jew allegedly led to the introduction of slavery, which was then used as a means of gaining profit and of dominating important institutions within the young country. A discussion on the newsgroup alt.skinhead illustrates this point. Here two users became engaged in dialogue, the first being Jewish, the second a radical subversive:

[User 1]:
This stuff is just so stupid that it's hard to take it seriously. I especially like the part where he accuses us Jews of bringing the slaves here in the first place. Hmmmm. How >did we do that? I'll tell you.

[User 2]:
I bet you could tell us, but you won't of course. The jew people invented slavery! Just read the old testament to learn the truth!

[User 1]:
And then we sold'em for a pretty penny, I'll tell you.

[User 2]:
It is a well known fact that the jew people will do anything for money.

[User 1]:
So, I think it's pretty clear that the only people who DO take these things seriously are brain-dead.

[User 2]:
So sure of yourself aren't you (I hate that about minorities)? So why don't you want anyone to respond to my personal statements? I can think of a couple of good reasons why a jewish person would not want people to talk about their involvement in history. I do not fear the truth! (Braun, 1996)

The assertion that the Jew initiated the slave trade ultimately transforms the African-American into a voiceless, objectified Other; they become a tool which the Jew ruthlessly used to inflict damage upon white, Christian Americans. This discourse demonstrates the polarity of demon figures used by subversives: one an unintelligent, animalistic force, the other a highly intelligent, evil manipulator which appropriates blacks in an objectified fashion. This supposed manipulation by the Jew surfaces in the supremacist narrative even as the radicals *themselves* reify and condense the Other into one malevolent Thing-like category. The distinction is best reflected by a belief structure which distinguishes between ethnic "mud people" as the *non*-humans and the Satanic Jew as the *super*humans. Together they function as the rancorous force which the sons of Adam must struggle against.

The historical context of anti-Semitism, extending back into medieval Europe, provides the ideological substance for many subversive texts. As the radicals define an all-powerful Jew, they are able to draw upon this extensive discursive history. Web pages and newsgroups have discussed the old anti-Semitic document the *Protocols of the Elders of Zion*. This document, forged at the turn of the century, was designed to oppress Jewish inhabitants. The narrative tells of the widespread design of Jewish leaders to control society, with the goal of ultimately destroying Christianity. Although the *Protocols* have been demasked as a fake, extremist groups still refer to this tale in order to prove the nefarious intentions of the world-dominating Jew. One man on alt.politics.nationalism.white called on other supremacists to download the tract, describing it as "a must read for those interested in furthering their understanding of the New World Order" (Mathis, 1996).

In addition to using this elaborate narrative history, each generation of subversives must redefine the Jew anew, constructing the Other within the parameters of contemporary ideology. In the most recent reconstruction, the Jew as Other is personified by the New World Order. Again the Other is intricately tied to the prevailing fear of an oppressive world government. The Jew within this radical narrative manipulates the world *openly* under the guise of the UN. *Surreptitiously*, the Jew functions at an even higher level: gaining control of the world's governments under the guise of ZOG. So impassioned do radicals feel about this world government, that one supremacist wrote on alt.politics.nationalism.white: "Death to ZOG and to all the traitors who work for them" (Shook, 1996). In radical literature the power of ZOG is so pervasive that it invades the very minds of white, Christian Americans through the use of government propaganda. White subversives view the US government as a tool of the conspiring Jew, one which promotes the liberal philosophy that has made the UN possible. This ideological weapon includes issues such as diversity and affirmative action as well. These policies, according to the subversives, have "brainwashed" society, thus enabling unqualified minorities and feminists to rise in stature over beleaguered white males.

As extremist ideologies depict the Jew as conspirators against the nation and the white race, they cannot praise any aspect of the Jew's entrepreneurial spirit. This can create a discursive tension, particularly in a capitalist society where economic success is deemed as positive. As vociferous anti-Communists, right-wing radicals generally support capitalism, often glorifying it as a form of America's economic heritage. In order to resolve this paradox, the subversives must distinguish the Jew from capitalists in general, demarcating specifically Jewish traits from those of the Christian entrepreneur.

This process requires a demonization which renders each individual Jew reprehensible. The subversives rigidly define Jews within their ethnic or cultural class, not allowing them to "pass" or become recognized members of society—despite the lack of distinctive physical markers. For example, one person on alt.politics.nationalism.white, under the title of "How to Spot a Jew," described the Jewish physiognomy: "Many prominent Jews (after centuries of pilfering European genes) have blue eyes and light coloring, which seems out of place with their basically tropical features. Large, sleepy, fish-like eyes Fat, square lips Pointy ears" ("Rad," 1996b). At the end of the category entitled JEWISH OCCUPATIONS, the author added "Anything which allows political or cultural control over Aryans." This discourse depicts an essentialized Jew and grants *carte blanche* to exclude individuals who might otherwise completely blend into society. The Jew here cannot become acceptable, cannot be converted, for their corruption lies essentialized within their cultural and genetic make-up. Thus in a way that is akin to the yellow star of the Nazi era, the radical subversives must make the Jew obvious, discursively marking the Other.

The Displacing of the Other   The discussion of diversity and affirmative action focuses upon one final dimension of the relationship between the subversives and the Other. Contemporary radicals in the cyber literature frequently deny the oppressed condition of the most disempowered groups. Instead members see *themselves* in this position. The discourse of displacing the Other has gained such prominence that it serves as another defining characteristic of the subversives as a culture.

Radical discourse typically depicts the dire condition of Caucasians. For example, the Web site for Resistance Records commented: "Look at global population levels. Whites account for openly 8% of the planet's population. Only 2% of the babies born last year were White. . . . It is the WHITE PEOPLE that are the true 'new' minority" (Hawthorne, 1996). According to these arguments, uncontrolled immigration and intermarriage are transforming the white sector of society into a "minority" race. Here the category of white-ness is also essentialized. The argument hearkens back to the "one drop" rule of the pre-civil rights era, where even the smallest amount of ethnic diversity in one's background rendered one "non-white." Subversives also argue that governmental regulations seek to impose—in the name of "multiculturalism"—what radicals depict as the "burden" of quotas and welfare payments, economic weights which are disproportionally carried by whites. A tract written by "Yggdrasil" (1996a), the German tree of life speaking through the National Alliance, articulated a list of "exploitations" which the white race must face:

> It is a long list. Burdensome racial preference schemes in hiring, racial preference schemes in university admissions, racial preference schemes in government contracting and small business loans. Beyond quotas there is the denial of rights

of free speech and of due process to Whites who are critical of these governmental policies. We have special punishments for assaults committed by Whites
if the motives might be racial. In addition, Whites pay a portion of the costs of
the welfare state that is disproportionate to what they receive in benefits.

This text argues that it is whites in reality who suffer in America, with
"successful minorities" controlling the media, forbidding "the dissemination of any message that calls attention to minority, racial, and ethnic
dominance. Only messages of minority victimization are allowed to pass"
("Yggdrasil," 1996b). This discourse of Othering oneself comes in part
from feelings of disassociation with society at large. Members frequently
comment on their loss of freedom of speech from censorship, imposed
both legally and through social norms. Such "restrictions" have turned
those who articulate "white pride" into outcasts. George Burdi—known as
"George Eric Hawthorne," the founder of Resistance Records—asserted on
the Resistance Records Home Page: "Look at how 'evil' pro-White individuals like myself are portrayed by the media. You would think that
being 'racist' was worse than being a 'rapist' nowadays. Just change one
little letter and *bing!* you have an instant headline for the nightly news"
(Hawthorne, 1996).

While persons of diverse backgrounds are given "unfair" advantage by
the government, these white radicals claim to be economically and socially
disenfranchised. The radicals thus articulate their identity as a dispossessed
and socially castigated Other. In this way the conflict the supremacists
have with oppressed group members may in part be aggravated by an
effort to expropriate their identity as the Other.

Interactive Relationships in Cyberspace

Radical cyberculture does not exist in a communicative vacuum. As
members discover more efficient ways to reach new recruits, non-racist
individuals can, concomitantly, contact the radicals. The interaction
spurred by Usenet newsgroups functions, in microcosm, as a conversation
between subversives and society as a whole. Although subversives occasionally present their views to the public, interactions occur daily online
via the Internet. Given their importance to the movement and the access
they provide to outside contacts, it is important to examine the patterns of
interaction and tendencies which make up the "language game" of the
subversive newsgroups.

The newsgroups operated by political extremists foster communication
between members of subversive groups and serve as a means of recruit-
ment. Yet upon analyzing the discourse I discovered an unexpected
phenomenon: the regular presence of outsiders. These non-members,
whom I shall designate by the term "antagonists," are a prominent component of the newsgroups. I choose the term "antagonists" for this label
because it most appropriately meets the stylistic attributes of many

(although not all) non-members. One person writing on alt.skinhead under the heading of "Nazi loser," exemplified the aversion some "antagonists" display toward the subversives:

> hey, you little Nazi-loser! . . . Just in case you haven't heard, Adolph [sic] is dead, the SS hanged and you white-trash are the sorry remnants of the panzer divisions! . . . Now that I have discovered your little hideout, I'm going to lead all of my buddies to ya. It will be fun! Swines like you should be placed in a cage and left with a traveling circus! (Membari, 1996)

While such rogue attacks should be expected, the importance of the antagonists in generating dialogue remains surprising. Most of the contributions encountered on alt.politics.nationalism.white, alt.politics.white-power, and alt.skinhead contain criticism from outside of the culture. Antagonistic messages play a key role in triggering a dialogue, providing a theme, or a sense of vivaciousness needed to continue a discussion.

These clashes between insiders and their antagonists function as an ideological dialectic. They result in an interplay between the subversives and non-subversives who browse newsgroups in order to dispute radicals. Such a discourse gains an almost Bakhtinian sense as it forms a dialogic relationship between rhetors (Sampson, 1993, pp. 97–110). In one such instance, two interlocutors on the alt.politics.white-power, the first, an Army officer, demonstrate the tendency for outsiders to critique racial claims:

> [User 1]:
> Well, I am proud and will not take crap from anyone. I hate niggers, spics, wops, kikes and yes, white trash.
>
> [User 2]:
> Such thoughtful, considered brilliance clearly show that the US special Forces only pick men of the highest caliber—intelligent and logical thinkers who scorn danger.
> I suggest the US military may need to rethink its recruiting policy.
> And by the way, your mother dresses you funny.
> Pip pip!
> Flipper. (1996)

This individual, "Flipper," also known as "Fingers McPhee," embodies the style of an antagonist as he inserts himself into radical conversations on the white supremacist and skinhead newsgroups. On one occasion another veteran antagonist formulated a racist survey for regular participants on a newsgroup. The entry begins by demonstrating a sense of personal intimacy, a form of friendliness used to augment the sarcasm of the textual message: "Les, you are indeed pretty renowned on the Internet! just do an Alta Vista search for 'Les Griswold' and behold! You are famous! Some even call you the premier Cybernazi! got a couple of questions for you if you would be so kind to answer" ("Carleton," 1996). This woman forwarded her answers to the survey, censoring part of the antagonist's message by noting: "(snip—rest of liberal noise-making deleted)." This interchange of critique and insult culminates with the antagonist disrupting the seriousness of the formal questionnaire to ask the woman why she did not shift to rec.music.white-power—a site which had recently been banished by a massive Internet vote—adding:

[User 1]:
Oh yeah I forgot, it got voted down,,hahahahahahha.
Losers!!!!!

[User 2]:
Gloat while you can asshole. . . . .
********SPEAK THE WORD********
          REVOLUTION
("Razorrogue," 1996)

This dialogue exemplifies a tension between familiarity and hostility which frequently surfaces on newsgroups. Such shifts from cordial recognition or warmth to ridicule also exist in discussions amongst supremacists themselves. Insiders, perhaps embracing more moderate levels of racist fervor, occasionally comment on posted notes. This internal critique may regulate what some supremacists view as the level of "acceptability" within the racial discourse.

The use of criticism and rebuke may function at yet another level. Respondents—from both the inside and the outside—write and appear to solicit insulting responses. This can become obvious even in the beginning when a user introduces a theme. The pattern of insult and rebuke may be part of the "language game" of these newsgroups. Respondents develop a form of call and response for verbal attacks, using *ad hominem* and hyperbole. While such discourse creates a climate of abuse, it also fosters a dimension of verbal sparring. Discussions turn into a limited linguistic warfare, limited in the sense that users seek not to end the interaction with the opponent, but to provoke the respondent to a stronger degree of extremism. In the following trifurcated response, an overlapping of messages blurs the issues supporting and opposing racial superiority. This obscures the distinct ideologies altogether within a single sparring language game:

[User 1]:
The white people must stick together to conquer all > the niggers.

[User 2]:
Evolved humans must band together to prevent simian vermin like this idiot from passing the [very rude epithet] gene on to another generation of imbeciles. Hey pal! Think you could try firing up your other neuron?

[User 3]:
Very nice sentiment, my friend, but could you please stop crossposting to groups in which Snowy's [author—respondent #1] racist rubbish and Whitey's [author—

respondent #2] mindless reply are completely redundant? We have no problems with racism here in Australia!
We are racists! No problem! (Hughes, 1996)

This pattern of call and response changes dramatically when alternative modes of communication enter the arena. The insertion of scholarly material serves as the best example. In one entry in an alternative newsgroup (misc.activism.militia) a researcher posted a query for further information on group membership. The request was met by a refusal to engage on the part of any participant. Similarly, an academic-sounding statement appeared on alt.skinhead. This posting began with language which contrasted greatly with the accepted patterns of the skinhead language game: "I am a female graduate student writing a thesis on women skins" (Megan, 1996). It continued with sophisticated language, concluding with a tone of cheerfulness rarely encountered in the newsgroup: "Thanks for your time and I look forward to your responses."
Although this query was met by several serious answers, group members mocked its style. Particularly problematic to some was the claim by the graduate student that women skinheads constituted "a movement." One female replied: "Joining a movement? I am very confused; I just *am* a skinhead. . . . I think that you are trying to artificially create some structured, hierarchical definition of skinhead that doesn't *really* exist" ("Schroedinger Cat," 1996). Another respondent strove to deconstruct the very notion of logic which the student had appropriated in formulating her inquiry:

If you want to write about the truth, why are you calling the whole skinhead thing a movement? Do you really know what a skinhead is? I doubt it. So i'll tell you what you want to hear, although it is absurdly untrue.
I'm a skinhead so I can breed with other whites and proliferate the Aryan race. (and for those of you who know me, you'll take this appropriately, as a JOKE). (Welch, 1996)

Finally, one woman posted a one-line rebuke of the academic after several women had provided serious replies to the query:

She iz EzTABLIzHMENT. IgnoR her sizterz. she iz Evl.

This response, perhaps most telling of all, isolated the academic as a "foreigner." Rather than seeking to attack the radical ideology, this graduate student strove to *study* it. As a result, her question initiated a very different kind of relationship with the users. This academic voice extended from the outside, from a culture that was foreign to the previously established parameters of the alt.skinhead newsgroup. The graduate student's goal, rather than to invite insult, was technical in nature. It sought to define the movement, objectifying it in the Foucauldian sense of turning a disciplined "gaze" upon it (Foucault, 1980). Rather than employing a language of insult and abuse, this discourse sought to redefine the group members in academic terms. Here a form of critique would occur, yet this critique would appear in a linguistic style and in a type of medium not accessible to the members. As a result, this academic request prohibited a sparring familial relationship that often occurred on the newsgroups. Within the insulting behavior there was an openness, a sense of full disclosure that would not be apparent in an academic work. For this reason, the academic—in her formal and polite language—became interpreted as "Evl."

Based on this analysis of the discourse of radical newsgroups, one can argue that while the antagonists are not part of the subversive community, their responses may serve an important function. Antagonists allow group members to counter-attack and to support their own peers, thus strengthening the internal cohesiveness. The language game of rudeness and insults allows the style of the radical culture to more forcefully emerge. This outlet can be discursively important to a culture that strives to be hyperbolic and confrontational. The participation of antagonists provides subversives with an audience and broadened access to the public, factors which increase the opportunities for the enactment of radical rhetoric.

Conclusion

This analysis has portrayed aspects of the subversive culture on the Internet as well as the delicate relationship between radicals, society, and the Other. The articulation of extremist ideas within cybertexts demonstrates that radicals are supportive of persecuting innocent members of society. Such ideas and actions *cannot* be sanctioned. I thus concur with the prevailing sentiment in our society which seeks to limit the power of such discourse. Nonetheless, we must also note that genuine ethical concerns could lead toward censorship. The case studies presented here reveal that a substantial infiltration from the outside may serve as an alternative to censorship. On the Internet a multiplicity of voices articulate a diversity of views. This differs substantially from the earlier "letters to the editor" columns in subversive magazines which featured only discourse from the converted. The openness of the Internet and its interactive options may make it less likely for supremacists to break away from society and to form isolated cultures completely outside the reach of moderating influences. I agree with the sentiment given by a Jewish man writing on alt.skinhead who confronted his radical opponent:

> Tell me, do you go up to your jewish neighbors an [sic] expound on the "ZOG", the "jewish invention of slavery", and etc.? . . . Go up to an elderly jew with a cane and tell them that the Holocaust was an exaggeration, and he would do his or her best to kill you with it. Weird sort of truth, that. Since you are the big white supremacist armed with the "truth", why don't you yell it from the rooftops? Afraid people will laugh at you?" (Braun, 1996)

While cyberspace cannot become a substitute for personal confrontation, to engage a radical on a newsgroup is, nonetheless, a step toward forcing subversives into an open interaction with society. Closed communities live in hermetic isolation, and may serve as breeding grounds for extremism with all its physical threats. The openness of cyberspace does not offer such seclusion. The Internet may thus endanger the very notion of a closed community. In doing so it could become an ally in the struggle against bigotry and racism.

References

After Oklahoma (2): The Wild West. (1995, May 13). *The Economist*. pp. 18–19.

Anderson B. (1983). *Imagined communities: Reflections on the origin and spread of nationalism*. London: Verso.

Barkun, M. (1994). *Religion and the racist right: The origins of the Christian Identity Movement*. Chapel Hill, NC: University of North Carolina Press.

Bennett, D.H. (1988). *The party of fear: The American far right from nativism to the militia movement*. New York: Vintage Books.

Bertleson, D.R. (1996, June 3). Civil war in America rages. Posted to alt.politics.white-power.

Black, E. (1983). The second persona. In J.R. Andrews (Ed.), *The practice of rhetorical criticism* (pp. 131–141). New York: Macmillan.

Boehmer, E. (1995). *Colonial and postcolonial literature*. Oxford: Oxford University Press.

Braun, D. (1996, June 3). Nazi loser. Posted to alt.skinhead.

Brenner, E. (1996, January 28). Censorship at issue on the Internet. *New York Times*, sec.13 wc, p. 1.

Carleton (1996, June 5). Les—you're famous! Posted to alt.politics.white-power.

Charland, M. (1987). Constitutive rhetoric: The case of the *Peuple Québecois*. *Quarterly Journal of Speech*, 73.

Charney, M.D. (1995, July 2). Word for word/The Skinhead International: Some music, it turns out, inflames the savage breast. *New York Times*, sec 4, p. 7.

Cyberhate (n.d.). http://www.io.com/~wlp/aryan-page/hate.html.

Dinnerstein, L. (1994). *Anti-semitism in America*. New York: Oxford University Press.

"Flipper" (1996, June 7). Who is McVey?????? Posted to alt.politics.white-power.

Foucault, M. (1980). The eye of power. In C. Gordon (Ed.), *Power and knowledge: Selected interventions and other writings, 1972–1977*. New York: Pantheon Books.

Germanica Online (n.d.). http://www.geocities.com/capitolhill/1343.

Hamm, M.S. (1993). *American skinheads: The criminology and control of hate crime*. Westport, CT: Praeger.

Hawthorne, G.E. (1996). Resistance Records Web home page. Accessed via the Aryan re-education links at http://www.cyberenet.net/%7Emicetrap/skinlinks.

Heidegger, M. (1962). *Being and time* (J. Macquarrie & E. Robinson, Trans.). San Francisco: Harper.

Hofstadter, R. (1965). *The paranoid style in American politics and other essays*. New York: Alfred A. Knopf.

Hughes, J.G. (1996, June 3). Get off our group! Posted to alt.skinhead.

Katz, W.L. (1987). *The invisible empire: The Ku Klux Klan impact on history*. Seattle: Open Hand Publishing.

Kovaleski, S.F. (1996, January 16). American skinheads: Fighting minorities and each other. *Washington Post*, sec A, p. 1.

Langer, E. (1990, July 16). The American neo-Nazi movement today. *Nation*, pp. 12, 85.

Lewis, P.H. (1996, July 30). Second ruling opposes rules on indecency on the Internet. *New York Times*, p. A7.

Lipset, S.M., & Raab, E. (1970). *The politics of unreason: Right-wing extremism in America, 1790–1970.* New York: Harper & Row.

Logsdon, R. (1995, September 17). Cyberhate Web Page.

Mail Order Catalogue (1996). NSDAP/AO, PO Box 6414, Lincoln, NE 68506. Accessed through the National Alliance Web link, http://www.io.com/~wlp/aryan-page/hate.html, the Web home page of Aryan Crusader's Library.

Mathis, A. (1996, June 8). Protocols of the Learned [*sic*] Elders of Zion. Posted to alt.politics.nationalism.white.

Megan (1996, June 3). Women skinheads. Posted to alt.skinhead.

Membari (1996, June 3). Nazi loser. Posted to alt.skinhead.

Myers, G. (1960). *History of bigotry in the United States.* New York: Capricorn Books.

Nationale Volkspartij/CP'86 (n.d.). http://www.nvp.com/partij/.

Neibuhr, R. (1937). Pawns for fascism: Our lower middle class. *The American Scholar,* 6, pp. 137–153.

Pierce, W.L. (1996). Freespeech: Skinheads and the law. National Alliance main Web page, accessed via http://www.io.com/~wlp/aryan-page/hate.html.

"Rad" (1996a, June 5). African Americans? Posted to alt.poltics.nationalism.white.

"Rad" (1996b, June 3). How to spot a Jew. Posted to alt.politics.nationalism.white.

"Razorrogue" (1996). Women skinheads. Posted to alt.skinhead.

Ridgeway, J. (1990). *Blood in the face.* New York: Thunder's Mouth Press.

Rosello, M. (1994). The screener's maps: Michel de Certeau's "Wandersmänner" and Paul Auster's hypertextual detective. In G.P. Landow (Ed.), *Hyper/Text/Theory.* Baltimore: Johns Hopkins University Press.

Sampson, E.E. (1993). *Celebrating the other: A dialogic account of human nature.* Boulder, CO: Westview Press.

Scarborough Skinheads (n.d.). Accessible via http://www.io.com/~wlp/aryan-page/hate.html.

Schoedel, R.C. (1996, June 7). Nazi/Third Reich items for sale! Posted to alt.politics.white-power.

"Schroedinger Cat" (1996, June 5). Women skinheads. Posted to alt.skinhead.

Schwartz, J. (1995, April 28). Advocates of Internet fear drive to restrict extremists' access. *Washington Post,* p. 22.

Shook, M. (1996, June 3). Wizard of ZOG. Posted to alt.politics.nationalism.white.

Stormfront (n.d.). http://www.stormfront.org/stormfront/german.html.

Strom, K.A. (1996, June 3). Racial feelings are natural and good. Posted on alt.politics.white-power.

Talty, S. (1996, February 25). The method of a neo-Nazi mogul. *New York Times,* sec. 6, p. 40.

Theunissen, M. (1984). *The other: Studies in the social ontology of Husserl, Heidegger, Sartre and Buber.* Cambridge, MA: The MIT Press.

Vos, J. (1996). The homosexual threat, Fact #10: Homosexuality is NOT Natural. CNG Web page, accessed via http://www.io.com/~wlp/aryan-page/hate.html.

Welch, J. (1996, June 6). Women skinheads. Posted to alt.skinhead.

Wittgenstein, L. (1953). *Philosophical investigations.* Oxford: Basil Blackwell.

"Yggdrasil" (1996a). The white nationalism FAQ. National Alliance Web page, accessed via http://www.io.com/~wlp/aryan-page/hate.html.

"Yggdrasil," (1996b). Ygg's white nationalism—key concepts. National Alliance Web page, accessed via http://www.io.com/~wlp/aryan-page/hate.html.

Zündelsite (n.d.). http://www.webcom.com/ezundel/

10

Punishing the Persona: Correctional Strategies for the Virtual Offender

Richard C. MacKinnon

What are "virtual crime" and "virtual punishment"? Intuitively, one knows the answers, but it is necessary to situate the original questions in the context or place where these crimes are allegedly occurring and where proper punishments are to be dealt. This leads to the more preliminary question "What is cybersociety?," for it is there where these phenomena are presently under study. Steven Jones (1995) coined the term to describe the "new forms of community" and "social formations" brought about by such "wonders of technology" as computer-mediated communication (CMC). Cybersociety is the emergence of community from a complex set of social formations in a space enacted by mediating technology. In the language of popular culture it is the society within virtual reality (VR) or "cyberspace" (Benedikt, 1991; Gibson, 1984; Rheingold, 1991, 1993).

It feels odd to state this definition so matter-of-factly when it has taken CMC and "cyberculture" researchers most of the 1990s to support the claim that cybersocieties even exist (Benedikt, 1991; Curtis, 1992; Dery, 1994; Hauben, 1993; Heim, 1993; Jones, 1995; MacKinnon, 1992, 1995, 1997; Reid, 1991, 1995; Rheingold, 1991, 1993). Only after these researchers were able to establish cybersociety's fundamental existence could they begin to study in-depth the nascent communities of which Jones speaks. Moreover, while researchers in this field had the additional burden of establishing the existence of the field itself, social developments within cybersociety outpaced the researchers' collective abilities to investigate them.

Cybersociety did not remain nascent for long. While it is easy to equate "nascence" with "innocence," it must be remembered that from the beginning cybersociety was populated by adults, not infants. Once Julian Dibbell (1993) reported what came to be known as the "first rape in cyberspace," it became apparent that "innocence" was no longer descriptive of a cybersociety which had matured enough to belie certain social developments or "social formations" which could only be properly identified as sociopathy.

While 1993 may be the year of the first *reported* incident of virtual rape, it is doubtfully the year of the first incidence of "net.rape," let alone the first instance of violence. And although the first studies of flaming or the general equivalent of virtual violence (MacKinnon, 1992; Reid, 1991) were not concluded until 1992, there is no doubt that the first flames were felt not long after the first virtual salutations were exchanged way back in the "ancient" Usenet year of 1979.

Indeed, as I argue in *Searching for the Leviathan in Usenet* (1992 and 1995, hereafter referred to as *Usenet Leviathan*; references to differences in the versions are cited by date), no sooner had the first virtual person in Usenet encountered the first stranger did he then have to face the possibility of fighting for his virtual life. As many can attest, survival in the wilds of Usenet is a trying experience—one that many have abandoned in favor of more civilized virtual environs. The flight or trend away from the free-for-all of the Usenet commons to the nominally governed environs of mailing lists and moderated newsgroups is something that I had anticipated while researching *Usenet Leviathan* (1995, p. 135); however, I cannot cite any supporting literature for this observation because I am unaware of any research investigating this shift. The point is that sociopathy has been a major part of our virtual interaction from the beginning, despite our inability or failure to comprehensively document and research it. It is abundantly clear that the "darker side" of virtual life merits considerable study. Fortunately, several projects help remedy this research gap (Karnow, 1997; MacKinnon, 1997; Reid, 1997; Smith, 1997; Smith, McLaughlin, & Osborne 1997).

The discussion and analysis leading to a theory of virtual punishment presumes that the reader is familiar with the growing literature which develops the notion of cybersociety or "virtual community" and its inhabitants (for instance, recently Hoberman, 1996; Overby, 1996). The argument developed herein, relying heavily upon groundwork established by this literature, is the final part of a trilogy (MacKinnon, 1995, 1997) using a politico-theoretical perspective for analyzing the origin and control of sociopathy in cybersociety. The cybergovernance trilogy is based on the "persona" as the unit of analysis. Life online is lived through the personae of the users of the technology, not the users themselves (MacKinnon, 1995, pp. 117–120). Within the society of personae, Jones' "social forma-tions" emerge from the newly developing norms, mores, tradition, or other standards of conduct (McLaughlin, Osborne, & Smith, 1995).

My interpretation of Thomas Hobbes' (1651/1962) social contract theory is that these putatively coercive standards of conduct constitute the "Leviathan" or authority phenomenon which forces the personae out of the anarchic "state of nature" into a state of self-imposed governance (MacKinnon, 1995). This virtual Leviathan defines and proscribes undesir-able or anti-social behavior as well as meting out the punishment of the violators. In the account of virtual rape which follows, it was the Leviathan in the form of the enraged community that accused the rapist of wrongdoing and threatened to punish him for his crime (MacKinnon, 1997). In effect, in a state of governance, the Leviathan enjoys a monopoly on the legitimate use of authoritative violence. All other violence is condemned and subject to retribution, which may include the exercise of legitimate violence. It is within the framework of the trilogy—virtual governance, crime, and punishment—that the discussion of the virtual Leviathan's power to punish is situated. And, while the examples of the online crimes to follow refer to specific types of VR-producing technology, the cybergovernance theories are developed broadly enough to account for technological implementations not yet imagined.

The Rogues' Gallery: Mitnick, Bungle, and Baker

It is my view that crimes involving computers have been often and wrongly conflated into a generalized category of "computer crime." Recognizing that categories of crimes tend to share categories of penalties, it follows that an over-broad category likely leads to unjustly adjudicated punishment. For the purposes of this chapter, "just adjudication" is defined as evaluating suspect actions in their local context, preserving the local context by the proper direction of punishment, and establishing a range of punishments appropriate to the local context and reflective of the relative seriousness of possible crimes.

Just Adjudication

Although "just" and "adjudication" have the same origin in *jus*, careless judicial procedure can stray from justice by failing to communicate and enforce clear social priorities. Justice is understood here as locally determined. While appeals to transcendent justice are possible, their discussion is beyond the scope of this argument. The major effort of this argument is to develop a standard of "just adjudication" by which one can recommend correctional or penal strategies to ensure that punishment for virtual offenses is commensurate to the crime. I establish this standard by identifying the facets of its three components:

1   Evaluating suspect actions in their local context.
2   Preserving the local context by the proper direction of punishment.
3   Establishing a range of punishments appropriate to the local context and reflective of the relative seriousness of the crime.

The first component, evaluating suspect actions in their local context, attempts to prevent someone from being judged according to external standards. For example, if the village of kissing-cousins permits marriages between first cousins, it would be unjust to judge those marriages according to the standards of a community that does not. Similarly, the united hamlets of rabbit-eaters would not want to be judged by a community that prohibits the consumption of meat.

The second component is preserving the local context by the proper direction of punishment. One way a community can preserve its local context is by developing and enforcing a legal jurisdiction over the criminal activities committed within them. This means that when a person commits a crime in a rabbit-eating hamlet, the people of that hamlet should prosecute that person for that crime. This seems obvious enough, but unfortunately is not how it has always happened. This will be illustrated in the case of a person who legally, though controversially, raped and murdered his victim in the city of sleazy-and-violent-sex, but was judged according to the standards of another community in which those activities were strictly prohibited.

The third component is establishing a range of punishments appropriate to the local context and reflective of the relative seriousness of possible crimes. This means that punishments should take into consideration the local history, customs, and other idiosyncratic considerations of a particular community. Public spanking is not very effective in a community of masochists. Further, the proper carriage of justice requires punishments which vary according to the seriousness of the crime. If murder is punishable by being changed into a toad, theft should not carry the same punishment. The severity of a penalty should determine the seriousness of a crime. Crimes with severe penalties should be more serious than crimes with less severe penalties. Crimes with the same penalties should be equal in seriousness. Establishing a stable set of graduated penalties makes the society's priorities clear. For example, the village of kissing-cousins prohibits the consumption of meat; however, the sale of meat is considered far more serious. To communicate this priority, meat-eating is punishable by fine and meat-selling is punishable by imprisonment.

The most important step toward establishing a standard of just adjudication is proposing that offenses involving computers should be divided into two primary categories: computer-related and computer-mediated, the latter being the domain of virtual punishment. This basic distinction goes a long way toward establishing the components of the just adjudication standard and is generally applicable to all societies. Additionally, since the scope of the argument is limited to the efficacy of virtual punishment, it allows us to eliminate cases from review which are not instances of virtual crime. Using the case studies of Kevin Mitnick, Mr Bungle, and Jake Baker, it is hoped that future cases will be properly categorized and justly adjudicated.

The Classification Scheme

Within the category of computer-related crimes are those which are "computer-incidental" and "computer-instrumental." Making the distinction among computer-related crimes becomes important when making just punishment decisions because computer-related crimes vary in seriousness and their penalties should vary accordingly.

Computer-incidental crimes are offenses in which the use of computers are involved only incidentally or tangentially to their perpetration. For example, the theft of computer equipment falls into this category, because the computers themselves are not involved in a significant way. Rather, they are the object of the crime. The involvement of computers should not obscure the fact that the crime is fundamentally a theft. Another example of this class of crime is a case in which a computer monitor is used to pummel a victim into unconsciousness. While computer equipment is involved in the crime, clearly its involvement should not obscure the fact that this is fundamentally an assault. Had the perpetrator used a portable television, we would not be tempted to categorize this as a "broadcast" or "electronic media" crime.

Theft and assault are well-defined crimes with a stable set of penalties. The mere presence of a computer should not obscure the underlying crime with an already stabilized set of penalties reflecting the social priority: crimes against people are worse than crimes against property. If the incidental presence of computers is allowed to shift the focus from the fundamental crimes, then the stability of their accompanying penalties is lost and the social priorities become confused.

Computer-instrumental crimes involve computers more directly. The computer becomes the "tool" or instrument of the crime. In contrast with the computer monitor used as a bludgeoning weapon, the operation of a computer to facilitate the commission of a theft is an example of instrumentality. This differs from a theft where a computer might be the object of the theft itself. Whereas the object and weapon of the theft could be anything, the use of a computer "as a computer," not as a blunt object, makes it instrumental to the crime. An example of computer-instrumental theft is gaining unauthorized electronic access to a computer database of credit card information in order to steal the account numbers. Note that if this information is gained without using a computer, it should be properly classified as incidental as opposed to instrumental. This is because the use of a computer is not necessary for committing the crime. Accordingly, coaxing or "conning" someone with computer access into providing database information is an example of computer-incidental crime because it is the coaxing which is the basis for the distinction, not the fact that a computer is involved.

A similar distinction is already made in differentiating between extortion and robbery. While both crimes result in the involuntary surrender of property, the distinction turns on how the surrender is induced. Therefore, recognizing the distinction among computer-related crimes is critical for determining punishment in accordance with the standard of just adjudication. Just as extortion is typically viewed as a less serious cousin to robbery, computer-incidental conning or theft ought to be the less serious cousin to computer-instrumental theft. Accordingly, the categories of punishment should reflect this priority as well. This is not to say that computer-instrumental theft is more serious than basic theft. Indeed, this social priority has yet to be established. Rather, the distinction is made to show that seriousness varies among the possible kinds of computer-related theft.

The category of computer-mediated offenses is more difficult to explain because it is more abstract. Whereas a computer in a computer-related offense is pertinent because it is in the foreground of the offense, a computer in a computer-mediated crime is pertinent because it provides the background. An example is entering a computer-generated environment and stealing a computer-representation of someone else's property. In this example, the computer provides the entire environment or virtual reality in which the crime takes place. In another example, a virtual assault is committed upon the representation of another person while inside a computer-generated environment. Once again, while a computer provides the environment for the crime, the crime does not turn on the instrumentality of the computer itself. The computer mediates every activity in this environment so much that to justly adjudicate offenses in this category, the computer must be properly understood *as* the environment rather than as the instrument. The computer's centrality makes it omnipresent and its use so pervasive as to be invisible. Allucquère Rosanne Stone (1995) calls this a "technosocial" environment in which "technology and nature are the same thing" (pp. 35, 38–39).

Understood in this way, the computer "as environment" seems somewhat similar to the earlier example of the computer "as incidental," yet an important difference between mediated and incidental offenses is physical intangibility. Intangibility makes for an uneasy equation between physical and virtual offenses. For example, an assault in a park does not seem the same as an assault in a computer-generated environment. On the other hand, enough victims of virtual assaults testify that the "felt" damage and pain is sometimes close enough to be tangible (MacKinnon, 1997). While common sense might tell us that they should not be treated the same, common practice threatens to hastily seek tangible recourse for intangible acts. I suggest that this is due to the lack of an alternative recourse with a set of stable virtual penalties which communicate the priorities of the cybercommunity. In other words, failing the "proper direction" component of the standard, justice has not been attained. As a result, virtual execution was the punishment for rape in one computer-generated environment, but physical arrest and scholastic expulsion was the punishment in another. It is clear that the absence of a standard for adjudication threatens the carriage of justice in physical and virtual reality.

Given the description for a standard of just adjudication, I turn now to actual cases of computer crimes to further clarify the boundaries of computer-related and computer-mediated offenses. The three case studies which follow were selected because of their high-profile media coverage and suitability as ideal types for laying down a classification scheme. The recurrent themes of rape and magic emerged only after their selection and during analysis. While these themes are discussed cursorily, they deserve further investigation in another forum. Finally, the standard of just adjudication calls for attentiveness to the local context of an offense. To illustrate the reasoning for this, the case studies are initially presented outside of their local contexts. Any disorientation experienced by the reader should make the context requirement of the standard clearer.

Kevin Mitnick

This description of Kevin Mitnick's activities dating back to the early 1980s relies heavily upon investigative journalist Jonathan Littman's (1996) account based on personal interviews and articles which appeared in various newspapers. The 17-year-old Mitnick's first publicized crime consisted of using unauthorized access to Pacific Bell's computers to alter telephone bills, gain entry to other machines, and steal $200,000 worth of data from a San Francisco corporation (p. 17). After serving a six-month sentence, his probation officer "found that her phone had been disconnected and the phone company had no record of it" (p. 17). In December 1988, Mitnick, then 25, was arrested for "causing $4 million damage to a Digital Equipment Corp. computer" and "stealing a highly secret computer system" (p. 17). A *New York Times* article on his arrest reported that a "judge's credit record at TRW, Inc. was inexplicably altered" (p. 17). US Magistrate Venetta Tassopulos "took the unusual step of ordering the young Panorama City computer whiz held without bail, ruling that when armed with a keyboard he posed a danger to the community" (p. 17). Afraid that Mitnick's capabilities were seemingly limitless, Tassopulos further ordered that Mitnick be held in solitary confinement (p. 19). Katie Hafner and co-author *New York Times* columnist John Markoff (1991) report that while Mitnick was confined he had "sharply restricted telephone access" because there was "no telling what havoc Mitnick might wreak from a telephone alone" (p. 342).

A frustrated employee of Digital Equipment Corporation wrote about his rape-like experience with Mitnick's repeated electronic incursions into corporate computers:

> We seem to be totally defenseless against these people. We have repeatedly rebuilt system after system and finally management has told the system support group to ignore the problem. As a good network citizen, I want to make sure someone at network security knows that we are being raped in broad daylight. These people freely walk into our systems and are taking restricted, confidential and proprietary information. (Hafner & Markoff, 1991, p. 120)

According to Littman (1996), shortly after Mitnick's arrest, additional allegations were made including investigators' belief that Mitnick "may have been the instigator of a false report released by a news service in April that Security Pacific National Bank lost $400 million in the first quarter of 1988" (p. 17).

Mitnick served his sentence, but he was arrested again on February 15, 1995 for violating the conditions of his parole and for committing a "crime spree that includes the theft of thousands of data files and at least 20,000 credit card numbers from computers around the nation" (p. 292). An assistant US attorney who helped coordinate the investigation from San Francisco said Mitnick was "clearly the most wanted hacker in the world. He allegedly had access to corporate trade secrets worth billions of dollars. He was a very big threat" (p. 292).

Mr Bungle

I rely on Julian Dibbell's (1993) account of "A Rape in Cyberspace" to describe Mr Bungle's alleged crimes. He is described as a "fat, oleaginous, Bisquick-faced clown dressed in cum-stained harlequin garb and girdled with a mistletoe-and-hemlock belt whose buckle bore the quaint inscription 'KISS ME UNDER THIS BITCH!'" (p. 239). Mr Bungle used a voodoo doll to force legba, a person of indeterminate gender, to "sexually service him in a variety of more or less conventional ways" (p. 239) whereupon Mr Bungle was "ejected bodily from the room" (p. 239); however, because the victims were still in range of the voodoo doll, he was able to force legba into "unwanted liaisons with other individuals present in the room" (p. 239). Further, as his actions grew progressively more violent, he forced legba to "eat his/her own pubic hair (p. 240), and forced Starsinger to "violate herself with a piece of kitchen cutlery" (p. 240). The assault ceased when Mr Bungle was "enveloped . . . in a cage impermeable even to a voodoo doll's powers" (p. 240).

Three days after the attack, the community members of LambdaMOO gathered to discuss Mr Bungle's fate. After a long discussion had ended without a resolution and everyone had left, the wizard Joe Feedback, acting alone and without witnesses, put Mr Bungle to death. Within days of the secret execution, Mr Bungle had apparently reincarnated as Dr Jest. The primary evidence leading the community to this conclusion was that Dr Jest had "developed the annoying habit of stuffing fellow players into a jar containing a tiny simulacrum of a certain deceased rapist" (p. 254). Almost immediately, members of the community called for another execution or "toading," but their resolve waned upon the realization that Bungle/Jest could simply reincarnate again. It soon became apparent that Bungle/Jest, although still not very likeable, was not as vile in the current incarnation. Apparently, his execution seemed to have mellowed his demeanor. He eventually left the community voluntarily and never returned (pp. 255, 257).

Jake Baker

The description of University of Michigan student Jake Baker's crime is drawn from the events detailed in his own published account entitled "Pamela's Ordeal" (Baker, 1995). Indeed, Baker's account constitutes much of the environment in which this computer-mediated crime took place. In the account, Baker and another male named Jerry apparently held a female victim captive in her own apartment. After some initial fondling, physical and verbal abuse, they forcefully removed her clothing and gagged her with her own undergarments. Jerry took several photographs, while Baker assaulted the victim in the face, eyes, nose, and ear with his penis. Following this, they taped her hands behind her back and suspended her by the hair from the ceiling fan. The assailants struck the suspended victim repeatedly with a "big spiky hair-brush," placed a "spreader bar" between her legs and applied "super-glue" and a "heavy clamp" to her genitals. After Baker photographed the still conscious and badly beaten victim, Jerry taunted her with a "hot curling iron" and then placed it against her buttocks while Baker observed and masturbated. After Baker removed the gag, he forced the victim to orally copulate him while Jerry forcefully inserted the curling iron into her rectum. After this, Jerry used a knife to sever one of her nipples. Then Baker paused to drink a beer while Jerry removed the curling iron and proceeded to sodomize her. Baker claimed he timed Jerry for ten minutes while the victim begged and pleaded with him to stop. They laughed, doused the apartment with gasoline, and set it afire with the victim still alive inside.

For his crime of virtual rape, torture, and murder, Baker was physically arrested for "the transmission in interstate or foreign commerce of a communication 'containing any threat to kidnap any person or any threat to injure the person of another'" (United States Attorney, 1995) and expelled from the university for endangering the "health, diligence, and order among the students" (Swanson, 1995). Jerry, on the other hand, was not apprehended because authorities were unable to identify a physical suspect. It is likely that Jerry was an additional persona of Baker's, in which case he was apprehended at the time of Baker's arrest. Further, although the victim's persona was definitely virtually raped and murdered, other than feeling "frightened and intimidated by [the event]" (United States Attorney, 1995), the victim was not harmed physically by Baker. In fact, other than being enrolled in the same course, any physical contact between them was minimal to none.

Corporal Punishment: Punishing the Body

The analysis of these three case studies requires the further development of the contours of the standard of just adjudication's second component—the proper direction of punishment.

Corporal punishment, literally, the punishment of the *corpus* or body, has a long history in our social development. Swedish criminologist Torsten Erikkson (1976) writes, "The history of justice is replete with violence and fear. Ever since the concept of law came into being, the authorities have been convinced that respect for the law mainly depends on the severity of the punishment" (p. 1). From the Hobbesian standpoint, that of the Leviathan's monopoly on legitimate violence, Erikkson's observation seems obvious. After all, it was the "fear of death, and wounds" (Hobbes, 1651/1962, p. 81) inflicted by one another which theoretically forced the "nasty, brutish," and short-lived people to leave the state of nature and enter into a social contract in the first place. In exchange for the peace and safety conferred by the contract, people surrendered to the Leviathan their individual rights to violence.

Hobbes' oft-called paranoid view of humanity was shaped during a period in which his people had feared an attack from the Spanish Armada—perhaps the most awesome and forceful display of human violence known at the time. It follows from reason that his situation would lead him to take a dim view of human nature; however, there are rosier alternatives to Hobbes' view of human nature. Indeed, while it may be characteristic of our human nature to mistrust one another—and for good reason—it also seems characteristic to feel ashamed of this predilection and to make strides towards a society based on "real" happiness—not happiness amounting to an enforced cease-fire by an all-powerful and dreadful Leviathan.

According to Erikkson (1976), just one among many reformers along the path to benevolence, "The history of the treatment of criminals is primarily the story of man's inhumanity to man. At the same time it contains innumerable examples of his compassion and of his will to lead the offender into a new life as a useful and responsible citizen" (Preface). In this sense, it is possible to look at our attempts to reform the penal process as an attempt to reform ourselves—the constituent elements of the Leviathan—and become more compassionate.

In his book *Discipline and Punish* (1979), Michel Foucault is critical of both levels of reform, but not because reform is undesirable or unneeded. On the contrary, he is critical because the reform actually hides the power which punishes rather than investigates the power's relationship to inhumanity. As a result, the treatment of criminals appears to be more compassionate because "man's inhumanity to man" has been hidden rather than reformed.

Foucault contrasts a graphic account of the mid-eighteenth-century public torture and execution of "Damiens the regicide" with the daily schedule for inmates sentenced to a Parisian "House of young prisoners" almost a hundred years later. Whereas the first account describes a type of punishment which Foucault calls the "spectacle of the scaffold," the latter shows how "modern" method removes or hides punishment from the public view. Perhaps the social importance of the public spectacle has been underestimated. George Ives (1914) comments on the pillory:

> This well-known instrument was made of all shapes and sizes, and varied from a forked post or a split pillor. . . . The hair of the head and beard was shaved off, and sometimes the victims were secured by being nailed through the ears to the framework, and might also be branded. With faces protruding through the strong beams, and with hands through two holes, secured and helpless, they were made to stand defenseless before the crowd as targets for any missiles that

might be thrown. To those who were hated, this was a serious ordeal, for they would be so pelted and knocked about by the mob as to be badly wounded, if not actually done to death. . . . The pillory was abolished . . . altogether in the year 1873. (p. 55)

It was not enough to simply imprison the offender. Nor was it sufficient to observe someone else deal the blows. Ives' account clearly reveals an interactive and intimate component of punishment which is built into the structure of the pillory itself. Foucault (1979, p. 9) explains that punishment's move behind prison walls and away from public view was a result of the "shame" of having to exercise violence to redress violence. Accordingly, the corresponding shift away from corporal punishment was justified by the ugliness and distastefulness of physically interacting with the punishment of a human body. Indeed, the recognition of punishment as "dirty work" resonates with Erikkson's call for compassion over brutality. Foucault writes:

> It was as if the punishment was thought to equal, if not to exceed, in savagery the crime itself, to accustom the spectators to a ferocity from which one wished to divert them, to show them the frequency of crime, to make the executioner resemble a criminal, judges murderers, to reverse roles at the last moment, to make the tortured criminal an object of pity or admiration. (p. 9)

It goes without saying that personally inflicting pain on another is an intensely intimate procedure. On this point, Ives (1914) writes:

> A remarkable illustration of the intensely individual and personal aspect of primitive penalties is furnished where—as it sometimes happened—the prosecutor had himself to execute his convicted assailant "or dwelle in prison with the felon unto the time that he wyll do that office or else find a hangman." (p. 57)

On the other hand, this personal relationship provides the vengeance desired when he notes, "At some of the American lynchings the injured woman applies a match to the wood upon which the offending negro [sic] is to be burned to death" (p. 57, n. 6).

Whatever the case, the relationship between the punisher and the punished changed. As Foucault (1979) puts it, "the body as the major target of penal repression disappeared" (p. 8), first from public view and then from under hand. The reform movement ended the public spectacle initially by shrouding the condemned in an effort to hide the vulgarity of the body and later by conducting the executions behind the walls of the prison (pp. 14–15). In LambdaMOO, the people were spared the intimacy and the spectacle of Mr Bungle's punishment for he was executed out of plain view. Despite the bodylessness of both the executioner and the executed, the lethal act was still intimate enough to leave the wizard-executioner "angst-ridden" (Dibbell, 1993, p. 253).

While reformers may argue that the distancing from or disappearance of the body was due to strides toward compassion, Foucault disagrees. Although penal reforms sought to end torture and distance the disciplinarian from the body by imposing non-physical penalties such as fines or restrictions on liberty, Foucault argues they could not be completely successful. By using the body as an intermediary, they hoped to effect a Cartesian split, in which they could "deprive a person of liberty that is regarded both as a right and as property" (Foucault, 1979, p. 11) while remaining convinced that the body was not the subject of the penalty. It was an attempt to separate the person from the body. "The body," writes Foucault, "is caught up in a system of constraints and privations, obligations and prohibitions. Physical pain, the pain of the body itself, is no longer the constituent element of the penalty" (p. 11). In other words, pain incidental to non-physical punishment was more acceptable than pain caused by corporal punishment because the object was not to cause it. Foucault notes that even "[f]orced labour or imprisonment—the mere loss of liberty—has never functioned without a certain additional element of punishment that certainly concerns the body itself: rationing of food, sexual deprivation, corporal punishment, solitary confinement" (p. 16). This was true for Jake Baker. His pain was incidental to the "non-physical" punishment of his person (arrest and expulsion) which was more acceptable than any "physical" pain meted out via virtual means, such as toading. Nonetheless, Foucault's point is well taken.

The phenomenon of the disappearing body seems well suited to the bodyless environments of VR, but, as Foucault points out, any attempt at restricting the body's liberties "certainly concerns the body itself." This observation reminds me of Stone's (1991) comments on the "old Cartesian trick" (p. 113) in response to the notion that "a time will come when [cyberspace developers] will be able to forget about the body" (p. 113). Reacting to this notion of unrestrained liberty once the body has been "decoupled" from the "subject" or persona, Stone turns Foucault on his head by reminding us, "No refigured body, no matter how beautiful, will slow the death of a cyberpunk with AIDS. Even in the age of the technosubject, life is lived through bodies" (p. 113). Indeed, whether we are trying to liberate the persona or restrict a person's liberties, it seems that we have yet to discover a way to completely lose the body. Nonetheless, as I observe in *Usenet Leviathan* (1995), "it is common and expedient to 'forget'" the coupling (p. 121). For now, the trick to losing the body is in the expediency of the forgetting. Presumably, this is what Foucault thinks most penal reformers are doing and what I believe most cyberspace inhabitants who think they can detach from their bodies *must* be doing.

Whereas I take the persona as my unit of analysis in the cyber-governance trilogy, Foucault, throughout his work, undertakes power as his. This approach permits Foucault a cross-sectional insight allowing him to view bodies as persons battling for power as well as the places where the battles are fought (Foucault, 1979, pp. 25–27). This perspective, which he calls the "political technology of the body" (p. 26), will be returned to repeatedly for it goes a long way toward fleshing out the virtual body and its punishment.

Non-corporal Punishment[1]

The purpose of this section is to see if anything can be learned from non-corporal punishment that can be applied to a community of bodiless beings. It is unlikely that Foucault had virtual reality in mind when he wrote his histories, but a fairly close reading shows us that the "political technology of the body" is certainly relevant to the production of virtual bodies. While the concept of virtual bodies may seem a bit ephemeral to some readers, I want to point out that Foucault did address non-corporal bodies while not dealing with virtual bodies *per se*. Of course, he was referring to the soul, a concept which may be even more (or less) ephemeral than virtual bodies, depending on your viewpoint.

In many cases, the soul rather than body was no doubt the target of punishment. If punishment of the soul was intended as the means of avoiding punishment of the body, it was ironically the site of extra-ordinarily painful episodes in the history of human torment. Some state-sanctioned actions bore a remarkable resemblance to the heinous actions perpetrated by both Mr Bungle and Baker. Let us revisit Damiens, who is in the process of having his flesh ripped away in a public spectacle:

> After these tearings with the pincers, Damiens, who cried out profusely, though without swearing, raised his head and looked at himself; the same executioner dipped an iron spoon in the pot containing boiling potion, which he poured liberally over each wound. Then the ropes that were to be harnessed to the horses were then attached with cords to the patient's body; the horses were then harnessed and placed alongside the arms and legs, one at each limb.
>
> Monsieur Le Breton, the clerk of the court, went up to the patient several times and asked him if he had anything to say. He said he had not; at each torment he cried out, as the damned in hell are supposed to cry out, "Pardon, my God! Pardon, Lord." Despite all this pain, he raised his head from time to time and looked at himself boldly. The cords had been tied so tightly by the men who pulled the ends that they caused him indescribable pain. Monsieur le [*sic*] Breton went up to him again and asked him if he had anything to say; he said no. Several confessors went up to him and spoke to him at length; he willingly kissed the crucifix that was held out to him; he opened his lips and repeated: "Pardon, Lord." (Foucault, 1979, p. 4)

First note that the reporter from the *Gazette d'Amsterdam* refers to Damiens as "the patient," presumably implying that he is being treated or cured. Yet, if his caretakers clearly intended to remove his four limbs by the most painful way possible, one must draw the conclusion that it was not Damiens's body that they were trying to cure. Also note that it is "Lord's" pardon which Damiens sought, not his executioner-caretakers'.

The treatment or salvation of the soul has been practiced throughout the centuries in nearly every culture with a concept of afterlife. Many societies, while believing in deities and divine retribution, still take it upon themselves to punish in the name of their god. In other words, just in case the patient or penitent escapes punishment in the afterlife, these societies make certain that he or she suffers as much as is mortally possible by way of "penal insurance" (MacKinnon, 1996).

The belief in divine retribution is very much a part of our own culture. "Solemnly swearing" to God is so ubiquitous a method for securing truthful testimony or loyalty that we rarely really think about the afterlife consequences. Chances are most people are more concerned with the mundane consequences for perjury or treason. Indeed, even the modern-day caretakers acknowledge this by allowing oath-makers to substitute "affirm" with "swear." This substitution is an affirmation in the knowledge that while divine punishment is to be feared, mortal punishment is a nearer certainty. In Damiens's case, his executioners went so far as to set him on fire, perhaps to insure against his less certain fate in Hell.

Penal reform's affect on non-corporal punishment delivered by physical means was the minimalization of pain and intimacy. Interestingly, the death penalty persisted as a method for punishing the soul. Foucault (1979) writes, "In France, the guillotine, that machine for the production of rapid and discreet deaths, represented a new ethic of legal death" (p. 15). The guillotine and other modern death-inducing systems serve the purpose of providing painless (thereby ethical) mortal punishment and rapid delivery of the soul to one's maker—often with the sentiment, "God have mercy on your soul." Perhaps the change came about from realizing that the proper place for administering non-corporal punishment was in the hands of God. Given this, non-corporal punishment became a means of transportation.

But not everyone believed that death was the best method for inducing divine retribution. According to anthropologist Bronislaw Malinowski (1932), the Melanesians used both lethal and non-lethal means for placing the punished in the hands of their deities. If they caught a rapist *in flagrante delicto*, he was put to death, otherwise "he was exposed to the danger of sorcery rather than to that of direct violence" (p. 387). The use of sorcery, voodoo, hexes, and curses are non-physical ways of meting out divine punishment. As a result, accident, disease, and death from natural causes are often credited to these methods (MacKinnon, 1996).

Of course, not all action taken against the soul must be painful or lethal. Recall the discussion of Damiens's session with God on earth. The reporter's use of the word "patient" implies that the prisoner's soul was being treated. The shift from punishment to treatment comports with the disappearing act of which Foucault speaks. This substitution allows both the criminal and the executioner to disappear behind the now medicalized curtain of penal reform. In effect, by drawing our attention to the magician's diversion, Foucault enables us to view with a critical eye penal reforms aimed at treatment and rehabilitation. Again, this is not an argument against these desirable and benevolent aims, but a call for the assessment of their implementations—we may not be as compassionate as we think.

Nonetheless, spiritual treatment abounds and, of course, it is not just available to criminals. Today it seems another kind of reform is

gaining popularity and this one is aimed at *remedying* a disappearance—
the disappearance of the soul in the corporate workplace and in the way
we conduct business. It is interesting to pause for a moment on the words
"corporate" and "incorporate" and to contemplate their implication—
to make a body. The incorporated body is an entity which embodies
and enlists the bodies of its constituent parts in the service of a greater
whole. Of course, the legal motivation behind incorporation is not to
make a body as much as it is to hide one—the principal business
owner's—from legal liability. Incorporation as a legally recognized body is
very much an example of the political technology of the body. The
corporate body or business-mediated body was a battle won in favor of
business people. The ramifications of this battle are evident whenever
people attempt to bring legal action against a corporation for injuring their
physical bodies.

In view of this, there is no doubt that corporations—bodies made for
business—lack a soul or *animus*. There is no business reason for—what
would the word be—animation? Yet this seems to be changing. Journalist
Jim Morrison (1995) gives several examples of how possessing or creating
a corporate soul can pay earthly dividends. In addition to superior
product, comfortable atmosphere, and brand identification, the business-
man behind Starbucks Coffee Company believes that the addition of
corporate soul will insure his company's competitiveness. Lotus Development Corporation has a "soul committee." The Boeing Company hired a
poet to "lift the spirits." Experts in the corporate soul movement have
written books such as David Whyte's best-seller *The Heart Aroused:
Poetry and the Preservation of the Soul in Corporate America* and Tom
Chappell's *The Soul of a Business: Managing for Profit and the Common
Good*. Chappell has a divinity degree from Harvard. Another book is
Leading with Soul: An Uncommon Journey, co-authored by Terrence Deal
and Lee Bolmon (Morrison, 1995, p. 94). We also have Thomas Moore's
*Care of the Soul: A Guide for Cultivating Depth and Sacredness in
Everyday Life* (1994), which ranked number one on the *New York Times*
best-seller list. Could it be possible that Moore is caring for the same soul
as the caretakers of the corporate soul?

Some people interchange the soul's relationship to the body with the
mind's relationship to the body. On this latter relationship, there is a
great deal of literature in psychology, philosophy, and other disciplines—
too much in too many divisive intellectual camps to formally list here
without going far astray from the argument. The Cartesian dichotomy
which places the body on one side of a theoretical gap necessarily, and
perhaps inaccurately, requires the placement of something else—mind,
spirit, or soul—on the other. If the computer interface places a virtual
body on one side of the gap, what, then, must be on the other? Is it
useful to think of the user as the "body" and the persona as the "mind"?
Or perhaps, the persona as the "body" and the user as the "mind"? Or
even the persona as the "body" and the user as the "soul"? A great

many words have been written by many people about this dichotomy, but, while fascinating, it cannot be satisfactorily resolved in this brief chapter.

Foucault (1979) obliquely calls the fascination with the soul the "reactivated remnants of an ideology" (p. 29). It seems to me that his word choice indicates his desire to maintain a safe distance from controversy—a strategy I admire and wish to duplicate here. He says that one should see the soul as the "present correlative of a certain technology of power over the body" (p. 29). In other words, the soul, like the body, is a battlefield upon which its definition and control are fought. But to define the soul as such implies that it really does not exist. On this point Foucault writes:

> It would be wrong to say the soul is an illusion, or an ideological effect. On the contrary, it exists, it has a reality, it is produced permanently around, on, within the body by the functioning of a power that is exercised on those punished. (p. 29)

By my interpretation, the Foucauldian soul is socially constructed, as is everything else in his universe. It is as "real" as anything else. Indeed, I will show later how the body, like the soul or the business body, is constructed in the same manner. Foucault wisely dodges rebuke, by differentiating the soul in his discussion—the "modern soul"—from the Christian soul, which he calls the "illusion of the theologians" (p. 30). He says that the political technology of body applies to the former. He does not comment on its applicability to the latter. I will leave an interpretation of the unsaid to more qualified Foucauldian scholars.

The controversial Cartesian split effected by the technology seemingly places something on one side and something else on the other. Since the production of the persona with its coupling to a virtual body inheres in it many physical, body-like qualities, it is arguable that if the persona-as-body sits on one side of the split, then the user-as-soul sits on the other. Such an argument paves the way for soul-oriented punishment (or treatment) of a persona to be directed toward the user. This approach seemingly solves the problem posed by the possibility of reincarnation, as exemplified by Mr Bungle's return as Dr Jest. On the other hand, misapplication of this approach, as in Baker's case, produces very unjust results. Indeed, the many-to-one relationship of personae to user challenges the development of theories of punishment for newly developing virtual communities.

Punishing the Person

If non-corporal punishment seems intangible due to its intertwining with an intangible soul, the regrounding of punishment in tangible bodies seems to be an obvious recourse even with penal reform's constraints taken into consideration. But regrounding punishment in tangible bodies seemingly takes me away from the goal of justly punishing intangible, virtual bodies. This is not the case. Physical bodies are not as tangible as they seem. Virtual and physical bodies have much in common.

Prior to punishment is the apprehension of the "person" or the juridical subject who must be held accountable for his or her actions. Without taking a side-trip into the burgeoning research area that answers the question "What is a person?", it is plain enough to recognize that a person is more than the mass and sum of his or her body. To greatly paraphrase the literature, a "person" is a complex mix of identity (negotiated, received, and cultivated), socially legitimated authority, and legal warrantability situated in a culturally legitimated body.

Stone (1995, p. 95) explains that warrantability is a political require-ment for effecting the social contract. In essence, one's body is warranted in good faith for keeping the tenets of the social contract. Should one fail to keep his or her end of the bargain with everyone else—the Leviathan—his or her body becomes warrantable and subject to arrest. It is because of warrantability, Stone concludes, that our political system reduces persons to their bodies. While not a wholly accurate reduction, up until recently it seemed that all of the traits of personage seemingly were found in the nexus of one's body. As a result, apprehension in our society, and most others, refers to the apprehension of the perpetrator's body. Although the discussion has shown how the focus of punishment has tended to shift away from the body, the body remains the focus of apprehension.

It makes sense that one should answer for misdeeds with one's body since it was the body which needed protection via the social contract in the first place. One could argue here that the contract was executed to safe-guard rights, not bodies, but it will be recalled that Foucault points out that it is impossible to apprehend or curtail one's rights without somehow affecting the body. Since in the physical world rights inhere and have context in bodies, then it follows that it is to bodies that accountability must attach. As a result, we—as government—go through great lengths to ensure the identifiability and uniqueness of each and every warrantable person in our society. This warranting process is accomplished by con-tinual and lifelong confirmation. When one seeks a social benefit, whether public or private, one can be expected to prove one's identity—an identity which describes a lifelong association with a particular body. Stone (1995) calls this association a "body unit grounded in a self," or a BUGS (p. 85). Therefore, law enforcement officials seeking to arrest misbehaving selves have little recourse but to arrest the bodies.

Although more tangible than selves, bodies are not as tangible as they seem. In fact, the constitution of a body is under constant change. Today's human body is very different from the prototype. The modern body incorporates contact lenses, dentures, hair plugs, hearing aids, artificial hearts, and synthetic limbs. When a self is frequently or permanently associated with any of these things they become a part of a body/identity.

In this way, a hacker can be seen as the prototypical incorporation of computers by humans. Mitnick was perceived as dangerous when "armed with a keyboard." It is possible to understand this perception in two ways: first, with the keyboard understood as an armament, but, second, with it understood as an arm, extra limb, or extension of his body.

Stone (1991) argues that the computer can be viewed as a type of incorporable prosthesis (p. 89). This line of thinking—that of challenging the boundaries of the body—is further developed in Donna Haraway's (1991) notion of the "cyborg" and Alexander Chislenko's (1995) cyborg-ization theory of "legacy systems." In effect, the boundaries of the human body are in constant flux by way of incorporation, extension, and augmentation.

The notion of the "culturally intelligible" or "culturally legible" body is one that harkens back to Foucault's battlefield. Subsequently developed by feminist theorists such as Judith Butler (1990) and Stone (1995), it essentially means that a bodily-associated identity is whatever society understands it or "writes" it to be. As a result, selves or owners of bodies with colored skins, traditionally female anatomy, physical disabilities, birth defects, transsexualized gender traits, disease, or advanced signs of aging have been written into the margins of the cultural text. Far from being a comprehensive list, it changes in length as the battle for intelligibility or legibility peaks and falls with some groups gaining recognition and understanding as "socially acceptable" identities while others are forced to remain on the fringes. The process of cultural intelligibility alters the social conception of what a person or body/identity is and whose body/identity matters.

Punishing the Persona: Bodyless Offenders and Virtual Penalties

The apparatus of punitive justice must now bite into this bodiless reality
—Michel Foucault, *Discipline and Punish* (1979), p. 17

What happens when Stone's "body units grounded in selves" meets Butler's "culturally intelligible bodies" and Foucault's "political technology of the self" is what I call the "battle of the BUGS." This battle has followed the human exploration into cyberspace, but persons cannot exist there because cyberspace is not habitable for physical bodies. Hence, the exploration and battle has been undertaken by personae—virtual bodies grounded in selves.

Although hacker bodies and identities, such as Mitnick's, have been the subject of much cultural construction, the boundaries of the virtual body and identity are even more flexible. The persona is the new site for coding cybercultural norms and establishing technosocial intelligibility. The relative decentralization of power in cybersocieties has permitted a variety of characteristics to be recognized as constitutive of one's persona. Examples include indeterminate or arbitrary gender; magical powers; teleportation ability; arbitrary physique, ethnicity, and sexual preference; non-human and inter-human species; regenerative abilities; and the ability to reincarnate. Yet, despite this vast array of difference with possibilities for new social configurations, we must not forget Stone's image of the super-persona tied to the dying body of a hacker with AIDS. To this day, virtual bodies remain coupled to selves which depend on physical bodies for existence. Until this relationship changes, the social configurations and possibilities in cyberspace will be constrained by it. With this in mind, I return to the remaining case studies and critique their dispositions in light of the standard of just adjudication. Afterwards, I will propose a model for establishing sentencing guidelines in accordance with the standard of just adjudication.

The adjudication of Kevin Mitnick: Computer-Related Offender

Mitnick's case shares much in common with the other two. All three committed crimes in which computers played an important role. All three crimes included actions which some people interpreted as rape. Seemingly without limit, Mitnick's technical abilities were reputed to be magic-like in nature. Similarly, Mr Bungle relied upon his technical skills to create a voodoo doll with magical abilities. Mitnick was accused of being deadly when armed with a computer. With computer-mediation, Jake Baker tortured and killed his victim's persona.

Despite these many similarities, Mitnick's case is different from the others in that his offenses were not computer-mediated. Mitnick's use of the computer was limited to incidental and instrumental roles. As much as I have to say regarding the disposition of his case, the just adjudication of computer-related offenses lies beyond the scope of this chapter, the purpose of which is to propose correctional strategies for virtual offenders. This is not to say that the study of Mitnick's case was not worthwhile. On the contrary, it serves as an important boundary marker between computer-related and computer-mediated offenses.

The adjudication of Mr Bungle: Computer-Mediated Offender

Mr Bungle's offenses are computer-mediated because they were committed in a computer-generated environment called LambdaMOO. The fact that the victims and other members of the community of LambdaMOO believed in the voodoo doll's magic and ascribed rape to the events which occurred is an interesting phenomenon in itself. The phenomenon, known as "attribution," occurred primarily as a result of the long socio-historical development of rape. The people of LambdaMOO had an understandable perspective given the set of events (MacKinnon, 1997). Indeed, it is arguable that their immersion in a technosocial environment gave them a stronger justification for believing in magic and "feeling" the rape than Mitnick's victims. In the interest of space, I will take the acceptance of rape and magic in LambdaMOO as a given; however, a complete discussion of the social construction of virtual rape and magic is taken up in the second part of the cybergovernance trilogy (MacKinnnon, 1997).

For his crimes, Mr Bungle was executed by a wizard. Wizards are personae who have the power to discipline. By "toading" or "recycling" Mr Bungle, the wizard destroyed him. It should be noted that the person in whom Mr Bungle "was grounded" was not disciplined in any way. This was a deliberate decision made by the community of LambdaMOO. "He had committed a MOO crime, and his punishment, if any, would be meted out via the MOO" (Dibbell, 1993, p. 249). Indeed, they had considered entreating his university to prosecute him for sexual harassment or seeking prosecution under California's laws prohibiting obscene phone calls. As Dibbell notes, despite the frequent references to Mr Bungle's misdeed as rape, the community's willingness to avoid conflating computer-mediated rape with physical rape "testifies both to the uniqueness of the crime and to the nimbleness with which the discussants were negotiating its idiosyncrasies" (p. 249).

I agree that the people of LambdaMOO should be commended for properly classifying the offense as computer-mediated and refraining from seeking tangible remedies (such as prohibitions against obscene phone calls) for an intangible act; however, the death penalty may have been too harsh. I appreciate the seriousness of Mr Bungle's crimes, but the virtual death penalty is the ultimate or most severe punishment available to cybersociety. To assign it to anything other than the most serious crime, such as murder, confuses the social priorities. While Mr Bungle did attack, torture, and sexually abuse several victims, he—unlike Jake Baker—fell short of murdering them.

It is not surprising that debates on the morality of the death penalty were played out on LambdaMOO—especially since virtual rape had not been criminalized by the time of the incident. To counter the anti-capital punishment concerns, the "toading" of personae on LambdaMOO was persuasively argued by some to be closer to banishment than decapitation; a "kind of turning of the communal back on the offending party" (Dibbell, 1993, p. 248). But as I explain in the first part of the cybergovernance trilogy, an important condition of virtual existence is "visible presence." A user whose persona is banished from a virtual community remains outside the "boundary of existence" for his or her actions go "unnoticed" until finally "the memory of that existence is forgotten by the other users" (MacKinnon, 1995, p. 120). Since one's virtual existence depends upon substantiation by others (MacKinnon, 1995, pp. 117–120), banishment from LambdaMOO is tantamount to death in LambdaMOO. If banishment implies being sent away, the rapid and discreet disposal of toaded individuals is a fairly close approximation of M. Guillotine's transportation machine.

The adjudication of Jake Baker: Computer-Mediated Offender

The place in which Jake Baker perpetrated his computer-mediated offenses is called alt.sex.stories—just one virtual community among thousands in a computer-based conferencing system known as Usenet. While the people of LambdaMOO decided against notifying Mr Bungle's university, Jake Baker's university was notified. As a result, the Baker case illustrates the legal challenge posed by "relationships between bodies and persona/selves/subjects, and the multiplicities of connections between them" (Stone, 1995, p. 86). As previously discussed, the coupling of the body and self makes any punishment of the self problematic for the body and vice versa. However, the relationship is just a coupling, not a merging nor an equation. Although the body is grounded in the self, it is not the self. The persistent relationship of the body with the self produces an identity known as a person which is the juridical or warrantable subject. The law must concern itself with warrantable subjects.

For alleged virtual torture, rape, and murder, the body of Jake Baker, as the warrantable part of his coupled person, was arrested and charged by the United States for the communication of a threat to injure the "person of another." Further, for the same offense, the officials of the University of Michigan banned Baker's person from the campus for endangering the "health, diligence, and order of the students." Practically speaking, this particular federal law aimed at protecting the "person of another" is really directed at protecting the "body of another." After all, being a physical component, the body is the more fragile component in the relationship. Theoretically speaking, the law is aimed at protecting the "person of another," but "another" what? Not "person," for that would be redundant. Surprisingly, even this awkwardly applied law seemingly recognizes the distinction between bodies and selves. The law was designed to protect the person of another self—not a body nor a self, but the two coupled together as a person.

Given the nuanced wording of the federal law, it is a shame it was not applied with the same subtlety. Jake Baker's persona, not his person, allegedly committed illegal acts against Jane Doe's persona, not her person. Seemingly, the law is capable of making this distinction. After all, it recognizes the difference between personal bodies and corporate or business bodies. Nonetheless, it is not yet ready to recognize the distinction between computer-mediated personae and persons. This is reflected in the rough application of the statute which prohibits the communication of a threat between persons, not personae. If virtual rape is to be taken seriously, was this the best way to proceed? Why not apply Michigan's rape statute to Jake Baker? The government was not ready to move the law in this direction either.

The case was dismissed because the government was unable to show Baker's person's intent to communicate the threat, further highlighting the distinction. Baker's persona's repeated assaults during the virtual rape and murder were clear indications of his intent in a computer-mediated environment, but his posting of a "sex fantasy" to a public forum and his minimal contact with the victim leaves his offline intent less clear. Was Baker's person threatening Jane Doe's person or was he making a fiction available for public comment? If he had wanted to threaten Jane Doe, why did he not use a more direct method?

The question of Baker's direction gives rise to the proper direction of his punishment. The dismissal was the right adjudication, but, arguably, the wrong jurisdiction. Neither the federal government nor the state had a law which it was ready to apply to the actions perpetrated by a persona. Arguably, LambdaMOO did. Had Jane Doe sought justice in cybersociety, the outcome might have been different, especially in LambdaMOO. But Baker's alleged crimes were committed in the Usenet community of alt.sex.stories, a place with very different social priorities from LambdaMOO. It is unlikely that it would have been possible to secure a conviction there either.

In alt.sex.stories, such activities as Baker's are not monolithically viewed as criminal. Similarly, discussions and plots of blackmail and murder are commonplace in another community called alt.evil (MacKinnon, 1992, pp. 43–48). In fact, Baker's "sex fantasy" was observed by thousands of spectators who congregate in that forum for that purpose. Certainly, the actions of Baker's persona were of questionable taste even to that community's standards, but they did not violate any written or formal statute of conduct in the local context. This is not to say that everyone in alt.sex.stories supported his conduct—after all, someone turned him in. But like LambdaMOO, no formal system of jurisprudence existed for evaluating Baker's persona's actions.

This would be more of a crisis for Jane Doe if she had a stake in the community of alt.sex.stories, but she was not aware of the actions taken against her persona until she was informed through third parties. Indeed, she may not have been aware of the community's existence at all. Given this, and her lack of intentional participation in the cybercommunity, it is arguable that Jane Doe did not have a persona to begin with. As a result, it seems that Jake Baker committed possibly permissible actions against his victim's persona which may not have been her persona at all. Was it all a misunderstanding?

Repugnant to the standard of just adjudication, the questionable actions of his persona placed Baker's person under the scrutiny of an outside community. Like a rabbit-eater being judged by vegetarians, his persona's murderous acts were nearly judged by the people of a less tolerant village. Because they are coupled to a common self, Baker's arrest suggests that his persona and person are viewed as interchangeably warrantable subjects. The ramifications of this view prompt serious concerns. Indeed, Stone (1995) suggests that as more people participate in computer-mediated environments, there will be more encounters with the problematic "relationships between bodies and persona/selves/subjects, and the multiplicities of connections between them" (p. 86).

Although the "neighboring village" let Baker go—albeit for the wrong reason (they lacked sufficient evidence to prosecute him)—the danger is quite clear when a person is held bodily accountable in one jurisdiction for non-bodily acts committed in another. Unlike Bungle, Baker's persona's actions were arguably permitted in the local context, yet Baker remains punished to this day. Despite the government's retreat, the University of Michigan still refuses to readmit him. This is a prime example of misadjudication and unjust punishment.

Sentencing guidelines for virtual offenses

Jake Baker never had his day in virtual court partly because formal jurisprudence had not yet arrived in alt.sex.stories—typical of a Usenet community which has barely emerged from the state of nature (MacKinnon, 1995). This is not the case in LambdaMOO. My critique of Mr Bungle's death sentence begins with the recognition that rape had not been criminalized on LambdaMOO by the time of the incident. This does not deny that the proscription of rape might be found in LambdaMOO's common law. Indeed, the ensuing discussion attracted record participation—a possible indication that a general notion of rape existed and could be supported by a common law argument. Nonetheless, the crowd disbanded without a resolution. On that day, the lone actions of the wizard-executioner constituted evidence that "might makes right." LambdaMOO had not evolved far out of the state of nature.

Subsequent to the Bungle affair, LambdaMOO citizen Nancy (#57980) arbitrated the drafting of a ballot measure which attempted to formally criminalize virtual rape by defining it and setting a penalty. Entitled "Virtual Rape Consequences (#60535)," it states in part,

> A virtual "rape," also known as a "MOOrape," is defined within LambdaMOO as a sexually-related act of a violent or acutely debasing or profounding [sic] humiliating nature against a character who has not explicitly consented to the interaction. Any act which explicitly references the non-consensual, involuntary exposure, manipulation, or touching of sexual organs of or by a character is considered an act of this nature. . . .
> The effect of this petition is to set a guideline for the appropriate penalty resulting from a single proven act of rape in this community at permanent expulsion; that is, @toading of the perpetrator and @recycling of their character and any secondary characters, and refusal of additional character registration requests known to originate from that individual. (Nancy [#57980] 1994)

By calling for "permanent expulsion," it asks for the most severe penalty available to LambdaMOO. Given his reincarnation, it is debatable whether Mr Bungle's banishment was tantamount to a death sentence, but the expulsion described in this petition applies to "any secondary characters" or personae as well. Further, it refuses "registration requests" of additional personae known to originate from that individual. In other words, the proposed law would apply to all personae, present and future, grounded in the same self. For a non-lethal alternative to the death penalty, it is effectively far more comprehensive than most implementations of the death penalty in the physical world—gas chambers and lethal injections do not aspire to make guarantees against reincarnation. In the physical world, at least this much is placed in "God's hands." Toading and recycling enforced in this way are euphemisms for the ultimate penalty virtually possible in LambdaMOO. By definition, the described penalty is capital punishment. Also, this law is aimed at the self, not the persona. This violates the "proper direction" component of the standard of just adjudication and threatens to be as unjust to virtual rapists as the University of Michigan was to Baker's person. Finally, this measure seeks to place rape among the most serious crimes possible because it assigns the most severe penalty available. As it happened, this placement was contentious. The measure was defeated, but approximately two weeks later a similar petition was presented to the community:

> Sexual harassment (particularly involving unsolicited acts which simulate rape against unwilling participants). Such behavior is not tolerated by the LambdaMOO community. A single incidence of such an act may, as a consequence of due process, result in permanent expulsion from LambdaMOO. . . .
> This petition makes no requirement on mediators that they recommend expulsion in every incident; if circumstances dictate, a lesser action may be designated. But if, after due consideration, the opinion of the mediator is that the situation was extreme enough to warrant expulsion, the effect of this petition is to confirm that the community thinks that expulsion is within the scope of reasonable penalties for an act of this kind. (Linnea [#58017], 1994)

While still calling for banishment, its rationale and references to "lesser actions" and a "scope of reasonable penalties" embraces the spirit of the standard's requirement for a range of punishments. Further, the expulsion is less comprehensive than the one in the earlier measure because it does not have a reincarnation proviso. The voters approved this measure. Since the measure provides for banishment, it is possible to say that LambdaMOO communicates as a social priority extreme intolerance towards sexual harassment.

The efficacy of virtual punishment

The effectiveness of virtual punishment depends on how well its implementation brings the actions of personae into accordance with the social priorities of a particular community. It is not my intention to enter into the debate on whether the role of corrections is to punish, reform, or serve as a deterrent. These value orientations can be adequately reflected in the development of correctional strategies while still meeting the standard of just adjudication. Regardless of this orientation, the sanction must have bearing on something "universally" valued within the community such as "life and liberty." In cyberspace, life and liberty are experienced by way of free and frequent communication among personae (MacKinnon, 1995, pp. 117–120). According to Tamir Maltz (1996), virtual punishment must therefore involve "controlling and disrupting the communication of others." In this way, efficacy is possible in cybersociety.

Based on the analysis of these measures alone, it seems that a range of "reasonable penalties" can exist in LambdaMOO to reflect the relative seriousness among crimes, and thereby clearly communicate the social priorities. While most of the discussion has focused on the upper ranges of punishment, not much has been said about the lower ranges. Jennifer Mnookin (1996) notes that the current LambdaMOO implementation of toading varies from other cybercommunities, where it is still "an unpleasant but far from fatal form of punishment in which the character's description is changed into that of a warty toad." Mnookin also notes that other punishments intended to humiliate include parading someone around or confining the persona in a public place. LambdaMOO effects a variant of the latter with temporary expulsion called a "time out box." Finally there is the "loss of quota," which represents the forfeiture of limited resources.

The classification of virtual penalties deduced from the preceding analysis extends from humiliation to death and corresponds to a basic structure perennially observed by anthropologists while conducting ethnographic research in representative societies (Brown, 1952). As I have shown that there are degrees of banishment, so too are there degrees of humiliation. While toading-as-transformation or public display may be the most severe form of humiliation, the forfeiture of property or status may constitute examples from the lower ranges. Precision is difficult because punishments are perceived differently in different local contexts—as in the ineffective spanking of masochists. In view of this, it is still possible to sketch out a hierarchy of general classifications which may serve as sentencing guidelines (Table 10.1).

The purpose of the general classification in Table 10.1 is to propose the hierarchy of culturally relevant punishments as it is understood in LambdaMOO. The general classification of punishments is intended to encompass the range of what is valued in LambdaMOO and the top-down ordering is intended to show the relative value among the classifications. Note that this is not an authoritative ordering of value within LambdaMOO. Nor is it a universal hierarchy because the relative values of status and property, for example, vary from culture to culture. Indeed, even the significance of death is culturally determined. Further, the role of divine retribution may not be significant at all. The precise ordering of value is left to justice practitioners within their respective cybercommunities.

Some examples of physical world punishment do not easily fit into this proposed hierarchy, such as mutilation or dismemberment, unless they are adapted to the local context. Given the construction of virtual bodies, such punishments would have to be reconceived as targeting participation, status, or even property. The loss of an arm or a leg can be viewed in this way in the physical world as well.

Table 10.1 *A hierarchy of punishment and sentencing guidelines*

General classification	Physical world implementations	Some virtual implementations
Divine retribution	Torture; sorcery, voodoo, hexes, and curses	Symbolic hexes and curses; virtual divinity; contacting a university or the police?
Deprivation/denial/ termination of existence	Death penalty, e.g. by guillotine	Comprehensive banishment (reincarnation proviso), e.g. toading and recycling of present and future personae
Deprivation of participation	Imprisonment	Temporary banishment; LambdaMOO's "time out box" or imprisonment
Deprivation of status	Demotion; public display, e.g. by pillory	Toading-as-transformation; loss of wizard status; being paraded around
Deprivation of property	Fines and seizures	Loss of quota on LambdaMOO; loss of objects

I have placed divine retribution at the top of this hierarchy because the threat of involving "the outside" in correctional matters is always looming. The earlier discussion of the user-as-soul *vis-à-vis* the persona makes possible the notion of literally appealing to a higher authority. Yet, such a recourse violates the local context preservation component of the standard of just adjudication. A divine appeal is misunderstood as such if it is *actually* a hotline to the heavens. To meet the standard, it is possible to conceive of virtual divinity bearing the same relationship to cybersociety as does the offline world to its deities.

While this general classification and the implied sentencing guidelines are derived from the socio-cultural priorities of LambdaMOO, a similar model may be constructed for any virtual community to assist with the development of punishments which meet the standard of just adjudication.

Conclusion

In short, it seems that virtual punishment can be an effective means for controlling the behavior of personae in virtual communities. It obviously depends upon the personae having a "stake," for example the pursuit of "life and liberty." This stake is typically safeguarded by belonging to a community which secures these values by way of emergent or formal governance. Further, the stake may be additionally protected by establishing a jurisprudence which adheres to the standard of just adjudication. This standard requires the evaluation of suspect actions in their local context, the preservation of the local context by the proper direction of punishment, and the establishment of a range of punishments appropriate to the local context and reflective of the relative seriousness of possible crimes.

The privileging of the local context is a normative requirement. Stone (1995) writes, "I want to see if cyberspace is a base camp for some kinds of cyborgs from which they might stage a coup on the rest of 'reality'" (p. 39). While not as radical, I had a similar vision for cyberspace while researching the *Usenet Leviathan* (MacKinnon, 1992), but to articulate it in late 1991 would have put me far out on the limb of academic credibility. Fortunately, others have since joined the base camp. Just four years later after I observed Usenet's emergence from the state of nature, John Perry Barlow (1996) declared cyberspace's independence:

> Governments of the Industrial World, you weary giants of flesh and steel, I come from Cyberspace, the new home of the Mind. On behalf of the future, I ask you of the past to leave us alone. You are not welcome among us. You have no sovereignty here. . . .

But perceiving of the development of cyberculture as formations of emergent states or the birth of a cyber-nation is the subject of much criticism. Geert Lovink and Patrice Riemens (1996) are among the scholars in the "net criticism" movement whose main point is to remind us of the relationship that binds "netizens" to the mortal and vulnerable bodies in an increasingly dangerous and unfair world. The reality of the "digital third world" is one not to be taken lightly.

Perhaps a reconciliation of these concerns causes some scholars to liken virtual communities, such as LambdaMOO, to a "role-playing game" (Mnookin, 1996). As opposed to being a village in a cyber-nation, Mnookin argues that the role-playing game metaphor avoids the complexity of overlapping, multiple legal jurisdictions. This approach seems to be particularly attractive when one wishes to confine personae's legal recourses to the rules of the game, but it is unsatisfactory when dealing with those situations when the "real world" intrudes into the game. Ironically, this was the case when the prototypical role-playing game, *Dungeons & Dragons*, was blamed for the bizarre behavior of its players. This point aside, how much of one's day does someone have to spend playing a game before it is fair to call it a "life"? How deep does a relationship with another player have to be before he or she can be called a spouse? How much money and respect must be earned before it can be called a profession? How much does it have to hurt before it can be called pain? Calling the interaction within LambdaMOO a game does not do justice to these questions. Perhaps, as more people spend more time in cyberspace, some jurisdictions of the physical world will retreat a little, just as they have left the arbitration of "roughing the passer" to the National Football League, the execution of Mr Bungle to LambdaMOO, and the governance of souls to "the church."

Note

1. In this section, I deliberately shift from the formal academic style of citation with regard to the soul. An attempt to present a comprehensive survey of the literature and authorities in the relevant fields seems pretentious in this case. For every person persuaded by the psychological approach, for instance—and there are many approaches—there is another who is unmoved. As much as I would be tempted to cite traditional religious texts, I am equally inclined to cite material published by the Rosicrucians. When it comes to the soul, it may be an omission to leave out references to certain types of music, art, and poetry. If it is possible to give the subject the care that it deserves, even a summary would certainly require more space than I have been allotted. As a result, I have decided to allude, rather than to cite. I trust that my discretion in this matter will be judged in this light.

References

Baker, J. (1995). Pamela's ordeal. Available electronically from http://www.eff.org/pub/Legal/Cases/Baker_UMich_case/baker.story.

Barlow, J. (1996). A declaration of the independence of cyberspace. Available electronically from http://www.cybermind.org.hk/archive/cybermind.0196/1636.html.

Benedikt, M. (Ed.) (1991). *Cyberspace: First steps*. Cambridge, MA: MIT Press.

Bolman, L., & Deal, T. (1995). *Leading with soul*. San Francisco: Jossey-Bass.

Brown, J. (1952). A comparative study of deviations from sexual mores. *American Sociological Review, 15*, 409–428.

Butler, J. (1990). *Gender trouble*. New York: Routledge.

Chappell, T. (1993). *The soul of a business: Managing for profit and the common good*. New York: Bantam Books.

Chislenko, S. (1995). Legacy systems and functional cyborgization of humans. Available electronically from http://www.lucifer.com/~sasha/articles/Cyborgs.html.

Curtis, P. (1992). Mudding: Social phenomena in text-based virtual realities. *Intertek, 3*(3), 26–34.

Dery, M. (Ed.) (1994). *Flame wars: The discourse of cyberculture*. Durham, NC and London: Duke University Press.

Dibbell, J. (1993). A rape in cyberspace or how an evil clown, a Haitian trickster spirit, two wizards, and a cast of dozens turned a database into a society. Available electronically from http://www.actlab.utexas.edu/~spartan/texts/dibbell.html.

Erikkson, T. (1976). *The reformers* (C. Djurklou, Trans.). New York: Elsevier.

Foucault, M. (1979). *Discipline and punish* (A. Sheridan, Trans.). New York: Vintage Books.

Gibson, W. (1984). Neuromancer. New York: Ace Books.

Hafner, K., & Markoff, M. (1991). *Cyberpunk*. New York: Touchstone.

Haraway, D.J. (1991). *Simians, cyborgs, and women: The reinvention of nature*. New York: Routledge.

Hauben, M. (1993). *The Net and netizens: The impact the Net has on people's lives*. Unpublished manuscript.

Heim, M. (1993). *The metaphysics of virtual reality*. New York: Oxford University Press.

Hobbes, T. (1962). *Leviathan* (M. Oakeshott, Ed.). New York: Macmillan. (Original work published 1651)

Hoberman, D. (1996). *Body, text and presence on the Internet*. Unpublished manuscript.

Ives, G. (1914). *A history of penal methods*. New York: Stokes.

Jones, S. (Ed.) (1995). *Cybersociety: Computer-mediated communication and community*. Thousand Oaks, CA: Sage.

Karnow, C. (1997). The encrypted self: Fleshing out the rights of electronic personalities. In P. Kollock & M. Smith (Eds.), *Communities in cyberspace: Perspectives on new forms of social organization*. Berkeley: University of California Press.

Linnea (#58017). (1994). Abuse by any other name. LambdaMOO object #68149. Available electronically from http://www.actlab.utexas.edu/~spartan/index.html/rape.

Littman, J. (1996). *The fugitive game.* Boston: Little, Brown and Co.

Lovink, G., & Riemens, P. (1996) "@fric@ or bust" in NetTime (nettime-l). September 1, 1996. Available electronically from http://www.cybermind.org.hk/archive/cybermind.0896/0967.html.

McLouglin, M., Osborne, K., & Smith, R. (1995). Standard of conduct on Usenet. In S.G. Jones, *Cybersociety: Computer-mediated communication and community* (pp. 90–111). Thousand Oaks, CA: Sage.

MacKinnon, R. (1992). *Searching for the Leviathan in Usenet.* Unpublished master's thesis, San Jose State University. Available electronically from http://www.actlab.utexas.edu/~spartan/index.html#leviathan.

MacKinnon, R. (1995). Searching for the Leviathan in Usenet. In S.G. Jones (Ed.), *Cybersociety: Computer-mediated communication and community* (pp. 112–137). Thousand Oaks, CA: Sage.

MacKinnon, R. (1997). The social construction of rape in virtual reality. In F. Sudweeks, M. McLaughlin, & S. Rafaeli (Eds.), *Network and netplay: Virtual groups on the Internet.* Menlo Park, CA: AAAI/MIT Press. Available electronically from http://www.portal.com/~rich/index.html#rape.

Malinowski, B. (1932). *The sexual life of savages in North-Western Melanesia.* London: Routledge.

Maltz, T. (1996). Customary law and power in Internet communities. *Journal of Computer-Mediated Communication, 2*(1). Available electronically from http://shum.cc.huji.ac.il/jcmc/vol2/issue1/custom.html.

Mnookin, J. (1996). Virtual(ly) law: The emergence of law in LambdaMOO. *Journal of Computer-Mediated Communication, 2*(1). Available electronically from http://shum.cc.huji.ac.il/jcmc/vol2/issue1/lambda.html.

Moore, T. (1994). *Care of the soul: A guide for cultivating depth and sacredness in everyday life.* New York: HarperPerennial.

Morrison, J. (1995, November 15). Corporate soul. *American Way,* pp. 94–98.

Nancy (#57980). (1994). Virtual rape consequences. LambdaMOO object #60535. Available electronically from http://www.actlab.utexas.edu/~spartan/index.html#rape.

Overby, B. (1996). *A societal model of the Usenet computer conferencing system.* Unpublished master's thesis. San José State University. Available electronically from http://www.well.com/user/deucer/thesis.html.

Reid, E. (1991). *Electropolis: Communication and community on Internet Relay Chat.* Unpublished master's thesis, University of Melbourne.

Reid, E. (1995). Virtual worlds: Culture and imagination. In S.G. Jones (Ed.), *Cybersociety: Computer-mediated communication and community* (pp. 164–183). Thousand Oaks, CA: Sage.

Reid, E. (1997). Hierarchy and power: Social control in cyberspace. In P. Kollock & M. Smith (Eds.), *Communities in cyberspace: Perspectives on new forms of social organization.* Berkeley: University of California Press.

Rheingold, H. (1991). *Virtual reality.* New York: Touchstone.

Rheingold, H. (1993). *The virtual community: Homesteading on the electronic frontier.* Reading, MA: Addison-Wesley.

Smith, A. (1997). Problems of conflict management in virtual communities. In P. Kollock & M. Smith (Eds.), *Communities in cyberspace: Perspectives on new forms of social organization.* Berkeley: University of California Press.

Smith, C., McLaughlin, M., & Osborne, K. (1997). From terminal ineptitude to virtual sociopathy: How conduct is regulated on Usenet. In F. Sudweeks, M. McLaughlin, & S. Rafaeli (Eds.), *Network and netplay: Virtual groups on the Internet.* Menlo Park, CA: AAAI/MIT Press.

Stone, A.R. (1991). Will the real body please stand up? Boundary stories about virtual cultures. In M. Benedikt (Ed.), *Cyberspace: First steps* (pp. 81–118). Cambridge, MA: MIT Press.

Stone, A.R. (1995). *The war of desire and technology at the close of the mechanical age.* Cambridge, MA: MIT Press.

Swanson, P. (1995). University of Michigan student suspended for pornographic writing on Net. Available electronically from http://www.eff.org/pub/Legal/Cases/Baker_UMich_case/baker_umich_case.notes.

United States Attorney (1995). Announcement of criminal complaint against Jake Baker (A.S. Brenner, Ed.). Available electronically from http://www.eff.org/pub/Legal/Cases/Baker_UMich_case/da_green_bake r_charges.announce.

Whyte, D. (1994). *The heart aroused: Poetry and preservation of the soul in corporate America.* New York: Doubleday.

Acknowledgements

For their helpful comments, I would like to thank kerry miller, RussOK, and Anna DuVal Smith. Perpetual thanks go to my mentors, Sandy Stone, Bill McCraw, T.K. Seung, and David Edwards. A special thank you to the netizens of the Cybermind community, of which I am proud to be a part. And finally, my thoughts extend to Timothy Leary, who tuned out during the completion of this chapter. A colorful and pioneering offender, his lead gives us good reason to question the eagerness to criminalize the mediation of reality.

11

Civil Society, Political Economy, and the Internet

Harris Breslow

One can discern three locations of arguments concerning the politics of the Internet as a system of communication. The first is that of the Internet itself: cybersociety, so to speak, the users of the Internet as they self-articulate the politics of their usage of the Net across the Net. Here one finds an effusive enthusiasm for the political implications of the exchange of information on the Net. As enthusiastic as it is naive, this line of thought argues that the computer-mediated communication of the Internet is necessarily anarchical, decentralized, and anti-state in its nature. For support arguments in this vein point to the nearly instantaneous nature of e-mail, newsgroup, and Web access, asserting that the immediacy of this access and the decentralization of both access to and production of electronic information allows activists of all stripes the opportunity to circumvent the centralized, bureaucratic, and location-bound state apparatus.

The second location is the college campus, the home of the Internet's critical analysis. One could say that this site is a potential location of more judicious criticisms; academics have long had access to one form of the Net or other, and as a result the novelty of the Net and the attendant optimism and fears—social, cultural, and political—which accompany the introduction of new technologies should have run their course. Contemporary academic criticism of the Internet tends to center itself upon questions concerning the nature of the politics of subjectivity, as opposed to the aforementioned discussions concerning the nature of the politics of the electronic apparatus which comprises the Internet. In much the way that Foucault (1991) argued that anonymity could afford the individual subject the opportunity to escape the socio-political and socio-cultural bonds which attempt to fix his or her identity, and thus his or her subjective potential, current analyses of the Internet tend to emphasize the nature of this anonymity, and the empowerment—both social and personal—which this allows individuals who use the Net.

The third location is "civil society," or rather the current political agenda of the state as it responds to a brief of civic morals charges against Internet users by preparing the Internet in general, and the Web in particular, for corporate commercialization via a wave of legislation, censorship, and regulatory control of content. In this respect the Internet is a disputed site; it is contested by, on the one hand, commercial and political forces that wish to define the Net in much the same way as television was construed—as both a commodified communications apparatus (which television accomplished through the economic valorization of air time) and a market (the display of commodities to viewers). On the other hand the Internet is contested by individuals and organizations who wish to preserve the Internet's status as a non-commercial communications system, since it is in this guise that the Net is seen as a progressive socio-political force.

The Communications Decency Act of 1996 exposed both sides of this debate. Regulators and commercial interests discussed the Act as a step toward bringing the Net into the mainstream of commerce by "cleaning it up" and making it "safe" for the majority of people (and their children) who wish to use the Net to browse for information, entertainment, etc. The Act thus presents entrepreneurs with a vast commercial opportunity: by maximizing "informational cleansing" regulators attempted to maximize the potential target audience available to commercial interests. They sought to accomplish this through the removal of a perceived blockage to the Internet's potential commercial exploitation, namely the hesitation on the part of many people who fear that access to the Net might be, in some way, corrupting (usually of their children) or otherwise immoral and/or obscene. Opponents to the Act saw it in terms of its effects upon the limitation of the freedom of speech, and of the potential of the Act to be used in ways which far exceed the perceived need to enforce "community standards" across the Net. In so doing, opponents of the Communications Decency Act described the Internet as a political space, one where the free electronic exchange of ideas allows for the improvement of the human condition. Thus we have what is tantamount to a debate concerning the nature of contemporary civil society; in principle at least, civil society is that space where individuals act socially, politically, and economically with one another outside of the private space of the home and according to the laws which establish the limits of "civil" behavior. An inherently public space, civil society is intimately related to the juridical principles, morals, and ethics which maintain its existence. More importantly, civil society is intimately integrated with the form and nature of social, political, and economic interaction. Indeed, one could say that civil society and the activities therein mutually define one another. In the remainder of this chapter I want to discuss what I believe to be the implications of the Internet for contemporary politics. In particular I want to address the effect of the presence of the Internet upon conceptions of civil society, the site of modern politics.

Civil Society: The Classical Model

At the end of the feudal period, Hobbes' terrifying vision of a society of individuals freed from feudal constraints and thus acting selfishly and violently—the war of all against all—was placated by his vision of a strong centralized government. This government, argued Hobbes (1651/1985), would abrogate the *ultimate* private freedom of an individual's powers, and in exchange provide for and maintain a set of commonly limited, socially viable freedoms—civil laws—which described the extent to which any citizen could act, and thus ensured the common prosperity (the "commonwealth") of all within the politically prescribed limits of society (pp. 227–229). Through the limitation and prescription of social, economic, and political interaction, he argued, government (the "Leviathan") established and pedagogically enforced a civility which delimits the interactions amongst its members (pp. 232–234). Richard MacKinnon (1995) identified a similar Leviathan on the Internet. In its classical conception, civil society was understood as a space—the site of political interaction, the marketplace—within which competing private interests— political and economic in nature for Hobbes—are peaceably mediated, negotiated if you will.

This mediatory function of civil society had—and continues to have— three dimensions. The *social* dimension of civil society is described by the juridical definition of civility, a space within which a specific behavioral latitude on the part of individual members of society is maintained. In this respect civil society is a space which is described by an ethos of conduct; out in public we behave in a certain fashion, whether to avoid legal or social sanctions, because we know that certain forms of behavior—even if they are permissible in private—are just not to be found in public. Thus civil society can be described as a space within which the impulses of the individual are limited by recognition of one's presence within a public environment (Rorty, 1989, pp. 44–73).

Politically, civil society exists as a space across which the private domain of the household—what Habermas (1962/1989, pp. 30–32) has called the intimate sphere—comes into contact with the politicized domain of the state. Here civil society acts as a threshold which, when crossed, causes one to enter the arena of public political debate within which the unlimited capacity of the private domain interacts with a politico-juridical apparatus—that is, the state—which functions to limit this capacity so as to maintain the orderly functioning of civil society. This should not be seen as unidirectional; as one crosses this threshold one's individual liberty and political will mediate the power of the state. In its classical conception, civil society, in its guise as the public sphere, is the site of what Habermas (1962/1989) has called the "rational–critical" function of the public (pp. 35–38). Through this function the public—the agglomeration of private citizens—retains the power to limit the state and direct the state's activities to public ends by means of an ongoing and politically effective public discourse concerning (1) the role of the state in public life, and (2) the limits to what the state may juridically define as the public sphere, and hence its realm of interest, given that the purpose of the modern state is to maintain civil society.

Economically, civil society exists in the guise of the free market, a space within which competing private economic actors "rationally negotiate" their interests with one another. In the marketplace, it is often argued, the mechanism by which people remain civil with one another is the invisible hand, the rationalized relationships of supply, demand, and price which govern the actions of those engaged in economic activities within a framework of reasonable conduct. The rational–critical function described of individuals as they act politically in the public sphere is relocated to the marketplace and redescribed as the capacity to rationally evaluate an item's exchange value against its use value in the public milieu of the market.

The classical model of civil society can be defined as a space of regulated social conduct, one which can be characterized according to the following four principles:

Spatio-social contiguity: Civil society is that space where private individuals interact, it is the space which bounds all private spaces and experiences, and across which they agglomerate. Through this process of agglomeration—which is, in essence one of congregation—civil society becomes a public realm (Habermas, 1983, p. 2; 1962/1989, p. 30). Moreover, civil society is that space across which the state, the public sphere, and the private sphere meet. It is the point of contact between the private and the public, between the individual and the social. Thus we will have to ask ourselves how this new form of communication affects spatio-social contiguity.

Socio-spatial density: Civil society is a site of social congregation. Indeed, it is active precisely at those moments when, and in those locales where, people have gathered. Skinner (1978) has argued that civil society was nascent as early as the thirteenth century in the Italian city-states, which were the first locations to have experienced a prototypical post-feudal emigration from the rural economies of feudalism toward embryonic urban economies of manufacture (pp. 3-6). For Skinner this is a nascent form of civil society for two reasons. First, precisely because of the fact of density. The large increase in the urban populations of the Italian city-states directly led to an entirely new social nomenclature which explicitly acknowledged the breakdown of the feudal system of ranks. Thus, argues Skinner, we see the beginning of an urban citizenry which understood itself simply as such, without reference to external systems of political, social, or religious ontology (pp. 35–41). Italy, then, is the origin of Hobbes' "nightmare" of a population free from externally imposed social, political, and economic obligation. Second, it is a nascent form of civil society because an entirely new form of conduct, one predicated upon the notion of proper individual comportment to match specific social, political, and economic settings, had begun to develop in response to the new social environment which the large and rapid increase in population engendered

(1978, pp. 35–40)—although it would be left to Castiglioni several hundred years later to express this "new" sensibility in its ideal form. Does the Internet affect socio-spatial density? This, in my opinion, is a very important question to consider.

Information/Communication: Habermas (1962/1989) made three points concerning the relevance of communication/media structures for the proper functioning of a civil society. His first point is that the ability of a public to function in a rational–critical manner with respect to the state rests upon its ability to properly assess the government's action (pp. 51–52). Thus the modern emphasis upon the political importance of the press, in particular, and the media in general as the watchdogs of government on behalf of the people. One can extrapolate from this and argue that as the form and availability of the media at hand have evolved over the course of the history of modern society, the ability to maintain an informed opinion, namely the public agenda, and the type of information which one uses to maintain this stance have changed as well. Thus we will have to ask ourselves what changes (if any) the Internet brings to the availability of publicly important information.

The second point Habermas makes concerns one's ability to act in a rational and timely manner in the marketplace. Habermas (1962/1989) has argued that timely and accurate information concerning commerce is the *sine qua non* for a rationalized and open economic market (pp. 73–78). In fact Habermas's imagery of the early bourgeois public sphere is explicitly oriented toward communication and commerce. Sitting in the coffee house, rapidly scanning the commercial postings in the early newspapers—which originally contained little else—members of the mercantile and industrial bourgeoisie openly debated the relevance of these notices *vis-à-vis* market conditions, which inevitably led to discussions concerning the relationship between the market and the government and the effect of governmental acts upon market conditions (pp. 15–17). How the Internet as a relatively novel commercial environment functions to redefine the marketplace in terms of the relationships amongst producers and sellers, along with those amongst sellers and buyers, not to mention its effect upon what is actually sold, is what the Communications Decency Act of 1996 addresses.

Habermas's third point is that the process of communication is the most important building block upon which the edifice of civil society is constructed. The inability on the part of members of a civil society to openly and accurately communicate with one another leads to a dysfunctional polity—one which cannot properly determine common political and social goals, one which cannot properly articulate a sense of shared common values—and to what Habermas has referred to as social trauma (1970a, p. 207; 1970b, p. 372). Thus we must ask ourselves how the Internet allows us to communicate, and whether or not this form of communication is inherently social. There is no doubt that, for Habermas, socially constructive communication begins with the basic speech-act, which is predicated upon an immediate, face-to-face process. I have no hesitation in saying that this is not the only form of communication which is, or which can be, socially constructive. Whether the Internet fosters sociability is another question entirely, and one which is in serious need of discussion.

Socio-economic struggle/competition: At first glance this might seem to be antithetical to the principles upon which civil society is said to exist; after all the notion of struggle is not usually associated with that of civility. Negri and Hardt (1994), however, have pointed to a direct relationship between the constitution of civil society and the formation and dynamics of socio-economic (class) struggle. For them class struggle and civil society are articulated to one another through a state's constitution, which juridically defines the parameters that delineate the limits of political, legal, and civil activities to be found in that state (pp. 28-29). Far from preventing class struggle, they argue, a state's constitution actually engenders it by describing the framework within which political action will occur. A constitution politically and socially legitimates the existence of specific socio-economic formations and describes to them how they may act in a legitimate political fashion, and what actions are extra-constitutional, and thus perhaps most effective. Most importantly, a constitution functions in a pedagogical manner; in juridically defining the limits to civil society a constitution teaches people what there is to be struggled for (p. 29). It describes to them the social, political, and economic spheres within which people function as members of a collectivity, and within which members of collective entities, such as economic classes, may come to be socially and economically exploited or otherwise disenfranchised. How the presence of a communications apparatus such as the Internet affects the conditions of this struggle is of deep social and political import.

Civil society, then, is tenuous; its social, political, and economic boundaries are subject to the shifting relationships amongst these same structures. Civil society is not an absolute space, it is not architectonic in nature. Two things may be said of the classical model with regards to this point. First, that civil society is a highly contingent and relational space. One does not enter civil society, rather one becomes active within it, and through one's activities and the actions of others—in aggregate—civil society is said to be active. Hence the notion that civil society constantly shifts locales. The coffee houses of the very early modern era, the salons of the eighteenth century (Zaret, 1992), the streets and barricades of the nineteenth and twentieth centuries (Gramsci, 1971a)—all were active locations of civil society. The second point which may be made with regards to the classical model of civil society is that as a contingently articulated space civil society is a flexible envelope which is subject to structural shifts. These shifts reconstitute not only the spatial dimensions of a civil society—where it is, the nature of socio-political and socio-economic enfranchisement, its relationship to other spaces such as the intimate sphere—but also the activities found within it. The Internet's existence as a truly novel form of communication, in both breadth and intensity, might very well be changing the structural parameters within which civil society—and hence political action—exists.

Civil Society: the Ties that Bind

From the early part of this century until some time late in the 1960s the social, cultural, political, and economic apparatus that is America articulated itself through the proliferation of a series of social spaces, cultural practices, political and economic institutions, and socio-economic arrangements which exemplified the classical principles of civil society; contiguity, density, information, and struggle.

Economically these structures articulated themselves through what Lash and Urry (1987, pp. 3–4) have called "organized capitalism," and what Lipietz (1987) has described as "the golden age of fordism." In either case what is being described is a corporatist national-political economic arrangement between labor and capital, politically managed by the state. This arrangement functioned to maintain both peaceful labor relations and expansive corporate profits through the establishment of a base salary rate and the linkage of increases in this rate to the rates of increase in corporate profits, price levels, and inflation. Fordist labor accords also managed the distribution of this increase across unionized industry based upon the specific nature of the industrial work performed. This model was functionally articulated during World War II, when the need for a highly managed industrial complex was of pressing importance. It articulated itself after the war through the politics of a managed relationship amongst diametrically opposed economic actors. In this regime, government, labor, and capital came together to form a strong centralized power managing the naturally competitive and potentially destructive relationship between a number of belligerent actors: a well-syncopated and well-regulated socio-economic mechanism which maintained harmony between its labor and capital components, a system of socio-economic relationships which found its way right down to the assembly line (Burawoy, 1985, p. 122) whose aim it was to keep continually running through fresh supplies of raw materials, productive capacity, and consumer consumption.

Politically this period ultimately understood itself to be witnessing what Bell (1960) called "the end of ideology." This was the belief that the various political factions in the United States (embodied for Bell by the Democratic and Republican parties) had moved to the political center and had come to occupy the middle ground, a political space of common agreement, rational deliberation, harmonious debate, and logical conclusion. Government and politics were thus seen mechanistically, as a system of functional rules, systemically applied, without prejudice. The imagery of

cerning the end of ideology, continental
ition of describing civil society in terms
g the ground upon which sociability is
ociety has also been described in the
contestation, one which sees socio-
ckey for political position which, once
to take political control of the state
he focus of much of twentieth-century
f with what Laclau and Mouffe (1985)
neity. Revolutionary spontaneity—the
roletariat to seize control of the state
ally effective general strike—concerns
to seize control of the urban spatial
city square and the street. The imagery
y coincidental, it calls to mind urban
n within a particular space, forming
d this space, concentrating its power
s well as contiguity (the ability on the
to quickly and effectively take control
non objective amongst the participants
ity to rationalize particular exigencies
with structural functionalism revolu-
-regulating social formation, although
tural crisis" (Laclau & Mouffe, 1985,
aneity concerns itself with functionally
rial conditions will lead to the "spon-
ss will. As with functionalist thought,
ionship between structure and subject
aalysis of subjective praxes which are
which exist within the space of civil

ns of civil society as a site of social
ver, a place to be seized—are basic
es, one of the larger bodies of pro-
tart Cultural Studies has presupposed
and one can see Hall's (1981) "Notes
one of the fullest expressions of this
are is defined as a site where popular
al identities, practices and representa-
npersonal, bureaucratically centralized
ratus of cultural production. Cultural
terms of density; it is composed of the
popular. It is made up of local insti-
. . . .—and social practices which are

a zero-sum political competition (which was never lost as *functional* principle by any member of either party) was temporarily displaced by metaphors of centrist agreement and impartial regulation, however tenuously maintained, and at the cost of witch-hunting those who did not want to sit at the center of the table.

Socially, this period saw the American city reach the apogee of its popularity and importance to the political economy and culture of the country. Indeed, the immediate post-war period saw the culmination of a century-long trend; it was at this point that the city reached the peak of its social and economic importance. A larger percentage of Americans had come to live in an urban environment than at any time before or since. Kerouac might have spent a great deal of time traveling, but *On the Road* opens in a tenement in New York City. In fact the road appears at interludes in between time spent in the big city. New York, Chicago, Denver, San Francisco, and LA—Sal's paradise comes to him in his dreams of the city and the thrill of becoming lost in the frenetic energy of a large crowd. This was the era of the space of public culture, a culture of the urban milieu; of the café, the city square, the corner bar, and the little doo-wop group singing in the alley just down the way. Everyone wanted to be in the city; it was the home of jazz, the place where the new painting, the new novel, the new music, and the new criticism were happening.[1] The city was where you could get a good job and make a good life amongst others of similar circumstance and like aspirations.

Indeed, we have lived within the shadows of the ideals of civil society for so long—its assumptions have imbued our actions so deeply—that it has penetrated our thoughts to the point where the principles of civil society have become a set of unspoken assumptions upon which, in part, the edifice of our language is built. This is particularly true of the language of much of American social thought of the twentieth century. It does not profit one to postulate a direct relationship between the evolution of structures of the intellect and the material structures of the apparatus of everyday life; ideas and thoughts live in their own sphere, on their own time, and are as autonomous as any other social structure. What I am describing is a conjuncture of a material apparatus and an apparatus of thought, one which informs a great deal of American social thought, and which was anticipated or otherwise understood by the most profound acts of enunciation which exemplified and explored one or more of the principles through which civil society functions.

Contiguity, for instance, is the principle through which civil society mediates the relationship between the individual subject and the greater social whole. In the classical model of civil society this principle was embodied in legalistic thought; the relationship between self and society was made possible through the establishment of a social contract. In *Leviathan*, for instance, civil society follows from an agreement amongst individuals to commonly cede one's ultimate freedom to do all to all in favor of the establishment and strict enforcement of a set of laws commonly applied to all. The initial source of conflict, argued Hobbes (1651/1985), and thus the most important feature of this initial agreement, was the establishment of a common language (pp. 227–229). This allowed the common perception and understanding of the world, and thus for peaceable social agreement concerning matters of social and political importance.

John Dewey, Charles Cooley, and Richard Rorty have based their social philosophies upon the idea that human communities are based upon the common perceptions and linguistic expressions of their subjects. Dewey saw education as the ground upon which civility is bred. For Dewey, education socially enables the subject. Education provides him or her with a common system of experiential reference and expression, which fosters communal bonds. In performing this function education performs a pragmatic social function; it provides a common basis for self-understanding and the portrayal of the self to the self and others within the community. Education provides the subject with a sense of purpose and place. As such education enables the subject to express him or herself to others, and thus to participate—socially, politically, culturally—within the community (Dewey, 1946). Through common education the communal dimension of a language—its intersubjective dimension—rests upon a relationship between a language and the contingent conditions which surround its articulation by a specific group, which becomes a linguistic community.

For Cooley and Rorty the articulation of a language not only gives members of a community the common ability to articulate themselves to one another within a common social framework, it also gives them a sense of individual identity. Language is that social structure which maintains contiguity, it mediates the relationship between the self and the social. Cooley understood this as a function particular to communication which dialogically establishes a social relationship amongst speakers and listeners, the parameters of which are drawn by the language being spoken. Rorty (1989) sees the existence of language in an equally functional fashion: language is the mechanism through which individuals articulate a common set of values. In this way a linguistic community becomes a moral community, and through regular linguistic interaction the ties which bind are formed (pp. 189–198).

Contiguity has also expressively manifested itself in the post-war structural functionalism of both Parsons and Easton. Post-war functionalism conceptualized social space as the functional intersection of material structures and social processes within which the subject is located. In doing it functionally explained and localized subjective experience in terms of the self-regulating system of society of which this experience is a part. The locale could vary in scale as the concept generically describes contiguity in a socio-functional fashion; located at the intersection of historico-material structures and self-regulating social processes, society functionally organizes itself as a self-regulating system around speci

The Politics of Civil Society

In contrast to Bell's predictions con writing has maintained its long tra of a field of struggle. Far from bei established and maintained, civil twentieth century as a terrain c political/socio-economic factions j achieved, allows for the attempt (Gramsci, 1971a, 1971b). This is marxism, which has concerned itse have termed revolutionary spont capacity of the urban–industrial through a spontaneous and polit itself with the proletariat's ability manifestations of civil society, the of the general strike is not merel density (the crowd rising up fro barricades to maintain and defer within the space of the uprising) a part of those involved in the strik of the mob and to generate a com which allows each person the ab with class objectives). Indeed, as tionary spontaneity assumes a se one which has experienced a "stru p. 18). As such, revolutionary spor understanding what historico–mat taneous" political expression of cl Western marxism postulates a rela which may be read through an a historico-materially determined an society.

Western marxist conceptualizati struggle—a place to be fought assumptions within Cultural Stud gressive academic work. From the social space to be a site of conflict on Deconstructing the Popular" a concern. In this essay popular cul traditions, local sayings, and cultu tions come into conflict with an i and industrially commodified appa Studies describes popular culture i mass of people who make up the tutions—the pub, the football pitc personal, responsive to localized needs, and which function to make representational sense of the world in a way that is both subjective and social. Popular culture is also idealized in terms of contiguity; it is what binds the people to one another within a structure of feeling. Structures of representation mediate the subjective and the social. They empower individual subjects by making the world sensible. At the same time these structures allow for the commonality of meaning, and the profundity of cultural solidarity amongst a culture's subjects. Thus we can see Radway's (1984) argument that it is incumbent upon cultural critics to tease out the kernels of revolution embedded within any cultural act[2] as a logic which originates within the very structure of the society which she wishes to see done away with.

Postcivil Society: The Spatial Dispersion of Social, Political, and Material Processes

Negri and Hardt (1994) say that we have entered a period which is witnessing the decline of civil society, arguing that "it is not modern society but civil society that has withered away, so that our world might be characterized not as postmodern but as postcivil" (p. 17). For them, this shift does not signal the end of the modern era, nor does it indicate the existence of an anti-modern movement on the part of the state. Rather, the shift to a postcivil society is an historically modern development, and they take pains to describe the political and constitutional origins of this shift, arguing that we can see the genesis of postcivil society in the work of Rawls and in the juridical challenge on the part of the state to redress the boundaries which delimit the private sphere. Recall my description of civil society as a flexible envelope which maintains a distance between the private sphere and the state while providing for a common social environment to which a society's private spaces are articulated. We can describe this challenge on the part of the state as one of several structural spatial shifts away from the dense and contiguous spaces which demarcate both civil society and modern sociability and toward an agglomeration of disarticulated, privatized, and highly regulated spaces. Moreover, this challenge to the integrity of the classical model of civil society consists, in actuality, of three mutually conversant trends, all of which function to further disarticulate the architectonics of civil society.

The juridical challenge to the space of civil society is of key importance because of the role which juridical structures play within the classical model. Insofar as civil society is a social space, it is just so because of the juridical limits which define civility and allow people to function sociably. These limits are not prescriptive in nature, but rather they are negative: We are not told *what* to do, rather we are told *what not* to do. In defining the limits of an individual's social freedom through a series of negative limits ("you can do anything you like so long as you don't . . ."), the classical model of civil society not only engendered both sociability and security, it also served to promote a sense of vitality and spontaneity within the public sphere.[3]

As a secure and social space, civil society promotes social density. Security promotes social interaction amongst individuals; it allows people to rest assured that they are safe when amongst others. This is accomplished through the juridical provision of a framework for the limits to tolerable social interaction which are reached and maintained through one's actions within the space of the public sphere. It is in this sense that Negri and Hardt argue that the space of the public sphere is pedagogic in nature. At the molecular level, being in public allows the individual to learn how to act amongst others and how to function as a discrete element within the public body. This pedagogy is not merely directed inwardly; we also learn how to anticipate the actions of others within the public environment, not in the sense that we can read each other like an open book and thus positively predict what someone *will do*, but rather that we learn to anticipate what others more than likely *will not* do. Familiarity, in this case, does not breed contempt, it cultivates both sociability and security.

Civil society, as a flexible envelope, is not simply vulnerable to assaults from the juridical realm. As a highly contingent and articulated space, civil society is open to incursions from either of its two limits. On the one hand, the limits to civil society can be rolled back on the part of the private spaces which comprise one of its two functional limits. In this sense the rational–critical function of the public, at particular moments and locales, generates an explosively critical mass of individual political subjects operating against the interests of the state. The destruction of the Berlin Wall in 1989 is one example of this phenomenon, but the popular occupation of the Russian White House in defiance of a (partially) state-sponsored coup against the popularly elected Duma and its executive is another such moment. In either instance what occurred was a delimitation of the limits of the state on the part of individual citizens acting *en masse* in a critically political fashion and should be understood as an expansion of civil society in the course of the reduction of the state.

On the other hand, civil society's envelope is also open to curtailment on the part of state, social and juridical mechanisms to pressure the limits which demarcate the boundary between the public and the private (Negri & Hardt, 1994, pp. 239–245). This process contains two key components: first, as described by Negri and Hardt, a juridical component which argues that it is the right of the state to legally dictate the limits of *all* private conduct. This is justified by recourse to arguments which describe the importance of the private sphere for the constitution of civil society. Thus we must be very wary of arguments which describe the home and those within it, for instance, as "resources" of social importance. In the classical model, civil society exists as the *limit* to the private sphere. In the postcivil model, the private sphere becomes an *extension* of civil society, an integral component which must be subject to the same control mechanisms as the private sphere proper lest the private sphere break down as a result of malignant actions on the part of the private. In the classical model, civil society insulates the private sphere from the state, whereas in the postcivil model the perceived legitimate needs of civil society serve to extend the state's power to observe and control into the intimate sphere.

The second component to the diminution of the space of civil society is moral in justification and quasi-governmental and public in function. This component consists of the semi-public morality squads—in America, for instance, the "Friends" of the American Way, the Parents' Music Resource Center, the so-called Moral Majority—which abrogate to themselves the right to stand in moral judgement of individual actions whether they be public or private. These groups further their cause by addressing the state as legitimate representatives of the public and as a functionaries who seek to maintain the public good. What is distressing about these groups is their dual capacity to articulate themselves to political parties[4] and governmental bodies[5] while articulating their interests to those of the state. Thus the moral standing of an individual's private conduct becomes of keen interest to the state because it is seen as critical to the state's ability to reproduce itself. In effect *private* morality becomes a *public* resource.

Respatializing Labor and Economic Processes

Carey (1989) has convincingly reminded us of Innis's most important point: that changes in the material structures of communication lead to shifts in political and economic capacity. This is the domain where the Internet is of primary importance, and where I want to situate the significance of the Internet's presence within the ongoing respatialization of the contemporary global political economy.

In terms of economic structures, the period since the late 1960s has witnessed a three-fold dispersion of the political–economic space of the fordist agreement. The centralized and harmonized space of economic production and labor relations has ceased to be of importance. Organizationally, corporations have begun to arrange themselves according to horizontal organizational algorithms rather than vertical algorithms. Simultaneously they have moved from being national to multinational/ global in scale. This should not be seen as a "natural" evolution of the industrial corporation. Lipietz (1987) has warned against this type of argument, pointing to the fact that at other times in their development industrial corporations have refused the move to go global. The evolution in corporate scale from national to global was the result of the inability of OECD corporations to maintain their rate of profit given: (1) their inability to increase their rate of relative exploitation of skilled Western labor given the limits of industrial technology; (2) a rapid rise in the cost of raw materials, engendered by the oil crisis of 1973; and (3) a product saturation of consumer markets, which signaled the end to the sense of limitless demand which had been the economic climate from the end of World War II until *circa. 1965*.[6]

Vertically organized corporations integrate the various processes required of industrial production within a specific productive and organizational algorithm. Typically this is accomplished through the purchase and organizational integration of companies involved in materials supply and parts manufacture. Lash and Urry (1987) have described this form of bureaucratic organization as typical of the national corporation. They argue that national corporations are the largest productive enterprises which can be contained by organized capitalism, for they have reached the spatial limits to the state's ability to govern their activities. They require economies of scale in order to maintain their relative regional economic advantage. So long as they remain national in scope the state can legislate or otherwise negotiate the limits to corporate initiative. Although the national corporation owns a variety of productive enterprises and extends itself across the economic space of the state, it tends to locate the majority of its interests within a single—or few—region(s). Typically the region(s) is (are) selected by the corporation as a result of the presence of resources such as raw materials or skilled labor, and the proximity of primary markets or ancillary enterprises (Malecki, 1986). *The most important manifestation of this process is the emphasis upon the urban locale as a productive center.* Indeed, the industrial city is the *sine qua non* for the national corporation. It is the home of the corporation's labor force, the site of economies of scale and the locale of ancillary and complementary enterprises which allow the corporation to concentrate its efforts upon the regional development of a national enterprise. Thus the need for a series of labor accords; the scale, diversity and concentration of labor involved in this type of organization requires a high degree of contractual and financial standardization—in other words "fair treatment"—and labor peace.

Multinational corporations have no use for the concept of a national region; an area of competitive economic advantage within a single country typically does not stand up to scrutiny when placed against the backdrop of a plethora of particular competitive advantages found across the entire world. As a result the multinational tends to forgo the advantages of spatial concentration in favor of geographical dispersion, for the extra costs involved in transporting finished and unfinished goods are far outweighed by the advantages of dispersion, such as vastly undervalued labor, which is non-unionized, and which continues to be the primary factor in multinational relocation (see Hansen, 1979; Massey, 1978, 1979; Rhodes, 1986).

Moreover, in moving to the multinational scale, corporations have found, for the most part, that vertical ownership/integration of all steps in a regionally based economy of scale is diseconomic. Of more economic sense is the ownership of those parts of a productive process which the corporation can profitably control, and which it manages best, the rest of the overall process being detailed through a series of local subcontracting arrangements, this coming to be spread across the globe (Alliez & Feher, 1990). Hence the emphasis upon a horizontal organization; by owning only the key components in the productive process—scaled down as a result of the use of international subcontractors—and nothing else, the contemporary industrial corporation minimizes organizational complexity, ancillary social costs arising from labor, and the huge, long-term economic risk involved in building a large-scale productive infrastructure.

This signifies the end of the concentration of large numbers of working bodies within a single enterprise, as well as the beginning of the end of the political import of the large-scale labor union: within the horizontally organized corporation, labor loses its political–economic advantage of scale (Alliez & Feher, 1990). When confronted with strikes, walkouts, or other pressure tactics, the corporation can simply relocate its productive capacity outside of the region—or country, if need be—affected by the labor strife (Hansen, 1979; Noyelle, 1983). This is of crucial importance to the nature of contemporary political structures, because it means that one key component of this process—the civil relationship between labor and capital—has been rendered unnecessary.

This is not the only effect that the spatial dispersion of industrial processes has upon civil society. The capacity of horizontally integrated multinational corporations to relocate signifies their ability to circumvent civil obligations—taxation rates, environmental standards, community relations—heretofore made upon the national corporation. As an "inhabitant" of a specific and singularly controlled environment, the national corporation has little to do but to act in good faith toward the other members of the civil milieu. Horizontal organization and international relocation make these obligations immaterial to the industrial multinational, an organization so large in scale that its departure from a region can have devastating effects which last for decades. Thus industrial corporations of scale have the ability to dictate the terms required of their continued economic presence (Strange, 1989). This is hardly a civil situation; the principles exemplified by density are under attack.

A Medium for Postcivil Society

This process is intensified by the Internet. Rapid site-to-site communication and the accurate relay of information are of key strategic importance to the multinational corporation, which requires vast telecommunications resources in order to maintain the logistics of operating a far-flung enterprise across the globe. Of key interest to me is the effect of this process upon fordist labor accords. The availability of telecommunications infrastructures, such as the Internet, is what affords industrial corporations the ability to de-emphasize strategies of vertical concentration in favor of those of horizontal dispersion. Without instantaneous communications capacity industrial corporations would simply not be able to run as efficiently in the horizontal algorithm as they can vertically. Indeed many corporations are using the Internet as a form of global internal communications network, supplanting their reliance upon the telephone and the fax. As multinational corporations move increasingly into Internet-based communications, their reliance upon, and costs derived from, commercial telecommunications utilities decreases. At the same time the ability to manage diversified interests and productive processes spread around the globe increases, given the fact that the Internet is an exclusively digital medium, capable of transmitting any form of data instantaneously with no loss of quality or accuracy due to the nature of the signal.

Another major shift within the political economy of civil society has been in the way industrial products are made. No less important than the new system of organization and location employed by multinational corporations, the introduction of digitally controlled machine tools has had significant effects. First, it allows for a flexible assembly line, as tools can be rapidly reprogrammed to produce different commodities. As well, the tools can be programmed to vary what they produce from a standard model, and thus give the cachet of a hand-tooled or otherwise low-volume product.

Second, the introduction of digital machine tools was articulated to a regional spatial shift away from the urban–industrial centers of much of the OECD in favor of suburban locales. The reasons, argue Massey and Meegan (1978), are three-fold. One, the introduction of digital machine tools allows plant managers to hire relatively unskilled labor, as the productive skill has been assigned to the machine. The implications of this phenomenon, known as "deskilling," are obvious: labor loses its most precious bargaining chip, the monopolization of productive skills. As a result the ability of labor to maintain its political position with respect to both capital and government is seriously diminished, and the socio-political fabric of civil society is rent.

Two, the introduction of this new technology has altered the scale of plant requirements. Once requiring large populations of skilled laborers, and housing huge machines requiring massive resources and a huge infrastructure, contemporary industrial production has seen itself down-sized without a concomitant reduction in plant capacity. The smaller-sized plants, requiring far less material resources and drawing upon much smaller, less skilled populations, have allowed industry to move away from urban–industrial agglomerations—which are crowded, require a high degree of infrastructural taxation, and are the home of high-priced, unionized labor—to the suburbs (Massey & Meegan, 1978). This is, in my opinion, a devastating development. Already made popular by inexpensive housing, the promise of a "healthy" social and physical environment, and the mass ownership of the automobile, the increasing trend to locate industrial processes to the suburbs is intensifying their growth; the process of industrial relocation serves to establish an economic base which is relatively autonomous from that of the city.

Three, the use of digital machine technology isolates laborers on the shop floor. In the taylorist mode of assembly line production workers on the line interacted with one another, passing the unfinished product from one to another, performing their work in syncopated rhythm. Much like the necessity of a dense social environment that requires social protocols and which fosters social solidarity, the assembly line and factory floor engender worker solidarity. This solidarity doesn't simply occur because of the common structure of experience; as with civil society's social consciousness, worker solidarity develops through communication amongst workers. Deleuze has argued that this was possible so long as the machines which were used on the floor were mechanical and analogue in nature. In this environment workers might have been slaves to the machine, but there was space and time for interaction made possible by the fact that the application of human skill to the operation of the machine—a process which mediates the social effects of the machine—caused temporal gaps in the productive process. The introduction of digital machine tools has changed all this. On the new shop floor the worker interacts constantly with the machine, maintaining the speed of its process, monitoring its operational parameters, feeding it the raw materials it requires to function. In this capacity the worker has become a machinic slave, operating at the device's pace, monitored by the device (it counts how many widgets they make, and it notes when the worker does not make the proper adjustments to the machine).

Matthews (1989) has argued that the new factory floor could be the home of a new form of politics of the productive subject. Free from the socio-productive obligations of the mechanical assembly line, workers on the new shop floor should be able to make their own schedules and decide what machine they are to manage for any given day, seeing as they are no longer the motor components which drive the shop's production. Subjective experience thus becomes more varied, open to varying routines, and ultimately—argues Matthews—much less alienating.

I disagree. Alienation has two dimensions: one can be alienated from oneself as well from others. I have no doubt that this type of work allows one to come into contact with one's inner child. Indeed, with no-one else to care for save the machine one is assigned to, all that is left is for one to get into touch with oneself. On the other hand, the alienation of the self from others is nowhere more profound than in this space. Burawoy (1985, p. 120) has argued that the institutional relationships found on the shop floor are homologically related to the nature of the political–economic apparatus of which the factory is a component. It is in this respect that he discusses the class solidarity which is engendered by the line, and which becomes politically effective on the line in the relationships between labor and management and outside the factory, in the union hall, the city square, and the ballot box. Mechanical assembly line work may not help one's sense of self, but it does foster a sense of class membership and social solidarity. On Matthews' assembly line the worker is an island, privately motivated, individually fulfilled. Each machine is a veritable suburb of the shop floor.

Civil society functions through the dense milieu of the public sphere; that space where all may congregate, where subjective identity and social membership are made palpably obvious. The wide-open spaces of the contemporary suburb are private by nature. Congregation occurs in use-specific sites, such as the mall, or the park, where the notions of spontaneous interaction and social congregation are all but designed out of the environment. The suburb is a purely private space, its design principles minimize the amount of area available to public use. As a result, and given the fact that a majority of people in Western societies now live in the suburbs, we are facing the evolution of our social space such that the socio-material structures of civil society—the great square, the union hall, the park bench, and, above all, the street—are being replaced by the apparatus of privatized life. Now we go to the shopping mall and the sports complex, and our children hang out at the Kwiki Mart. Our homes are fully detached, and the backyards fenced in. Joy; now I don't have to see anyone at all.

It is in this sense that I worry about the time which we devote to social interaction over the Internet. I am not trying to argue that the Net is a bad thing. What I am trying to say is that it tends to amplify the sense of isolation which is a preponderant effect of postcivil society. In this sense the Internet is contributing to the dispersion of the social processes which make up civil society; immediate and spontaneous face-to-face social interaction of necessity does not occur within the suburb. The distances are too great, the spaces too spare, the architectonic milieu too bare and unwelcoming. There is a great deal of speculation that the Internet will eventually replace the shopping mall. Soon one will be able to access the Web site of any vendor, manufacturer, or provider one needs, find a full-color, full-motion catalogue of all goods and services offered, and arrange for purchase and delivery. Increasingly social interaction is becoming a mediated practice. After we shop we will be able to visit our friends' Web sites, do a little chatting (perhaps even over the phone), and watch a little television. The Internet's presence does not cause, although it does enable, this heightened sense of privacy and social detachment.

Moreover, the Net promotes a sense of sociability, but it remains to be seen whether this sociability translates into solidarity. Political and social change over the course of this century have occurred as a result of solidarity, both social and physical; people get together to protest. They do so with their friends, people whom they meet regularly, and with whom they have built a storehouse of memories. These memories do not tend to be disembodied and private, but rather fully of the body and social in nature. Guattari and Negri (1990, pp. 38–46) have argued that the emergence of new structures of communication (Guattari, 1995, pp. 33–36) engenders potentially revolutionary possibilities for subjectivity and for the political alliances which these new subjectivities might be able to engender. I am wary of claims of this nature. It would seem to me that political solidarity is a function of density—we will fight for our friends, die for our friends, rise up with our friends, precisely because we know them and we share a commonality with them. To be sure, there are many friendships and systems of alliance which are daily being made through the Internet. However, the Net's lack of spatiality, its lack of density and its ability to maintain distance between people would appear to be counterproductive to solidarity. Moreover, the Net allows people to maintain their anonymity and it is often this quality which attracts a great many people to it. How should I know who is at the other end, and when the chips are down, will people actually strip off their electronic guises to stand and be counted?

Conclusion

At this point I find myself unable to predict how society will reconceptualize—if at all—social solidarity and communal identity. If one thing is clear it is that theory and praxis are not in sync. Contemporary political and social thought still operates according to logics more properly part of principles of density and contiguity as opposed to dispersion and isolation. For nigh on two hundred years the ideals of solidarity, community, and identity—born as much out of the satanic mills as they were of the city square—have informed our sense of political ethics, our understanding of the language we speak and the identities we occupy. I am not at all convinced of arguments which lobby for the end of the modern. Like Negri I believe that what is coming to the end is the civil, not the modern. To be modern is to embrace change, to exalt in one's ability to move freely, suddenly, and swiftly (Berman, 1988). These are principles which inform the Internet, and which the Internet reinforces, and I'm not sure what we are able to say about the Net, since we all live in the shadow of civil society.

I now find the thought of this century to be both attractive and inadequate. Attractive because I am a child of the fordist era, and I hold ideals such as solidarity and community quite dear. Inadequate because I find these terms and the values they are associated with wholly incapable of explaining the spatial dispersion which is increasingly a part of contemporary culture.

Notes

1. Thus one is tempted to describe Jacoby (1987) as nostalgic for civil society.
2. "If we do not, we have already admitted the impossibility of creating a world where the vicarious pleasure supplied by [the practices found within popular culture] . . . would be unnecessary" (Radway, 1984, p. 222).
3. Thus we can regard Laclau's and Mouffe's discussion of Western marxism's continual confrontation with the concept of revolutionary spontaneity in a new light. Indeed, as with Negri, one can see the pedagogic genesis of an entire body of revolutionary doctrine at

precisely the moment when civil society begins to engender spontaneous and free social interaction.

4. The Christian Coalition, for instance, has in effect taken minority control of the policy process within the Republican Party.

5. The PMRC's ability to make its crusade a matter of congressional and senatorial importance is a disturbing example of this.

6. Kolko (1988) discusses these factors in excellent detail. See also Lipietz (1986).

References

Alliez, E., & Feher, M. (1990). The luster of Capital. *Zone, 1/2,* 314–359.

Bell, D. (1960). *The end of ideology.* New York: Free Press.

Berman, M. (1988). *All that is solid melts into air: The experience of modernity.* New York: Penguin.

Burawoy, M. (1985). *The politics of production: Factory regimes under capitalism and socialism.* London: Verso.

Carey, J.W. (1989). *Communication as culture: Essays on media and society.* Boston: Unwin Hyman.

Dewey, J. (1946). *Problems of men.* New York: Philosophical Library.

Foucault, M. (1991). *Remarks on Marx: Conversations with Duccio Trombadori.* New York: Semiotext(e).

Gramsci, A. (1971a). State and civil society. In Q. Hoare & G.N. Smith (Eds.), *Selections from the prison notebooks* (pp. 206–276). New York: International Publishers.

Gramsci, A. (1971b). The modern prince. In Q. Hoare & G.N. Smith (Eds.), *Selections from the prison notebooks* (pp. 135–205). New York: International Publishers.

Guattari, F. (1995). *Chaosmosis: An ethico-aesthetic paradigm* (P. Burns and J. Pefouis, Trans.). Bloomington: Indiana University Press.

Guattari, F., & Negri, T. (1990). *Communists like us: New spaces of liberty, new lines of alliance.* New York: Semiotext(e).

Habermas, J. (1970a). On systematically distorted communication. *Inquiry, 13*(3), 205–218.

Habermas, J. (1970b). Towards a theory of communicative competence. *Inquiry, 13*(4), 360–375.

Habermas, J. (1983). Modernity, an incomplete project. In H. Foster (Ed.), *The anti-aesthetic: Essays on postmodern culture* (pp. 3–15). Seattle: Bay Press.

Habermas, J. (1989). *The structural transformation of the public sphere: An inquiry into a category of bourgeois society* (T. Burger & F. Lawrence, Trans.). Cambridge, MA: MIT Press. (Original work published 1962)

Hall, S. (1981). Notes on deconstructing the popular. In R. Samuel (Ed.), *People's history and socialist theory* (pp. 227–240). London: Routledge & Kegan Paul.

Hansen, N. (1979). The new international division of labour and manufacturing decentralisation in the U.S. *Review of Regional Studies, 9*(1), 1–11.

Hobbes, T. (1985). *Leviathan: Or the matter, forme and power of a commonwealth ecclesiastical and civil.* London: Penguin. (Original work published 1651)

Jacoby, R. (1987). *The last intellectuals: American culture in the age of academe.* New York: Basic Books.

Kolko, J. (1988). *Restructuring the world economy.* New York: Pantheon Books.

Laclau, E., & Mouffe, M. (1985). *Hegemony and socialist strategy: Towards a radical democratic politics.* London: Verso.

Lash, S., & Urry, J. (1987). *The end of organized capitalism.* Madison: University of Wisconsin Press.

Lipietz, A. (1986). New tendencies in the international division of labour: Regimes of accumulation and modes of regulation. In A.J. Scott and M. Storper (Eds.), *Production, work, territory: The geographical anatomy of industrial capitalism* (pp. 16–40). Boston: Allen & Unwin.

Lipietz, A. (1987). *Mirages and miracles: The crisis of global fordism.* London: Verso.

MacKinnon, R. (1995). Searching for the Leviathan on Usenet. In S.G. Jones (Ed.), *CyberSociety: Computer-mediated communication and community* (pp. 112–137). Thousand Oaks, CA: Sage.

Malecki, E.J. (1986). Technological imperatives and modern corporate strategy. In A.J. Scott & M. Storper (Eds.), *Production, work, territory: The geographical anatomy of industrial capitalism* (pp. 67–79). Boston: Allen & Unwin.

Massey, D. (1978). Regionalism: Some current issues. *Capital and Class, 6,* 106–125.

Massey, D. (1979). In what sense a regional problem? *Regional Studies, 13,* 233–243.

Massey, D., & Meegan, R. (1978). Industrial restructuring versus the cities. *Urban Studies, 15,* 273–288.

Matthews, J. (1989). *Age of democracy: The politics of post-fordism.* New York: Oxford University Press.

Negri, A., & Hardt, M. (1994). *The labor of Dionysus: A critique of the state form.* Minneapolis: University of Minnesota Press.

Noyelle, T. (1983). The implications of industry restructuring for spatial organization in the United States. In F. Moulaert & P.W. Salinas (Eds.), *Regional analysis and the new international division of labor* (pp. 113–134). Boston: Kluwer.

Radway, J. (1984). *Reading the romance: Women, patriarchy and popular literature.* Chapel Hill, NC: University of North Carolina Press.

Rhodes, J. (1986). Regional dimensions of industrial decline. In R. Martin & B. Rowthorn (Eds.), *The geography of de-industrialisation.* Basingstoke: Macmillan.

Rorty, R. (1989). *Contingency, irony, and solidarity.* Cambridge: Cambridge University Press.

Skinner, Q. (1978). *The foundations of modern political thought (vols. 1 & 2).* London: Cambridge University Press.

Strange, S. (1989). Supranationals and the state. In J. Hall (Ed.), *States in history* (pp. 289–305). Oxford: Blackwell.

Zaret, D. (1992). Defining the public sphere in eighteenth-century France: Variations on a theme by Habermas. In C. Calhoun (Ed.), *Habermas and the public sphere* (pp. 212–235). Cambridge, MA: MIT Press.

Index